JOURNEY
TO
THE NORTH OF INDIA

JOURNEY
TO
THE NORTH OF INDIA,

OVERLAND FROM ENGLAND,

THROUGH RUSSIA, PERSIA, AND AFFGHAUNISTAUN.

BY
LIEUT. ARTHUR CONOLLY.

IN TWO VOLUMES.

VOL. I

SECOND EDITION, REVISED

GYAN

Published by

Gyan Publishing House
5, Ansari Road
Daryaganj, New Delhi-110002
Phone: 011-47034999, 9811692060
E-mail: books@gyanbooks.com

Distribution Network
gyanbooks.com
India, USA, Canada, UK, Australia, France

ISBN : 978-81-212-3656-0 (Set)
ISBN : 978-81-212-4887-7 (HB)
First Published, 1838

2nd Impression 2020

Printed at: Gyan Press, Delhi.

Journey to The North of India
Author: Lieut Arthur Conolly

JOURNEY

TO

THE NORTH OF INDIA,

OVERLAND FROM ENGLAND,

THROUGH RUSSIA, PERSIA, AND AFFGHAUNISTAUN.

BY LIEUT. ARTHUR CONOLLY.

IN TWO VOLUMES.

VOL. I.

SECOND EDITION, REVISED.

LONDON:
RICHARD BENTLEY, NEW BURLINGTON STREET,
Publisher in Ordinary to Her Majesty.
1838.

TOORKMUN CAMP.

PREFACE

TO THE SECOND EDITION.

In this new edition I have put together, and occasionally condensed, some matter which was scattered and repeated in my first impression. Mr. J. Arrowsmith has been good enough to superintend the arrangement of a new Map, which fully illustrates the political questions on which I have ventured, and the further kindness of amateur artists, has enabled me to introduce to my readers the two native friends who give prominent interest to the Narrative.

London, November, 1838.

PREFACE

TO THE FIRST EDITION.

My apology for submitting this Work to the notice of the public, must rest upon the circumstance of my having travelled, by a new route, through very interesting countries. The journey was undertaken upon a few days' resolve; I had not the means of procuring any scientific information, did not always enjoy opportunity of committing my observations to paper, and lost some of my notes; I trust, therefore, that my Journal will be received with the indulgence that it needs.

For the accompanying sketches of a Toorkmun Camp, and the Affghaun National Dance, I am indebted to the kindness of the talented friends whose names they bear. The Map was constructed from my own notes.

CONTENTS

OF

THE FIRST VOLUME.

LIST OF PLATES.

NARRATIVE

OF AN

OVERLAND JOURNEY

TO THE

NORTH OF INDIA.

CHAPTER I.

St Petersburgh.—Moscow.—Journey over the Caucasus to Tiflis and thence to Tabreez.

QUITTING London on the 10th of August, 1829, I travelled through France and the North of Germany to Hamburg, and, embarking on board a steam-vessel at Travemunde on the 1st of September, sailed up the Baltic and the Gulf of Finland in four days to St. Petersburg.

In this capital I was joined by two friends and fellow-travellers to Persia, Captain Strong, of the Bombay military service, and Captain Willock, R.N., who had come from Hamburg *viâ* Denmark and Sweden. We spent a pleasant month here, being enabled, through the kindness of the premier, Count Nesselrode, and other gentlemen to whom we brought letters of introduction, to see much of what is interesting in this wonderful and ever new-looking city of palaces;* then, as winter was fast approaching, and as our journey was to be a long one, we prepared to journey on to Persia. My friend S. and I purchased, for 900 roubles, a light britchka on four springs, which we provisioned, and fitted up for day and night travelling; and for 550 roubles we bought a smaller carriage to contain our baggage, of which we gave charge to our French valet. Captain W. bought a good English-built carriage for himself; and, at the cost of 1000 roubles, we jointly engaged the services of an Englishman many years resident in Russia, who, as servant and interpreter, accompanied us to Tiflis.

The last things that we provided for our journey were sable caps, and soft leather jack-boots lined with wool, to keep our extremities warm, and racoon skin *shoobes,* huge cloaks worn with the fur inside, which are a defence against old Hyems himself. Our money we carried in bills upon Moscow, and, provided with necessary letters of introduction as far as Tiflis, we drove out of St. Petersburg on the noon of the 8th of October, and travelled, in five days and nights, 727 verstes to the city of Moscow.

On our route we passed through the once great city of Novgorod, which is now only remarkable for

* For a good sketch of St. Petersburg, I recommend the travels of Captain Jones, R.N., a work from the perusal of which much information and amusement may be gained.

the decayed vestiges of its former magnificence, and for being the head-quarters of the first military colony, established by the therefore famed Count Arrachief. There was little in the general appearance of the country to interest the eye: we saw parts of a very fine macadamised highway, which it was said would be thrown open the next year; but our road was a very bad one, sandy, muddy, or over the trunks of trees which had been laid across it, and we experienced so much weariness from the jolting, that we were very glad to see the spires of the ancient capital of the Muscovites.

At Moscow we remained only four days, for the first snow of the season falling on the second day after our arrival, we became anxious to be across the Caucasus: we made the most of our time however,—ascended heights to survey the city in its different aspects, and wandered, with intelligent guides, through its quarters, which are fast rising, phœnix-like, from their ashes, though they still bear many traces of the conflagration which was so heroically fanned. We saw the Kremlin, and the curiosities that its walls contain—were shown splendid modern buildings, with churches and convents of most ancient, strange, and varied architecture, and had reason to be delighted with all that we witnessed among the semi-Asiatic people of this extraordinary city, except a gross and idolatrous superstition, which can scarcely be imagined by a Protestant, and which cannot be too deeply lamented by any Christian.

Here we cashed our bills for Russian ducats, which I believe are a good remittance to most parts of the world, and on the 17th of October resumed our route. From the last of a succession of hills, which rise gradually above each other in a distance of four verstes, we looked back upon the painted and gilded roofs and cupolas of "the city of forty times forty churches," which lay *en masse* on either side of the river Moskva, backed by a deep blue sky that told of snow: while we looked the flakes began to fall thick about us; so, wrapping ourselves in our fur cloaks, we set our faces resolutely towards Asia, and bade the Isvoschtshicks give the rein and whip to their horses.

The thermometer this afternoon stood at 34° F^t; a week later, when, after travelling day and night, *via* Toula and Eletz, we reached the town of Veronetz, at nine in the morning it was 6° below zero. As we ran south, we seemed just to keep ahead of the snow; whenever we halted it overtook us, and we hurried on day and night with as little intermission as possible.

On the night of the 24th we crossed the Don into the Cossack country; halted the 26th and 27th at Tcherkask, the recent capital of the Don Cossacks, on the 28th again crossed this noble river into Asia, and continued our rapid journey over the steppes to the Caucasus.

We chose our own road upon the turf of these vast plains, and galloped across them with six sturdy orses attached to each vehicle, halting only an hour, morning or evening, to refresh ourselves with ablutions and food, or occasionally for a few minutes during the day, to get a shot at bustard, florican, or wild fowl. There was nothing else on the face of the country to invite our stay, and the less we entered houses, the less we suffered from the attacks of the vermin which have taken a lease of Russia; the road was as safe as easy, and after rolling smoothly along all day, we used to put a board between the seats of our carriage, and, buried in our furs, sleep soundly, if not very comfortably, through the bright cold nights.

During this part of our journey, we saw no people except those inhabiting the small villages at the government posts, and the few Cossack guards connecting them, links in the chain of communication thrown over this vast empire, through which the mandates of the Czar are conducted to their point as by electricity, and to which *kootoo* is performed as reverentially as to the indisputable decrees of the Emperor of China.

Our onward route lay through the towns of Stavrapol, Alexandrof, and Georgevsk, to Ekaterinegrade, where we arrived on the 3rd of November, and were detained until the 8th, when, a sufficient party of travellers having assembled, we were allowed to proceed slowly under escort of some Terek Cossacks, a party of infantry, and a twelve-pounder, to defend us against attack from any of the yet unsubdued Circassian tribes. In this manner, we travelled to Vladi Caucase, which we reached in three days: this is the last station on the northern side of the Caucasus, and, as the key to the pass into Georgia, a military post of importance. On the 12th of November we set out again, still escorted by soldiers, and marching under their protection through and over these stupendous mountains in five days, in the course of two more we drove to Tiflis.

We had two rather laborious days' journey over the snow in the Caucasus; our carriages however were not much injured. On our route we met a troop of horse artillery coming from the war, the soldiers attached to which seemed to make light of every difficulty, assisting the horses where the road was heavy, and occasionally unharnessing them, while with ropes they drew or lowered the guns up and down the slippery steeps. As a specimen of Russian soldiership, I may mention that, early one morning, we came upon a regiment of infantry bivouacked in regular order upon the snow.

The Russians do not yet command free passage through the Caucasus; for they are obliged to be very vigilant against surprise by the Circassian sons of the mist, who still cherish the bitterest hatred against them. In some instances, the Russian posts on the right of the defile, were opposed to little stone eyries perched upon the opposite heights; and when any number of the Caucasians were observed descending the goat-paths on the mountain's side, the Russian guards would turn out and be on the alert. We learned that not very long before our arrival a party of Circassians had, in the sheer spirit of hatred, lain in ambush for a return guard of some sixteen Cossacks, and killed every man.

Such facts seem to argue much weakness on the part of the Russians; but great have been the difficulties they have contended with in keeping the upper hand over enemies whose haunts are almost inaccessible to any but themselves. Several colonies of these ferocious mountaineers have been captured and transplanted to villages of their own in the plains, where they are guarded, and live as sulkily as wild beasts; and a general crusade, if I may be allowed the expression, has been talked of for some years past, to sweep such untameable enemies from the mountains, and settle them on the plains in the interior of Russia. Whatever policy is now adopted towards this people, the Russians will find it an easy task, comparatively with former times, to reduce them to obedience, since they have obtained possession of Anapa and Poti, on the east shore of the Black Sea, where the Turks used to furnish their friends with supplies which enabled them to sustain the war.

At Tiflis we rested a week, during which time we experienced much civility and kindness at the hands of General Count Paskovitch, and the Russian officers under his command; nor must I omit to acknowledge the very polite attentions for which we remain indebted to that excellent gentleman, the Chevalier Gamba, French consul. Here we saw some of the hardy-looking soldiers who had gained Paskovitch's victories; among them a regiment of dragoons, who the count said had taken a fort by galloping into it before the gates could be closed; and also a large irregular corps of Russo-Persians, chiefly men of the ceded province of Karabaugh, who had done good service against the Turks. Though we arrived just too late for a ball which had been given to the Turkish pashas made prisoners during the war, we danced at another, given to the army by the Georgian merchants of the city. Our lodging was in a tumble-down house kept by a French sutler, who had set up as an innkeeper; but we had the entrée at government-house, and were hospitably entertained by the different chiefs to whom we were introduced, and, in short, amused ourselves so well that we were sorry to depart.

Here we sold our carriages for about two-thirds of the money that they had cost us at St. Petersburg, and, purchasing horses, marched along the Kur, *viâ* Gunja, or, as it has been christened, *Elizabeth-pol*, to the curious hill-fortress of Sheesha, which a handful of brave Russians kept in defiance of Abbas Meerza's army during the last war. Thence our route lay across the Arras into Persia, and reaching Tabreez about Christmas-day, we spent the winter in the very pleasant society of the ladies and gentlemen who were with the British mission there.

SYUD KERAMUT ALI.

CHAPTER II.

Syud Karamut Ali—Journey to Tehraun on through Mazenderan to Astrabad—Toorkmuns—Assumed character—Toorkmun hospitality on the river Goorgaun.

My original intention had been to travel on to the south of Persia, and to embark at Bushire for Bombay; but now, thinking that I might get to India by an overland route, and being desirous of adding to the information obtained respecting the interesting and little travelled countries of the Toorkmuns and Affghauns, I determined to attempt a journey either *viâ* Khiva, Bokhara, and Caubul, or through Khorassân and Affghaunistaun, to the Indus. I had the good fortune to engage as my companion, Syud Karamut Ali, an unprejudiced, very clever, and gentlemanly native of Hindoostân, who had resided many years in Persia, and was held in great esteem by the English there. I had afterwards much reason to congratulate myself upon having so agreeable a companion, and it was chiefly owing to his assistance that I safely completed the journey.

Sir John Macdonald, who was at this time British envoy to the Persian court, gave my design every assistance, furnished me with letters likely to be of service to me, and most kindly authorized me to draw bills upon him during my journey. We engaged two servants, purchased three ambling galloways, and hired two mules; and all our preparations being completed in a few days, on the 6th of March, 1830, I took leave of many kind friends, and rode from Tabreez.

We made fourteen marches to Tehraun, by the well-known high-road through Meeana, Zunjan, and Casbine. Deep snow covered the ground nearly all the way, and our road was a narrow footpath, which if we missed we were plunged up to the horses' girths in the drifts on either side. Altogether it was rather an unpleasant journey, for we were exposed to much bad weather, and our eyes suffered greatly from the glare of the snow, which tanned our faces as black as a scorching sun would have done. We, however, always got comfortable lodging at night, in the houses of the village "Ketkhodas," and my companion and the servants reconciled themselves to the annoyances of the journey, by reflecting that they were excused from the strict fast enjoined upon all who remained at home in this month (Ramazân). Although we left Tabreez yet in the depth of winter, such was the difference of climate, that a fortnight afterwards, when we reached Tehraun, the trees were bursting into blossom! We took up our abode in the English residency, a building after the European style enclosed in a walled garden.

At Tehraun, our object was to obtain bills for the road. Sir John Macdonald had referred me to a Hindoo, his banker, in the city; but unfortunately the man was at this time absent at Yezd, and while we were endeavouring to find some merchant who would arrange our affair, the city was visited by a severe earthquake, which drove the inhabitants from their houses, and business was consequently at a stand.

Though earthquakes are events of common occurrence in Persia, the panic struck by this one was great. Several houses were thrown down, and part of the arched brick bazaar fell in; and so sudden was the visitation, that many of the inhabitants ran from their dwellings without caring for their property. As we rode through the bazaar after the first shocks, we saw the deserted shops open, with the various goods left on the boards as they had been displayed for sale. In gardens and all open places, families were grouped with their most valuable portable effects; in some cases the sick had been hurried from their dwellings, and mournful salutations and anxious inquiries were exchanged by those who met each other in the streets. We heard of a man who having gone to a house-top to say his prayers, had been left there by the falling of the stairs by which he had ascended; and many were the instances related of tragical deaths and providential escapes.

The Prince Governor gave me audience a few days

afterwards in a garden of the palace, seated in one of a suite of tents that had been pitched for his accommodation; and the chief officers of the Court were encamped in the open courts of the citadel, transacting business.

This unfortunate event delayed us longer than we intended to have stayed at Tehraun. My companion busied himself in seeking for a merchant who would give us bills, and in making inquiries about the different roads; there was a good library in the Residency, and I had an acquaintance who frequently visited me, to prevent, as he said, the hours passing heavily. This was an Italian youth, named Signor Turconi, who was by profession an Esculapius, and attached to the service of one or two great men about the court.

This gentleman was dressed in a long red cloth vest of Asiatic cut, pantaloons, and Persian slippers, *gills*, and a silk neckcloth, and a Persian cap, covering long auburn locks which flowed half-way down his back. His account of himself was as extraordinary as his appearance. He said that he had travelled from Naples to London, and at the latter city had taken his passage for America. He embarked on board a vessel laden with coals, and, after having been tossed about for six weeks, and fed with nothing but potatoes, was landed at Liverpool, and told to amuse himself there awhile. Not understanding this, and having acquired a distaste for the sea, he had gone over to France, and wandered across the continent from place to place, until he found himself at Constantinople, whence he had travelled on to Persia.

The labels of some medicine bottles that I had brought from Tabreez having been wetted on the journey, I requested my acquaintance to look at the phials and relabel them. After a few excuses about the difference of English and Italian practice and medicaments, &c., the Signor was frank enough to confess that he had not received a college education, but that he was a sort of amateur practitioner. "When I first came to Irân, *voyez vous*," said he, "every body asked me for physic; and seeing that they only considered me ill-natured when I refused to doctor them, I ventured upon a gentle experimental treatment, and succeeded so wonderfully well, that I began to think lightly of the difficulties with which professors have encompassed the science. The constitution of a man is a very simple thing! I do assure you, that you have only to —— and to —— to get the better of any of the common maladies that afflict people. I have some treatises upon the fundamental principles of medicine, as taught by the earliest sages, to which I refer in difficult cases, and you have no idea how many of these Persians I have cured! The secret of my success, *voyez vous*, is this: *J'ai beaucoup beaucoup de courage;* I never let a disease keep quiet possession of a body, but instantly attack it with something or other."

We visited our friend's quarters one day, and found

him drowning two vipers in a large bottle in order to form a decoction, "according to a receipt of Galen's," which he intended to administer to one of the ladies of the royal harem. "*Voyez!*" said he, uncovering a tray on which were some small articles of embroidery, and cakes of sugar-candy, "this is how the ladies pay. Did you see an old woman muffled up in her veil as you came in? That is an old 'white head' of another female inmate of the Shah's harem, to whom I am going to send this little box. I am in favour there, and receive mountains of sugar-candy. I take no other fee but sweets from *le beau sexe*, for Hossein Khan sirdar and others give me as much gold as I need." At parting I gave my acquaintance a lancet, and received the present of a box of his own pills, which I was cautioned only to administer to men, and not more than three at a time. Some time after, I tried two upon a sick muleteer, and as they were nearly strong enough to kill him, I thought it prudent to throw the rest away.

Syud Karamut Ali failed in his endeavours to obtain bills for the road, but he met with a worthy Guebre merchant, Moollâ Bairam, who offered to cash a bill upon the envoy, and, assuring us that there were no regular bankers on the roads we proposed travelling, recommended us to carry what we required with us. Suffering ourselves to be guided by his advice, we drew for a sum that, added to our stock, we calculated would pay our expenses all the way to India, and converted the whole into gold ducats (of

Russian coinage), which we secured in belts round our waists. Moollâ Bairam further gave us letters to some Astrabad merchants, who, we were assured, would render us any assistance in their power. Every thing else being now arranged for our departure, I went to the bath and submitted my head to the razor: my beard had been growing for two months, so that when I came out dressed in Persian apparel, my companion declared that as soon as the weather had tanned my neck, I should pass very good muster for a Kuzzilbâsh.

On the 6th of April we took our departure from the capital, and rode out fifteen miles easterly to Jujjer-rood, a rapid stream in a narrow barren glen, which we forded with some difficulty, by reason of the loose stones in its bed. On the other bank was a brick caravânsera, a solitary instance of the reigning monarch's extravagance. As part of this building appeared to have lately fallen, we did not venture to lodge in any of its cells, but spread our beds in the centre of the square. Well was it that we did so; for about midnight we were awakened by a heavy rumbling sound that seemed to pass under the ground we lay upon, and, starting up in alarm, we saw the bricks of the different apartments falling all round us.

I have not recovered my notes of our journey from Tehraun to Astrabad, but I remember that we made three marches of a distance between sixty and seventy miles, from Jujjer-rood to Ferooz-koh, a town of three hundred houses, romantically built on and at the foot of a sweeping hill, opposed to which is a very high rock, crowned with the ruins of a castle, which in the history of Ameer Timour is styled,—"the mother of Persian forts, whose height is to the sky, and whose strength is a proverb." Four days' more march took us a distance of about ninety miles to Sâri, the capital of Mazenderaun, which, though termed a fortress, is a place of no strength, but a moderate-sized town, surrounded with a brick wall, breast high. Here we crossed the river Tedjen, by a once fine bridge of seventeen arches, some of which were nearly broken away from each other.

We were told that his majesty Futteh Ali Shah, Geetee Sooltaun (the Lord of the Universe), had sent 1500 tomauns for the repair of this bridge; but that his son Mohummud Kouli Meerza, Moolkara (the Ornament of the Land), had caused a few boards to be laid over the broken arches, and kept the money to pay the Ghazeeaun-e-Islam (the warriors of Islam—his soldiers); a courtier-like mode of expressing that the prince had put the money into his own pocket.

It may be imagined that the roads in the province of such a governor were not of the best. Once a public-spirited individual began to repair the fine causeway that Shah Abbas made, but a stop was presently put to his undertaking by a message from the capital, intimating that if he had any spare cash the prince would be glad of it. Our road up many of the ascents was worn into steps by the feet of beasts of burden, and the old one over parts of the low grounds had been converted into a morass, so that the day we rode into Sâri, we nearly lost one of our horses in a bog, and wandered in all directions seeking a path, until we happened to meet a person who knew the country.

Our journey through Mazenderaun was delightful. It is a province of high mountains, which are clothed from base to summit with the forest and fruit trees of Europe and Asia. Wild vines of gigantic growth twine round the large trees, and drop their tendrils from the highest branches. The walnut, mulberry, pear, and pomegranate trees were in profusion, and their blossoms were in beautiful relief to the dark foliage of the forest trees; the turf was green and elastic, and covered with flowers; we enjoyed lovely weather, and the fresh air was always perfumed with the scent of the wild rose, jasmine, and hawthorn.

The narrow valleys between the high mountains are cut in steps, like the hanging gardens of Lahore. Through each one flows a stream, the water of which, being raised to the level of the highest step, is made to fall successively upon the others into its bed again. On these ridges is grown rice, the staple food of the people, and an article of considerable export. A great quantity of coarse sugar is also grown in Mazenderaun, and exported; and the province is famed for the manufacture of grass cloths, which are taken to all parts of Persia. Though the mulberry-tree is common, the silkworm is less attended to than in the adjoining province of Ghilan, the capital of which, Reshdt, is still a great mart for silk. Mazenderaun, though a beautiful and productive province, has a very unhealthy climate during half the year; for in summer a malaria, caused by the thick damp forests and saturated rice-grounds, renders the valleys uninhabitable, and it is said that the prodigious quantity of vermin engendered in them at this season is beyond belief.

The villages are built high up in the mountains, and a few only of the men come down into the valleys, where they reside in sheds, to look after their rice and sugar plantations, and to profit by the travellers who pass during the favourable months. On the sides and crests of the mountains, wheat and barley are partially cultivated, but so little do the people use the former grain, that it is a saying among other Persians, "An unruly Mazenderaun boy threatens his mother, that if his wish be not complied with, he will go into Irâk and eat bread."

We travelled about twenty-four miles east, through a forest, from Sâri to Ashruff, where we spent a day among the still magnificent ruins of Shah Abbas's palace. Hence we looked across a thick forest to the Caspian sea, which we first distinguished from the sky, by noticing a little sloop that was sailing outside a long tongue of land which forms a sort of bay in the south-east corner of this sea. From Ashruff we travelled still east to Astrabad, which we reached on the 21st of April, and took up our lodgings in the merchants' caravânsera.

Astrabad is a moderate-sized town of no strength, situated close under the richly-wooded mountains of Elborz. It is chiefly inhabited by Cujjers,* and being a frontier town, is governed by a prince of the blood royal. Ten miles north of Astrabad is the river Goorgaun, on the fertile banks of which are seated Toorkmuns, who are nominally tributary to the Shah of Persia, but they pay so little respect to his Majesty's authority, that they catch and sell his Persian subjects when they can, and the two people are continually upon the watch against each other.

We lost no time in presenting the Guebre merchants' letters to three traders of the town, named Hossein Kouli Aga, Hajee Motallib, and Aga Mohummud Tucky, his son; they were very civil, begged us to consider all that they had as our own, and to be sure that they would satisfactorily arrange all our affairs. Some of the Astrabadees, who trade constantly with the Toorkmuns, are known to, and go freely among them. Hossein Kouli Aga was one of these, and when we signified our wish to go to Khiva, he said that he would enable us to get there safely:

* The tribe from which the present Shah of Persia has his origin.

he accordingly sent to Goorgaun for a Toorkmun friend of his, named Orauz Kouli, who assured us that he would provide a trusty guide for us. We were just in time, he said, for several persons were assembling at Goorgaun for the purpose of travelling to Khiva together, therefore he would hire camels for us, and arrange so that we might accompany them. Thinking it necessary to have a pretence for our journey to Khiva, I assumed the character of a merchant; the Syud was to call himself my partner, and, at our friends' suggestion we purchased for the Khiva market, red silk scarfs, Kerman shawls, furs, and some large bags of pepper, ginger, and other spices. For our own use on the road, we provided some rice and a small bag of raisins, tea and sugar, and a bottle of vinegar; and our friends most kindly sent us a large supply of biscuit, prepared in their own "Anderoons."*

On the 24th, Orauz Kouli Toorkmun came into Astrabad to report that a caravan was about to start to Khiva; so, with our two Persian friends, we accompanied him that afternoon on his return to Goorgaun. We had difficulty in persuading our muleteer to convey our baggage out, for, though an old man of seventy, he feared lest the Toorkmuns should take a fancy to him, and a Persian lad, our servant, seemed to think that they would eat him. Our

* Inner or women's apartments.

other servant, however, Meshedee Norooz, who spoke Toorkish, agreed to take his chance with us, and he assumed the alias of Abdoollah, as better sounding in Soonnee ears.

As we were riding out of the town, we met a Cujjer friend, who, in taking leave, whispered in my ear, " I don't like those dogs you're going amongst; give me a word by which I may know that you have safely reached Khiva." Thinking that the Khan was merely affecting a particular interest in our welfare, and pretty sure of not shocking his ears, I said in joke, "*Shraub*"—wine; and receiving his adieus in a puff of tobacco (the last of a water-pipe which had gone round in the place of a stirrup-cup), we rode from the gate.

The commencement of our journey was marked by a very prosperous omen;—a snake crossing the road in front of us, Hossein Kouli Aga dismounted, and cut it in two with his sword. He then, with a fervent Bismillah!* threw one-half on either side of the road, and such a happy effect had the feat upon his spirits, that on remounting, he dashed off at full speed, flourishing his sword and shouting, while he careered about and charged as if engaged in mowing down whole hosts of foes, nor did he rejoin us until both he and his steed were out of breath. "*Moobarick ust,*" said the rest, "it is propitious; ride on

* In the name of the Lord!

under God's protection; no fear for your journey now, *the enemy* has been killed." I could obtain no other account of this remarkable superstition than that it probably was as old as the days of "Huzrut Adam:" an instance of it is related in the life of Aga Mohummud Khan, Cujjer, who, when at the death of Kerreem Khan Zund he fled up from Shiraz to this very Astrabad, had the good fortune to be crossed by a snake, which he killed with his own hand, and so infused much confidence into the minds of the party which had collected to support his pretensions to the throne of Persia.

Four miles of our road from Astrabad were through an open wood, in which there was a vast lake,* and our path lay for the most part over the heads of many strong dams, raised to divide the water, so that portions of it might be drawn off at pleasure for rice-grounds. Then we rode for six miles across a very rich meadow to the river Goorgaun. The grass in some places grew so luxuriantly, that at a distance we mistook it for grain. The Toorkmun tents, in camps of from sixty to eighty families, were thickly dotted over this green plain; troops of mares and foals, herds of oxen and camels, and numerous flocks of sheep and goats, were ranging in all directions to choose their

* This lake has been erroneously laid down in some maps as a gulf of the Caspian. It extends, I believe, from a point three miles north-east of Astrabad, to within as many miles of the sea. The water, being confined, stagnates in summer, and the inhabitants of Astrabad suffer much from the malaria that is caused by it.

pasture, watched here and there by a dog or a ragged Tartar child, and when at evening they all came into their camps, we were at a loss whether to be most struck with the beauty or the wildness of the scene.

Orauz Kouli's tent was one of twenty-eight, pitched about a stone's throw from the river; at the door of it we were cordially welcomed by his wife, who hastened to set before us bread, and bowls of rice-milk. A tent was allotted to us and our Persian friends; we spent some hours of the night in listening to their wild stories about the wars of the Persians and Tartars, and the feats of both parties, and then, spreading our beds upon the ground, we put our feet to the embers, and slept soundly till morning.

25th.—This day was passed in finishing a few letters, and in making arrangements for our journey to Khiva. Our host introduced us to one "Peerwullee, brother to Bábek, and son to Daoudi," who, for 22 tomauns, engaged to furnish us with four camels to carry ourselves and our merchandise to Khiva, and either himself to guide us thither, or to bring us safely back (God willing). These were the terms of the agreement, and as all declared Peerwullee to be a very worthy person, we felt perfectly satisfied. The tent was crowded during the whole of the day, for a sheep had been killed in honour of our visit, and the incomers busied themselves in roasting kabobs on ramrods. The women too passed freely in and out to see the strangers, and did not conceal their faces: they were not very beautiful, but it was a pleasure to look upon them after having so long been debarred the sight of female countenances. I was particularly struck with the softness of the Toorkish language as spoken by these people; so much so, that the first persons whom I heard speak it appeared to me to lisp. The manner also of those who visited us was so frank and kind, so totally different from what we had been taught to expect, that we were inclined to think them a much belied people.

The family of our host consisted of one wife and two children; and he was master of two slaves, an old negro-woman and a Kalmuck Tartar girl. The latter had just been sold into his hands by a young Khivian, who was a guest in the tent, waiting the departure of the caravan to return to his home. Orauz Kellije being introduced to us, took our hands between his own, and promised to serve us on the road, as well as to show us kindness when we should reach Khiva.

Before proceeding further with the account of our journey into the desert, it may be well to describe the people who inhabit it: the pages of Pallas, Moravieff, and Meyendorff, have furnished information about the northerly tribes, and Mr. Fraser has been beforehand with me in treating of the Toorkmuns in advance of the Persian frontier; but as my information was collected without reference to the above authorities, and as it is connected with my narrative, I state it as I obtained it; happy when it agrees with that detailed by Mr. Fraser, to the great accuracy of whose statements regarding Khorassaun, I am able in many cases to bear witness.

CHAPTER III.

Tribes of the Caspian desert—Their ranges—Genealogical tree—Modes of Nomade life—River Goorgaun—Frontier Toorkmuns—Tartar and Persian differences.

THE Nomade people inhabiting the desert which stretches north and east from the Caspian sea, are divided into separate tribes, some of which are at variance with each other. All clans have their understood ranges,* and, residing under tents the year round, they rove over their several portions of the steppe, in camps proportioned to its fertility in different parts. Within each range are many halting-stations (places where forage is mostplentiful), and they march from one to another as the herbage becomes exhausted, not staying more than from six to ten days at each, except in winter, when snow is on the ground. At some stations there are pools, which retain the winter and spring rains; at others there are wells, the sides of which are strengthened by thick wattle frames.

* Some of the tribes ally themselves with each other, and have common ranges. Pasturage being very scanty, they are particular in preventing encroachments upon their limits, and have frequent quarrels on this score.

The Toorkmuns are first met with on the river Goorgaun. They range north till they meet the Aralian tribes and the Kirghiz, and I will take the Oxus, on the east, as the boundary of those tribes whom my narrative concerns.

The large tribe of Yimoot occupy the banks of the Goorgaun river, fifty miles east from the sea, to a brook tributary to the Goorgaun, called Kara-soo, or blackwater; and they extend up the right coast of the Caspian to above Balkan Bay, when, meeting the small tribe of Attah, they turn, and range the desert east to near Khiva.

The Gôklans are a smaller tribe: a few miles of neutral ground are left on Goorgaun between them and their enemies the Yimoots, and they then possess the banks of the river for about ninety miles, till they meet the Koords, who were removed from the Turkish frontier to the border of Persian Khorassaun, by Shah Abbas, that they might be between his people and the Toorkmuns. The Gôklans do not at furthest range more than forty miles north; greatly inferior to the Yimoots, and to the strong tribe of Tekkah, who are both at enmity with them, they are obliged to keep back upon Persian Khorassaun, and may be considered as subservient to the Shah.* Living a more settled life than other tribes,

* The Shah retains three or four hundred Toorkmuns at Tehraun, half troops, half hostages. The majority of these are Gôklans, the rest Yimoots from the neighbourhood of Astrabad. They bring their families with them, and are relieved every year or so.

and having fine lands, they employ themselves much in agriculture, and they possess large herds and flocks.

The Tekkahs range from north of the Gôklans up to Khiva, and beyond Merve Shah Jehan they are found upon the bank of the Oxus. They are the most warlike and powerful tribe, and they render feudal allegiance to the Khan of Khiva.*

Below Merve are found several small clans, chiefly branching from the tribe of Saulour. They are better known by the name of Serruxees, from the circumstance of their being thickly seated about Serrux. These clans form a confederacy, and occasionally take a part in the quarrels of the Persian Khorassaun chieftains: they hold the fort of Serrux, and keep the road eastward from Meshed to Bulkh. Near Serrux they cultivate grain for their own use, and they are said to be rich in cattle, which they drive into the desert when threatened with attack.

Every great tribe is divided and subdivided into smaller clans, which retaining the common name, have each a distinguishing one, that generally of a patriarch who went out from a large society to head a smaller set. The following Yimoot genealogical tree, though imperfect, will afford an idea of the order of their societies.

* The Khan of Khiva, we learned, has twelve thousand Toorkmun horse in regular pay. They receive each 20 tillas (13*l.*) yearly, and pay their own expenses. They are for the most part Tekkahs, the rest are from the Yimoot clans seated near to Khiva. Besides these, the Khan, it is said, can raise 30,000 feudal horse on emergency.

YIMOOT.

Yimoot, who was the son of Arsári, the son of Saulour Kazán, had four sons, Chooni̇, Sherruff, Cowjuck Tartar, and Bairam Shalli.

- **CHOONI,**
  - Auk,
    - Kiskeh,
      - Sheer Mohummud-lee, or loo (*a genitive.*)
      - Gooz Mohummud-lee.
      - Kooch Mohummud-lee.
      - Khojesh-lee.
      - Kuzzilgeh.
      - Boi-lur.
    - Oozeem,
      - Hubbeeb-lee.
      - Sukkauvee.
      - Goog.
      - Soort.
  - Otaboi,
    - Khaunum-lee,
      - Oodamish-lee.
      - Tauneh.
      - Kushkulkur.
      - Kusseh.
      - Doogoonchee.
      - Ashoor-goog.
      - Kara-zaurtic.
    - Auk Sukkaulee,
      - Sunnah,
      - Sookee. }
      - Sooklur. }
      - Yámpee.
      - Serjelli̇.
      - Tummick.
      - Mohummud Ali-look.
  - Dauz,
    - Haunkeh,
      - Nuzzur Kouli.
      - Yeshman Kouli.
      - Kussick.
      - Baukee.
      - Hussan Moollah.
      - Beg-lur.
      - Ali Kouli.
    - Paunkeh,
      - Soozmeh.
      - Kizzil-lur.
      - Khaun-lur.
      - Cheen-sooppoolee.
  - Budrauk, Eegdir, Koucheck, — No information about their descendants.
  - Eimur, — Eermunnee, Aux Mooslim, Kara Mooslim. (Degrees of propinquity not ascertained.)
  - Mushreck, Yoolmah, Kaun Kirmiz, — No information about their descendants.
  - Kaun Yaikmuz, — Kuzzil-jur, Pushmuck, Ali Yar-lee, Hullakee, Iskundur-lee. (Degrees of propinquity not ascertained.)

SHERUFF.

- Jaffer Bi,
  - Yarlee,
    - Aurookh,... Kul.
    - Shukkaulee, Onôk.
    - Toomaugh .
      - Ish Mohummud-lee.
      - Dowlut Verdi-lee.
      - Poorkhaus.
    - Chookaun.
    - Kuzzil.
    - Koosullee.
  - Noor Ali,
    - Kooor.................
    - Punk *
      - (Kooor and Punk *:) Kootook.
        - Hussan Kouli,
          - Neaz Kellije.
          - Peere Kouli [Sooltän.
          - Khirdar.
          - Koolgheeruk.
          - Kum.
        - Toorjah, ...
        - Koort, ...
    - Kulteh,
      - Karajeh.
    - Kara Yenjick.—(Seated near Mangishlauk.)
- Eelghi, ...
  - Onök,
    - Kullur.
    - Choorooshlur.
  - Eeree,
    - Sukkaur.
    - Meerzaulee.
    - Vakeel.
    - Kehyer.
    - Orauz-lee.
- Dévechee, (*i.e.*) *camel-grazier.*
  - Khiva-lee, Kara daug-lee, Oduk Mayööt, Choobaush, Ogerjelli,
    - (Ogerjelli:) Abdaul, Gerraie Summudun, Terrukmeh.
- Kurravee,
  - Yaupunk, Serrunsee, Toorunj, Koollauk, Baushlee-kurra. (Degrees of propinquity not ascertained.)
- Behtekkeh, Behghur,
  - No information about their descendants.

BAIRAM SHALLI.

- Okuz, ...
  - Kara Okuz.
  - Auk Okuz,...
    - Chuncheh.
    - Otelboï.
    - Yerkï.
    - Koor.
    - Goorveh.
    - Yeghr.
    - Kara Yenick.
    - Kara Komaun.
    - Kullur.
- Saulook,...
- Oortejji,...
- Ooshauk,

* The immediate descendants of Punk (of some others the same) were not numerous enough to go out and form new societies, but remained some years with the paternal name. Then, perhaps their sons, or their sons' sons, went out. It is very difficult for one not bred among the Toorkmuns to trace their pedigrees: it appears from the names of the branches said to come from the Dévechees, that they do not confine themselves to patronymics, and pro-

Only of the first two sons have we full accounts. —The descendants of the Cowjuck Tartars are not many, and the Bairam Shallis are still less numerous: the latter are seated towards Khiva, and therefore perhaps less was known about them by those who gave us information. The space of twelve fursukhs, which is between the Yimoot boundary of Kara-soo and the sea, may be loosely divided into three tracts: the most easterly one is occupied by the Cowjuck Tartars; the Choonïs (3000 tents) are found in the middle one; and the Sherruffs (4500 tents) inhabit the third, to the coast of the sea. The boundary line on the north of these three great divisions may be imagined to cross the desert at the parallel latitude of Balkan bay.

The Toorkmuns are classed under the heads of Charwar and Choomoor, that is, rovers and settlers, and the first are considered to be in the proportion of three to one of the last. The terms are not arbitrary, for many become settlers for a while, and

bably any remarkable circumstance happening to a man, frequently gives him an *agnomen* which descends to his issue. Hossein Kouli Aga told me that the clan of the Cujjers, to which he belonged, *Kuzzil Aiyaug*, took its name from the following incident: In former years, the Cujjers were "chader nisheen," or abiders in tents, and they inhabited a part of the desert beyond Astrabad, now occupied by the Yimoots. The head of this clan comingin to Astrabad to see a friend, was taken to the bath, and his host paid him the compliment of giving him a smart dress, and of dying his feet with *henna*. When he returned to his brethren in the desert, they were struck with his appearance, and gave him the name of Kuzzil Aiyaug, *red* or *gold foot*.

then return to the desert again; but there is a great difference in the mode of life of the two.

The settlers (I describe those near Astrabad), who seldom change their ground, need but few camels; they occupy themselves in pasturing large herds and flocks, from the produce of which they reap a good profit.* They also rear fowls, and they cultivate much grain on the banks of the Goorgaun.

The rovers, on the contrary, chiefly estimate their wealth by the number of camels they possess: they have flocks of sheep and goats, but no oxen, neither have they any fowls: a few dogs are kept to watch their flocks, but we did not even see a cat among them.

Both Charwars and Choomoors breed horses: preference is given to those reared in the desert, as being most hardy. Some of these animals rise to the height of sixteen hands; they are remarkable for bone and sinew, but they have very long backs, and large coarse heads: these characteristics, however, are ameliorated by a mixture of Arab blood. The wealthiest Toorkmuns possess Arab stallions and mares, and the produce of the two castes is very good.

The rovers and settlers both share in the culti-

* It was said among the Yimoots on Goorgaun, that one man, the wealthiest among them, possessed seven hundred camels, five thousand sheep and goats, and two hundred mares; to wit, several *neckful* of money. The Toorkmuns keep their money and little valuable etceteras in large purses made of the skins of camels' necks.

vated lands on Goorgaun, parties of the Yimoots from as far as Balkan coming in at sowing and reaping seasons. Part of their produce of wheat and barley is exchanged with the Persians for Mazenderaun rice. The rovers take with them only grain sufficient for two months' consumption; the overplus they sell at Astrabad, and come in from the desert and repurchase as they require it. They are losers by this arrangement, but they cannot well carry much with them on their marches, and on the whole they calculate that they obtain the supply they yearly require, for the labour of cultivating about twice as much.

The river Goorgaun measures about sixty yards from bank to bank: its bed is deep, and in spring, when the snows of the Elborz melt, there is much water in it; but in summer (except when occasionally swelled by the rains which the mountains attract) it is shallow. The water, though not clear, is sweet, and very drinkable when its mud has been allowed to settle. The Toorkmuns swear by it. Nothing can exceed the richness of the land through which this river flows. About three miles' breadth on either side of it is cultivated with the finest wheat and barley: the ground is turned up with a wooden share, to which is yoked a horse, bullock, or camel, and it is loosely said to give an increase of from seventy to one hundred fold.

For the privileges of pasture and cultivation, the Goorgaun Yimoots affect allegiance to the Shah of Persia; and their brethren as far as Balkan, being dependent upon this quarter for their supplies, also call themselves Astrabad Yimoots:* but they are very independent liegemen, pay their slight tribute only when it suits them, and carry off their fellow-subjects the Persians whenever they can catch them. An Astrabadee dares not go to Goorgaun without the safeguard of a Toorkmun, neither do the Toorkmuns venture to Astrabad unguaranteed. The Cujjer prince himself hardly affected to have much control over them, and indeed he had a short time before our arrival been taught how lightly his authority was regarded; for on his going to Goorgaun to honour the wedding of his Meer Akor's† brother, an old Toorkmun rated him soundly before the assembled guests, and carried off one of his suite, as they were returning to Astrabad, to balance a wrong which he conceived the prince had done to a party connected with him.

The Toorkmuns have proved themselves such galling neighbours as enemies, that the Persians are glad to keep any terms with them; still this state of affairs arises entirely from the insufficiency of the Shah's government; for though a few families may strike their tents and retire into the desert at will, the bulk of the Yimoots, even if they could obtain the necessaries of life elsewhere, could not afford to abandon the lands on Goorgaun by which they profit

* Twelve thousand tents were on the roll of the Astrabad governor, and each tent was rated to pay four Persian reals; but this must have been a flourish of the Meerza in charge of the records, or else copied from a very old census.

† Master of Horse.

so largely; and, under a proper government, they might not only be brought to respect the persons of his majesty's natural subjects, but themselves become profitable members of the state. At present these Yimoots will appeal to the Astrabad Hákim, if they find themselves the weakest party in a dispute with the Persians, as the following incident will show. Kutool is a district in the province of Astrabad on the Khorassaun side, and its inhabitants render a very imperfect allegiance to the Shah. Their chief chuppaoed a clan of Dévechee Yimoots, and took many sheep. The Dévechees deeming it inexpedient to cross the border, recollected that they were Persian subjects, and petitioned the Shahzadeh, who recommended them just to satisfy themselves by retaliation. They tried his receipt, but could only kill two men and capture three others; however they met a party of Astrabad Persians who had gone out to try some horses, and attacking *them*, killed one man (a Cujjer Khan), and carried off the rest. It was now the Persians' turn, and they laid an embargo upon several Toorkmuns who unsuspiciously came to the town. The difference was unadjusted when we quitted Astrabad, the parties not being able to agree about the comparative value of their prisoners, and the Kutoollees refusing to restore the sheep they had taken.

All our arrangements for the journey being completed, it was determined that we should set out the next day for the river Attruk, to join the caravan said to be assembling on its bank. Every thing looked well for our journey; Hossein Kouli Aga answered for Orauz Kouli, and Orauz Kouli for Peerwullee, and we could not help congratulating ourselves upon having found such friends, and on having come among them at such good season. We had endeavoured to sell our horses at Astrabad, but not succeeding, we reserved them as presents to our Persian friends. Hossein Kouli Aga accepted my horse and furniture complete, and in return gave me much of that cheap commodity—good advice. I was too generous, he said, and among the people we were going to visit, I must carefully guard against the indulgence of a liberal feeling.

The view south from hence was very beautiful. Far across the meadow, on a rising ground, was the town of Astrabad, faintly marked out in all its angles like a fortification on a map, and at the back of it rose to a great height the richly-wooded Elborz mountains. We lay on the grass at sunset enjoying this scene, while the Syud was going through the Soonnee forms of prayer with much ostentation. "You are a *Mooselmaun* then," said a Toorkmun to him (for Soonnees will not allow Sheahs the name). "Alhumdoolillah!"—I thank God! was the reply. "Hei Kaufir!" muttered the Persian at my side,—Ah infidel! Then turning to me he said with much earnestness, "Friend of mine, you have a *treasure* in that Syud, for God is witness that he goes through the Soonnee forms with the veriest dog among them." My friend, however, kept his disgust to himself when near Toorkmuns, for whose creed he hinted much toleration, if not a considerable penchant; such hypocrisy does their religious system enjoin.

The Soonnee, or (as they call themselves) the orthodox Mohummudans, reverence Abu Bukr, Omar, and Oosman, the three men who were successively made caliphs after the death of the great impostor. The Sheahs protest against these, as being merely men raised by the caprice of the people to a sacred office which was the right of Ali, the prophet's son-in-law, and in the excess of their zeal, they look upon the first three caliphs as usurpers, and imprecate curses upon them. "'May God curse Abu Bukr, Omar, and Oosman, and shed his peace upon the blessed Ali!' is the form of speech commonly used (said a reverend Sheah to me); but there is no strict injunction to use *words* of cursing, so long as a man holds them accursed in his *heart*." The names of the original caliphs are commonly introduced into the phrases of gross abuse in which the Persians deal so largely: "May the face of the father and the father's father of *your Omar* be defiled," will a mule-driver say in correcting an unruly beast, and without entertaining a particular regard for either sect, I think that the Soonnees have the best excuse for their enmity, for it must be galling to a man to hear the fathers of his creed cursed in the grossest terms. One reason for preferring the Soonnees is, that they are the most sociable sect of the two. They will eat, drink, and bathe with you; while the most scrupulous among the Sheahs will even send their clothes to be washed if you brush up against them in the street. The Sheahs, being the weaker party, are enjoined to protect themselves from the enmity of the Soonnees by any means of deceit that appear expedient, and accordingly, when they travel in a Soonnee country, they deny their religion, and learn to say their prayers after their adversaries' forms. "We know no sin," they argue, "in defending the lives which God has given us; and if there be any, He will visit it on those who force us to it:" forgetting that their bitter and uncalled for maledictions have provoked the enmity.

CHAPTER IV.

Ford the rivers Goorgaun and Attruk, and advance into the desert—Ruined city—Toorkish forays—Camps in the desert—Deserted river-bed—Supposed branch of the Oxus—Aujeree and Balkan hills—Mirage—Barren plain—Halting-place for caravans.

April 26th.—About ten o'clock in the morning we quitted Orauz Kouli's tent. It would have been insulting our host to have offered payment for lodging and cheer, but we presented his wife with a silk scarf and a small shawl. She accepted them with many smiles, and when she had feasted her own eyes upon them, and excited the envy of her female friends, she inquired of Hossein Kouli Aga the cost of the scarf, and at his valuation made it over to Orauz Kellije, in part payment for the Kalmuck girl. This compromise with scruples that we had heard so much about surprised us, but it seemed to be a matter of course. The lady dismissed us with "Khosh Geldin! Allah Yârin!" "You are welcome! God be with you!" and her brother, in repeating these expressions, added, "May you come again! may you come often!"

We forded the Goorgaun where the water was not up to our saddle-girths, and rode two miles beyond to a large oubeh,* where we were introduced to *Odekka*, the father of our host. Here Peerwullee joined us with three camels; the fourth, he said, he would get from the caravan at the Attruk river. One camel carried a pair of kajavahs (open cribs slung loosely on a camel's sides, like panniers), in which the Syud and I stowed our bedding, and sat or lay upon it. On the other two beasts our merchandise was laden, and Meshedee-Norouz, alias Abdoollah, found a place for himself upon the spice-bags. At starting, Hossein Kouli Aga placed what little beard Peerwullee had within the Syud's hand, to signify that he was bound to guard and cherish us, even as he would this precious part of his own person. With some difficulty we adjusted our weights on the kajavahs, and then, bidding adieu to our Persian and Toorkish friends, commenced our journey, with many kind wishes shouted after us.

Peerwullee led the march on foot, and Orauz Kellije, mounted on his own horse, made angles with all elevated bits of land, to look out, he said, for Gôklans, who occasionally rode far from their stations to surprise the Yimoots. He was armed with a sword, and a light spear twelve feet long. Peerwullee had two of the strangest-looking weapons imaginable; a pistol with a blunderbuss mouth, and about two-thirds of an European gun-barrel mounted on a Persian stock: however he seemed to think himself very

* Camp.

well armed, and when we halted always made a show of examining the state of his locks.

We took a northerly direction, and after six miles, losing the meadow-land, we entered upon a dry light soil where, save occasional patches of good grass, grew only small thorns and weedy bushes. We halted at evening from five till eight, and a great relief was this respite from the distressing motion of the kajavahs. These cribs were but four feet by two, and when we had contrived to dispose of our bodies in this small space so as not to be in torture, our remaining skill was needed to preserve the centre of gravity; for the kajavahs were only loosely slung over the camel's back, and the very act of rising to draw a cramped leg from under one might have sufficed to destroy the balance. The motion had the effect of giving me a severe headach, which I should have minded more had I not been kept in laughter at the alarm of my friend in the other pannier. We were frequently obliged to spring up and clutch each other, as one or other crib leaned over, and he took infinite pains to show, upon philosophical principles, how by my giving too much of my weight to one side, he might be made to fly over my head and break his bones. At eight o'clock we continued our march for two hours and a half, and then halted till four in the morning.

27th.—At half-past five forded the Attruk, distant by our computation about 27½ miles from Goorgaun. Orauz Kellije walked ahead to feel the way for the camels, and the water was up to the middle of his thigh. This river is a third less broad than the Goorgaun: in spring its banks are overflowed, and the Toorkmuns sow melon and jowgan* seed in the alluvial soil. The water was so muddy, that we thought we should dirty ourselves by washing with it; the Toorkmuns however took it up in their palms, and drank it with apparent relish. The sight determined me not to trust to a Toorkmun's account of water.

There was not a tent in view, and, contrary to what we had imagined, we were told that the Yimoots do not settle themselves on the bank of this river as on the Goorgaun. The soil is good, but it is not the rich loam of the frontier meadow, which produces such excellent pasture. We halted about an hour, and Peerwullee went up the bank to look for traces of the caravan: he decided that it had gone on, and in the hope of overtaking it we marched on without intermission all day, our course due north. At five in the evening, we halted at a long pool of rain-water: it was deep enough to bathe in, and our guides said that it did not quite dry up in the hottest weather. Here we collected a heap of weedy bushes, and made a sort of fire, at which we boiled some rice and tea. The latter the Toorkmuns drank with much gusto, and behaved quite like children, asking for sugar to their tea, and tea to their sugar, till the patience of our steward Abdoollah was exhausted; and they ended by taking each a lump of sugar and a mouthful of

* Holcus sorghum.—(Jawarree.)

tea-leaves to chew at leisure. The Oosbegs, who live in a great measure upon tea, keep the leaves in their mouths to prevent thirst. The latter Tartars actually stew their tea, with bread, butter, and salt. At eight we resumed our march, and kept on a northerly course, over a very bare country, till four in the morning.

28th.—Halted one hour, and then marched on. Between nine and ten we passed between two hills (or rather mounds) about seven miles apart, on one of which there appeared to be vestiges of buildings, but they were so wrapped in vapour that we could distinguish nothing clearly. These mounds are called Roostum-e Zal's forts.* Then our road lay over the remains of a town, once apparently of good extent, and, as it seemed, systematically laid in ruin. Not one stone was upon another to mark the form of a building, but square well-burnt bricks lay in detached low mounds over a considerable space. We could get no better information from our guides about these ruins, than that a long time ago they formed a city: "just a city," as a Scotchman would have said. About one we came to twenty-two Eelghï Yimoot tents, and got some camel's *chaal*,† the acid of which was very refreshing in the heat. The tents were pitched under a broad ridge of sandhills, about six miles east of the ruins of a city called Meshed-e Misreaun. Two tall minârs and a mosque were distin-

* Roostum the son of Zal—the Hercules of Persian history.

† Butter-milk.

guishable, hanging as if in air above a cloud of vapour, like Aladdin's palace. We got no tidings of the caravan, and after a few minutes' halt resumed our route. After winding about among hillocks of loose sand till near five in the evening, partly in search of water, we halted to give the camels rest. Luckily we had water enough in our mushk* to boil some rice; at eight o'clock we marched on, and, after two hours and a half, halted again till three in the morning.

29th.—From five to six o'clock we stayed at a camp of twenty-four Otaboï Yimoot tents, where they put before us the usual Toorkmun fare, boiled rice mixed with sour milk, a very unpalatable mess to those unused to it. Again, about noon, we took refuge from the sun in one of five tents belonging to the family of a man who roved apart from his other kindred, because he had "much substance."†

We halted one hour and marched on. There were other tents at some distance, to which Orauz Kouli rode on his unwearied horse to seek tidings of the caravan: he returned without any, but it was agreed that, as we had got over the most dangerous part of the road, we need not concern ourselves about convoy.

Orauz Kellije's horse excited our astonishment: for two days we saw that he got no water, and fed only upon what he could pick up (coarse grass or weeds) as we went along, or when we halted: corn he did not taste a grain of, "nor should he, please God," said his master, "till he reached home, when he

* Water-skin. † Gen. xiii. 6.

should lie down before a hill of it." He explained this expression by saying, that it was their custom when they had no foray in view, to allow their horses entire discretion as to their food. "We tether them," he said, "within reach of abundance, and they know better than to eat too much." I would rather state the Toorkmuns' own accounts of some of their customs, than my entire belief in them, for some of their stories were only just within the bounds of credibility; but it cannot be doubted that both they and their horses perform astonishing feats; and as they are themselves as lazy at home, as active when abroad, what Orauz Kellije said about their mode of treating horses may be true. The Toorkmuns roll a piece of fat round their snaffles, to keep their horses' mouths moist on a long march. Some said that they bled their steeds to relieve them when they were much fatigued, and others spoke of drinking the blood in case of their being themselves short of water; but as some of the latter, in allusion to their own great prowess, hinted that they were "man-eaters," I learned to consider the first account as hyperbolical.

They train their horses for a long march, and when they are going beyond the plain country they shoe them, which they do not at other times. Their longest expeditions are undertaken in spring and autumn. With a bag of flour, some oil-cakes, a few *kooroot** balls, and a water-skin, for their own use, and a small bag of barley or jawarree for their horses, they set

* Hard pressed cheese.

out on a distant foray. Their pace is alternately a yoortmah (or gentle jog-trot) and a long walk; every hour or two they halt, and let their horses graze if there be herbage (themselves perhaps snatching a few moments' sleep), and occasionally they give them a handful of corn. Marching on thus unceasingly to the point they have in view, they get over much ground in a few days, and their horses', and indeed their own, steady endurance of fatigue is wonderful. They have the excitement which attends a dangerous service to keep up their spirits, and pretty sure of booty if they can get within the reach of Persians, they forget their fatigues in thinking of their probable gains. It is a chance if their enemies hear any thing of them till they have crossed the border, and then they are more likely to get out of the way than to muster to oppose them. "*Chacun pour soi*" is a Persian's motto, and if an accident befalls his neighbour, he says, "It is his fate." The Persians have been so long afraid of these Tartars that they will hardly make an effort to defend themselves. "*Oonha bisseaur jungee hustund, wo má ser né dareem,*" is their apology: "They are very warlike, and we've no head." In the last three words the Persian has shown the cause of all the evils that afflict his countrymen—they have no head.

If the foraging party be numerous, they make for a village, and if they can get within it, they slay those who resist, and the aged, and carry off the strong and beautiful into slavery: when the walls of a village keep them out, they content themselves with "driving" the cattle. A smaller party waits near a high road for kafilahs, as on the one between Shahrood and Meshed, which is travelled yearly by fifty or sixty thousand pilgrims. Their custom has been to post a reserve at a little distance from the road, to support the advanced party in their retreat, and, upon the strength of the belief that they always do so, they sometimes push forward their whole force, and capture a stronger party than themselves; for the sight of one Toorkmun induces a Persian to suppose that he has a thousand others at his beck, and the feeling, if it does not frighten him into an incapacity to defend himself, certainly operates to dissuade him from attempting the rescue of his friends. It is generally in the gray of the morning that the Toorkmuns wait for the pilgrims, when half asleep, after a weary night's march, they have dispersed for prayers; then, with a ho! ho! they dart down upon them, make haste to cut down a few of the least valuable persons, and do not find it very difficult to drive off the greater part of the rest. A few of the kafilah escape at the first onset, and hastening to the nearest station with the news of their friends' capture, give perhaps the first intimation that the Toorkmuns are out. "They come," to use a Persian's own expression, "like the whirlwind, and are only known by the traces of their devastation."

Great must be the merriment of these freebooters when, beyond reach of pursuit, they proceed to share the strange mass of Mohummudans who get together on pilgrimage; and great their satisfaction when, after their profitable labours, they return to a life of idleness. They sell or retain their captives, according to their worth: they complain that they are often deceived in the Persians, getting as they think a hale strong man, and seeing his black beard grow out quite gray in the course of a few days.—But to return to our route:

Quitting the Eelghï camp, we marched on till five in the evening. Orauz Kellije found a puddle of rain-water, and, though it was so bad as to disguise the taste of our food, we contrived to make a meal. On again from nine to eleven; then halted for the sake of the camels, in a large patch of high coarse grass. In the centre of this was a pool of water, but it was so bad, that only with the addition of vinegar could we drink it. We remained here till morning, but the night was close, and swarms of hungry musquitoes, who probably but seldom tasted animal food, determined to make the most of us, so we were glad to march away after a sleepless night.

30th.—About six we halted in sight of eight tents. One of our camels had a sore wound upon its back, and we insisted upon Peerwullee's getting a fourth, pursuant to his engagement. He went for the purpose, and was absent till noon, when he returned with the master of one of the tents, bringing with him a skin of chaal, a great treat, for the thermometer rose to 97° in the sun, and not a breath of air was stirring.

From this man we purchased a lamb for a sahibkoran.* Looking hard at my European complexion, he accused me of being a Russian spy; and when I affected anger at the insinuation, he merely said that it would be well for me if I was not, but that I had much the look of one. He confessed, however, that he had never met a Russian, nor did he wish to do, except for the opportunity of cutting his head off and making kabaubs of it. From him Peerwullee had taken a camel, for which he was to bring from Khiva a mare, an iron cooking-pot, and an auftauba (a vessel for holding water, in shape something like the one which the stork is represented as feeding from, when she asked the fox to dinner). The mare appears a large item in the exchange, but as the selection of her was left to Peerwullee's conscience, she would probably have been the least valuable article of the three.

We marched hence N.N.E. for two hours, then coming to the bank of a dry nullah, we kept along it till we found a place of descent into the bed. This, after a while, led us into deep ravines, and from them we passed into what appeared to be the deserted bed of a once very large river. We journeyed N.E. up its centre for two hours, then a little before sunset halted to prepare a meal.

The Syud and I, parting from the centre, walked each to a bank, and measured jointly about a thousand paces. The soil differed from that above, having

* About 1*s.* 3*d.*

gravel and pebbles, and against the right* bank, to which I walked, many large stones were collected, and the earth near it was coned up, as if by the strong force of water. The banks, which were very high and much worn, would run for some distance at a breadth about equal to that we measured; then they would be broken into a succession of deep parallel ravines, each the size of a nullah.

We wished to believe ourselves in the bed of the Oxus, and indeed we calculated that we had come far enough north to meet with the supposed ancient course of that river; but we feared lest the very wish to decide so interesting and long controverted a question might influence our opinions. That it was the bed of a very large river was apparent,† though at what period deserted, and from what cause, there was little to show. Moravieff speaks of an earthquake which happened five hundred years ago; we were told of a great flood about that time: all agree in saying that at such period the face of the country was materially altered, but the Toorkmuns have no books, neither have they very positive notions about time or events.

Moravieff, more than once on his journey to Khiva, met with apparently the continuation of this bed; and whatever obscurity rests upon the cause or the period of its secession, there seems no great reason to doubt that a branch of the Oxus formerly flowed

* Presuming that the river ran to the Caspian.

† The Toorkmuns call the bed *marsullee*: the meaning of the word I know not.

west to the Caspian. One of the strongest reasons for supposing that it did, is found in the writings of Mirkhoond, author of the Rowzutusuffa, who, in his account of the descendants of Oguz Khan, the great Tartar, says, that they spread themselves not only over Mawâra-oon-nuhr, that is, the country on that side of the river Jihoon which bounds Persia on the north,—but also to the south of that river, and along the borders of Khorassaun, a province of Irân. Now, to bound Persia on the north, and to have Khorassaun on its south, the Jihoon must have flowed west. Abulghazi Khan also, in his History of the Tartars, speaks of the Amou as separating Karazm from Khorassaun, to the northward of the latter province; and in the writings of many old eastern historians Karazm is treated of as part of Mawara-oon-nuhr.

My friend the Syud carried his speculations much further; for he not only saw no reason why this great bed, which could be traced so far east, should not be admitted to prove the ancient historian's account of the Oxus, but he was inclined to think that, if the water of one of a river's two arms was turned off (as it is traditionary that one stream of the Jihoon was) by human agency, it might by the same means be conducted back again, so as to afford the Russians water communication between the Caspian and the capital of Karazm. This would indeed be revolutionizing Asia.

A single Toorkmun horseman, who was riding south, met us and sat down to share our lamb, which was prepared *à la Tartare,* grilled on ramrods over the embers of the stump of a tree. The Toorkmuns had much the advantage of us, for they tore the hot flesh in pieces with their horny fingers, and had nearly made an end of the meat before we could venture upon it. I learned from this a fact which is perhaps not generally understood by civilized people—that the mouth can bear a much greater heat than the fingers. It is on record that at the death of one of the Bunnee Abbas caliphs, his upper robes were all found to be greased on the right sleeve; the reason of which was, that the Commander of the Faithful, being always impatient for his dinner, could not wait till it cooled, and so, rather than burn his fingers, he used to cover his hand with the loose sleeve of his abba, and thus feed himself.

The night set in dark and rainy. At eight o'clock we loaded the camels and marched up the bed for an hour and a half, when we got into a narrow path between rocks. Not a star shone out to guide us, and the rain making the path slippery, the camels moved unwillingly on, steadying themselves at every step. We lost our way more than once, but at last our guide found the spot he was in search of, and from two till five in the morning we halted at a spring of delicious water, rising from a plateau of fine grass. We marched away hence N.E. and getting on the plain again after an hour, halted near some high tamarisk bushes, with which we made a fire to dry our clothes and bedding. From this point we viewed the hills which we had left, running in a segment of a circle nearly N.E. by S.W. and touching either horizon. They are named Aujeree, and are apparently of volcanic origin, being formed of differently-composed rocky strata, set very irregularly in various coloured earths. On some of the narrow flats between the rocks grew excellent grass, and here and there a small tree.

Close to where we halted was a small water-course, lately dried, and Orauz Kellije said that a rivulet ran in the great bed when the snow melted and the spring rains fell. Thirty miles or so distant on our left was a higher range of hills, named Balkan, running E.N.E. by W.S.W. from horizon to horizon. We learned that there are several springs, and much verdure in them, and that many Toorkmuns pitch their tents there in summer. Of their height or distance we could not form a correct notion, for they were enveloped in mirage, which in this desert distorts the appearance of every distant thing. This "Fata Morgana" was ever round us, now showing the appearance of a lake of water, with whatever was near distinctly reflected in it; and in another view, not only heightening distant objects, but seeming to separate and raise them from the earth. I shall not forget seeing a man in the distance leading two camels; the figures were lengthened out to spectral height, and any body might have been excused for fancying them beings of another world. These magical appearances occurred at all times of day; they were strongest when the air was still; in cloudy or windy weather there were only patches of thick vapour visible here and there.

We were *en route* again at half-past ten, and journeyed all day over a barren white plain, on which there was not a blade of herbage—not a weed. In parts it was strongly impregnated with salt, and portions of soil on which the mineral lay in a thin crust, when refracted in the extreme distance, had the appearance of white buildings. The hard earth sounded under the horses' feet, but some tracks of deep camel footmarks, which crossed the plain, showed that earlier in the season it had been watered. These, and the bones of a camel which lay bleaching in the sun, were the only signs we had of any other living thing having passed over so waste a place. Before us was apparently a forest, but when we neared it at evening, we found only large bushes growing in deep sand, with here and there a small tree; so much did the mirage deceive us, after all our experience of its illusions. A cuckoo was singing on the decayed branch of a small tree; we saw some beautifully-coloured paroquets (the body green, head and wings of a rich brown), as well as a flight of birds like the Indian minas; and, desolate as the scene was, there was a beauty about it in the stillness of broad twilight. Occasionally, during our journey from Goorgaun, we had started a hare from her form; many antelopes bounded across the plain, and the desert rat (an animal rather slighter than a common rat, with a tuft on the tip of its tail, and which springs with four feet, like a kangaroo) was every where common. The Toorkmuns are more particular than the Arabs, who, Burckhardt says, eat this little animal as a dainty: "but," observed my companion, who has travelled in Arabia, "no reptile comes amiss to an Arab, from a snake to a lizard:—and why should it?—Europeans eat frogs!"

We got off the plain after sunset, and travelled for an hour, by a heavy sandy road between weedy jungle, to a large pond of water called Cheen Mohummud, where we rested all night. This is a great halting-place for caravans, and moreover, much esteemed by the Toorkmuns, as the reputed burial-place of one Mohummud Choonee, a Soonnee who succeeded in gaining such influence over these superstitious Tartars, that he thought he could make successful war upon the Persians, but who fell a martyr to his ambition, or as the Toorkmuns have it, his holy zeal. "Thyud Aga," said Peerwullee, "recite a fâteheh! this is sacred ground."

It was now decided that we were ahead of the caravan, because it must come by this road, and there were no late footmarks. Habit enables these sons of the desert to determine with great exactness, by the traces of a caravan, the time that has elapsed since it was at any place; and with regard to route, old Peerwullee, who certainly was not among the most sagacious of his tribe, led us day and night in as true a direction as if he had laid his points down by a compass.

CHAPTER V.

Overtaken by a party from Goorgaun, and obliged to quit the Khiva route.—Led suspiciously about the desert.—Traces of former habitation in this waste.—Meshed-e-Misreaun.—Ill treated, robbed, and quitted by the Goorgaun party.—Gain refuge in a friendly Oubeh.

May 2nd.—Peerwullee arose much refreshed by an unbroken night's rest. I put him at the head of a chapter, because I wish, in justice to ourselves, to contrast our kindness to him with his subsequent rascality. Our servant Abdoollah had frequently given him up his seat on the camel, and taken the leading-string; our stores were always open to him (and he was never tired of asking for sugar or raisins), and this night in particular, thinking him ill from fatigue, we had made tea for him, lent him covering, and in short, put him to bed as one would a sick child.

Early in the morning Orauz Kellije had baked bread in embers, after the Toorkmun fashion,* and we were preparing to resume our route, when four horsemen came upon us at a gallop: a sand-

* The Toorkmuns burn sticks or weeds to ashes, and cover up a cake of unleavened dough in them, turning it every now and then to prevent its burning. Bread thus prepared is excellent.

bank, under which we lay, concealed the road from us, and we had only just time to run to our arms. Seeing that they had no hostile intention, we at first supposed them to be an advanced party from the caravan, but when they came forward and saluted Peerwullee, we recognised two of them; one, Mohummud Kouli, brother to our Goorgaun host, and the second, Bábek, the worthy mentioned in the articles of agreement as brother to our guide. These took Peerwullee aside and conversed with him, while the other two led their foaming horses to the pond, and when they had watered them, galloped them about at speed (their usual practice when the animals are heated). The behaviour of the new comers was any thing but friendly: they took no direct notice of us, but spoke to Peerwullee with much earnestness, in a low tone, turning their eyes upon us every now and then in a manner that plainly showed we were the subject of their conversation, and it may be imagined that we did not feel very comfortable the while.

The conference ended, I plied Bábek with salaam alekooms; but without looking up, he busied himself in wetting earth and drawing a string through it, to make a channel for tobacco-smoke,* and the only word that I could distinguish among the few that he muttered was—*Jehannum.*† He was an ill-looking

* This is the Toorkmaun travelling-pipe; on one end of it they put a pinch of tobacco, and to the other their mouths, and inhale, what my friends described as—" a draught cool as the breath of Paradise."

† H——.

old fellow, for leprosy had whitened parts of his face, and left the others of their original swarthy colour. Mohummud Kouli was a large, bull-necked man, with a good-humoured face, and he had the civility to ask after the state of our brains. "By the extremity of your favour, good," was the Syud's answer, though how far he was justified in saying so is doubtful. The other two were just Toorkmuns; ragged little fellows with small elliptic eyes, and very little either of nose or beard. They were all armed with swords: three of the party had guns of all calibres and fashions, and Bábek carried a light spear. Mohummud Kouli was the leading man of the party: he had been in the service of the Koord chief, and had learned Persian, in which language he mostly addressed us.

To the Syud's question why they had honoured us by coming, they answered, purely to serve us; that one Sooltaun Mohummud Khan, of the Jaffer Bï tribe, had set out with a party to murder and rob us, on the report that our camels were laden with gold ducats; that they had ridden day and night to the defence of their guests, and that we must turn aside with them to a place of safety. Then, leaving us to make up our minds upon words which their countenances belied, they sat themselves down to the contents of our table-cloth, which Abdoollah unrolled before them with a forced alacrity that would have excited mirth in a moment of less alarm.

We were all naturally much flurried by this surprise, and for some time were by no means certain that the new comers would not proceed to direct hostility, so very sour were the looks that they turned upon us: however my friend the Syud was not long in recovering his presence of mind, and in deciding what course to follow, upon reasons which he partly then, and subsequently fully explained to me. There could be no doubt, he said, that these men either suspected our character, or were treacherously disposed towards us; that in the first case there might be truth in their story, yet that they might still be inclined to protect us, as their received guests; while, if they were treacherously minded, we should be as well situated in their hands, as when left to the tender mercies of the said pursuing or any other party, since if we went on our own way, in opposition to our hosts' advice, they would consider themselves absolved from all claims upon their protection; that perhaps indeed they wished for such an excuse to cast us off and then set some of their allies upon us. Although we were a match for these, reasoned my friend, they doubtless knew where to obtain an addition to their numbers; and even supposing that we could dispose of *them*, we had advanced so far into the desert that we could not hope to make good our escape from it, since the first person who met us in our wanderings would consider us in the light of a Godsend, and use means to secure us. Our best plan therefore, he concluded, was, to be guided by our captors, and keep on terms with them as long as possible; to be strictly on our guard, yet endeavour to conceal our distrust, and find out their real intentions. Upon this determination, we told Mohummud Kouli and his party that, being their guests, we would of course go where they chose to take us; and accordingly, when they had broken their fast upon what remained of our bread, we mounted our camel, and allowed them to conduct us back the road we had come.

Peerwullee, I should have observed, kept out of the way, on pretence of watering his camels: when at last the Syud got an opportunity of conferring with him, he said, with a downcast look and shuffling manner, that there was great danger on the road; that if we insisted upon risking it, he would lead us on, but that we had better be advised by our friends, who were good men and meant us well. It was evident that he had been talked over, and that we could place no dependence upon him.

Orauz Kellije several times earnestly requested leave to depart. The Syud told him that it depended upon himself to desert us, but that we would not virtually release him from his pledged word to accompany us to Khiva; and, on the other hand, promised him a good reward if he abided by his engagement. He replied that, having promised to travel with us to his home, he would not go unless we acquitted him; but that as he could not interfere with our hosts' arrangements, he could not much serve us,—while they threatened to take his life if he remained. We could then no longer refuse to release the lad, and therefore gave him some money for his past labours, and declared him free from his promise. Orauz Kellije, as he said, would have been little able to serve us while our captors were averse to his remaining, but we had become good friends upon the road, and I believe we all experienced an increased feeling of helplessness when he said his Allah Yârin, and rode off.

The anxiety of the whole party to get rid of this young man boded us no good; but we felt a security in the possession of our arms, of which they had not attempted to deprive us. When upon the plain again, we struck off west, skirting the jungle, and marched for an hour, until we saw a few camels grazing upon weedy bushes, tended by a half-naked Toorkmun with whom our party held some conversation. We asked if it was in this person's oubeh that we were to take refuge; they answered no, and led us on again still west. Towards evening, they halted and asked for food: of course our stores were produced for our hosts; indeed we were glad to see their thoughts turn upon eating, for we were not without fear that they had led us off the track in order to despatch us quietly. Water they had forgotten to bring, but the deficiency was made up by clarified butter, of which we carried a large pot, and they dressed some rice and raisins after a manner probably unheard of in cookery, making Abdoollah bestir himself to wait upon them; a foretaste, as he ruefully observed, fo the servitude which we might expect for the remaining years of our life.

The long line of the caravan we thought to have travelled with was just in sight at sunset, far off across the plain; they had doubtless passed it and led us west to avoid it. The Syud then addressing our hosts, as they were pleased to call themselves, said, that it was impossible to doubt the goodness of their motive, but that we did not exactly comprehend their intentions regarding us;—that we wished to go to Khiva, not to retrace our route. They answered vaguely, that I was said to be a Russian spy, in Abbas Meerza's confidence, travelling with books, instruments, and much money, on my master's service; and that they must satisfy themselves how far the report was true. We told them to examine our baggage, and convince themselves that we had no wealth, and then escort us to the caravan, where there was force enough to resist the party said to be out against us; or two of their number might come on with us to Khiva, where Russians would certify that I was not of their country, and Indians, that I came from Hindoostân. No!—we must absolutely go with them to Bábek's "oubeh!"—Our friends required an assurance of our safety;—Bábek had killed a horse worth a hundred tomauns in his hurry to serve us;—our baggage would be examined in due season; and finally they would themselves escort us to Allee Kouli Khan at Khiva. It now struck us that they were agents of a higher party; for books and instruments, we felt sure, were not their own thought, and we had expressed no sort of wish to be introduced to Allee Kouli Khan. The dialogue ended with their telling us not to fear, and though we could not exactly do as they bade us, we felt that we had no voice in the matter, and so resolved to await the upshot philosophically.

Our next march was to the spring of clear water in the Aujeree hills, where we halted for two hours; and again marching on till noon, our conductors found another small spring to the right of the road, where they halted and cooked food. Here I was astonished at an instance of Bábek's politeness; he actually took his jubba off, and spread it over a bush, inviting me to repose under the slight shade that it cast. This was comforting, for it looked as if we were not going to be killed; but as a set-off to the civility, one of the others found means to introduce his hand into the pocket of my dress, and to extract a small pocket-compass, before I was even aware of his vicinity. This familiarity was resisted, and, on the Syud's remonstrating, he apologized, saying that he was a Toorkmun, and that their customs were freer than other people's;—a truth of which we could not but feel the force. On the march, our friends usually preceded us, and when they had ridden some distance ahead, they would picket their horses, and stretch themselves to sleep. Though very scantily clothed, they were all excellently mounted; Bábek's horse (a chestnut, that he said he had hired at the death of his own) was a perfect model, and altogether we should have made a very pretty picture.

We deviated a little from our former course through the bed,—ascending the left bank sooner, and keeping along it, we passed over an old burying-ground. The Syud thought that it was Mohummudan, but the head-stones of the graves had fallen, and he did not think it prudent to stay the camel and descend, as we wished to appear as incurious as possible.

This evening they took money from us, and went to purchase a lamb; but they kept us out of sight of the camp from which they obtained this provision. When they returned, they brought with them another brother of our Goorgaun host's, a young man who, according to his story had been obliged to remain behind, in consequence of his horse falling lame; he would now however accompany us, they said, and we might therefore pay the fourth man of their party two tomauns for the trouble he had incurred, and dismiss him. Seeing that we were nearly retracing our steps, we proposed going to Astrabad, as our provision was exhausted. We might fare as Toorkmuns did, they said; and then, in atonement for this lapsus of their real feeling, they put on an affectionate manner. We were on strange terms with them, for while treating us so capriciously, they were in some measure afraid of the Syud. He had in this short time acquired an influence over these superstitious men, though unfortunately it only worked when not opposed to their immediate interests; they thought him a Soonnee, and a great devotee, and always after the first day addressed him by the respectful title of Syud Aga, or as they lispingly pronounced it, *Thyud Aga!*—my lord Syud. Though they never thought of saying their prayers, they seemed much edified when he went through the forms; and being from ignorance very superstitious, they were affected by some obscure words that he here and there threw out. He impressed them with the idea that he was a conjurer, and I an Hakeem: Peerwullee, on whose face we now read every species of villany, had the impudence to request the Syud not to conjure down evil upon him and his family, for that he was our friend; and Bábek, coming to me, bared his arm, and with a piteous look begged me to cure his leprosy, which had come upon him some years before, in consequence of his grief at having been taken prisoner by the Gôklans. I promised to cure him at Astrabad, but he was too old a rat to be caught so easily.

They were anxious to know what could induce such an intimacy between a descendant of the Prophet and an unbeliever, and asked the Syud whether we were on those terms that he would not separate himself from me. He replied, on no account, for that I was one of the good sort of Kaufirs, who read books, and did not pray to images, and that he had taken me for a brother. The last expression relates to a Mohummudan custom (chiefly however observed by the

Sheah sect), by which a man entertaining an excessive friendship for another, makes a solemn vow of it. On the 18th day of the twelfth month (Zehedja), two such friends meet in a mosque, and after the recital of an Arabic formula, bind themselves to be to each other "as brothers in this world and in the next." Such a vow, the Persians say, should be very binding; for they hold with Jeremy Taylor, that fraternity is but a cognation of bodies, but friendship, a union of souls; it is not however rare to see such cronies become bitter enemies, inasmuch as the poorest of the pair is often inclined to pay too little regard to the distinctions of *meum* and *tuum*.

4th.—This morning early, a white-bearded old man, mounted on a pony, overtook us. Him the Syud addressed, appealing to the wisdom that belonged to his years, whether it was fair treatment to guests to lead them about against their will. The old man was flattered by an appeal to what perhaps few had given him credit for, and spoke a few words of remonstrance to our conductors, who deeming it advisable to quiet his sympathy, discovered that our camels were overloaded, and proposed to hire his pony at a good rate. A few trifling things were accordingly put behind his saddle, and in a short time he became the most forward of the party. This old person never failed to halt five times a day for the purpose of saying his prayers, and evidently looked upon himself as a religious, good man. This morning, when Abdoollah put common bread before them, they refused it, and desired him to produce sweet biscuit and raisins. This, from fellows who had lived upon rice and sour milk all their lives, was rather *de trop*, and showed us in what situation we really stood. They seemed to be only restrained by some uncertainty from treating us with indignity, and we judged from their conduct that they were awaiting intelligence from Astrabad.

On remounting, they took our water-skin and rode away with it in a different direction, saying that they would join us at even-fall with water. We kept on till past sunset without seeing them; it then began to rain, and as there was an oubeh in our course, which Peerwullee wished to steer wide of, we exerted our temporary superiority, and threatened to shoot him if he deviated from the route. Hardly knowing whether we were in earnest or not, he led sulkily in the direction of the tents, which he still would have passed, but Abdoollah, jumping down from his camel, seized the leading-string and took us up to them. The whole oubeh had turned out on our approach, and the men coming forward in a body, reproached Peerwullee for wishing to avoid their camp, looking upon the act as a slight to their hospitality. Peerwullee excused himself by saying that we were anxious to join our friends, who were awaiting us, but we gladly accepted the offer of shelter from the rain, and all hands were shortly employed in removing our baggage to the nearest tent.

We recognised the camp as the one at which we

had breakfasted early on the 29th. They boiled sweet rice-milk, and baked bread, and set a meal before us, three brothers of our host, and one or two others, remaining to partake. The Syud's sword (a very good Khorassaun blade) was missing: the master wearied us with protesting that it had not been brought over the threshold of his tent, and the Syud at last begged him not to afflict himself, since it had been doubtless taken by some one curious in sword-blades, who would shortly return it. Peerwullee hastened to prevent our answering their inquiries as to the reason of our return, by saying that Orauz Kouli had sent for us back, there being danger on our road. The repast ended, the Syud took upon himself to say a long Arabic grace, at the conclusion of which all passed their hands down their beards, and said, Allah Ho Acber!* "We'll remain as your guests," said my companion. "You're God's guests," was the reply, "and welcome as long as you choose to remain."—"We may need your shelter; you'll not put us forth?" All exclaimed at the very idea;—we felt saved, and stretched ourselves securely to sleep. We shared the tent with our host *Istalour*, his wife, two children, and an old slave woman. Heavy rain fell at night; once I awoke at the sound of it beating on the tent above us, and felt additionally grateful for shelter from an inclement night that possibly would have decided our fate.

* God is great.

It had been some time day when Peerwullee awoke us to propose a start. The Syud positively declared that he would not budge a step until he should hear from his friends; that we were now guests of Istakour's, and that he, Peerwullee, and his party, might go where they pleased, since tired of being led about the desert, without knowing the why or the wherefore, we released them from their hostship. I shall never forget the tone or the self-satisfied air with which my friend delivered himself of this speech; it sent Peerwullee off in a hurry to communicate the state of affairs to his party, and we enjoyed a delicious breakfast of hot bread and fresh milk, congratulating ourselves upon our great dexterity in having, as we thought, turned tables upon our captors. In about an hour they came in, bringing with them another very ill-looking fellow, who sat down and stared at us. He took up my sword: "Is it a good blade?" I asked him, as he looked alternately at it and me. "It would be better if it were mine," was his laconic answer. The rest seated themselves sulkily to the food that was set before them, not deigning a reply to the Syud's salutation. It was known in camp that we were averse to proceeding with them, and as soon as they came our tent was crowded. I counted thirty-one heads. By degrees their sulkiness wore off, and they talked earnestly with our host's brother, our servant (who alone well understood the language) translating their conversation, from time to time, in a low tone to us.

They wished to take us away. "There must be no force used," said one brother, "it would bring discredit upon our oubeh; if you can persuade them, well." Istakour was then called out to private conference. On his return, the Syud addressed him to the following effect:—"You said last night that we were welcome to remain in your tent; do we now intrude?"—"No; you are welcome."—"Then we're your guests, and will remain here till we hear from our friends at Astrabad;—these men have broken their faith, and we will not go with them; we are your guests." Istakour seemed at a loss how to answer, and spoke a few words in a low tone. Our servant, who was all attention, caught their meaning, and exclaimed, "He says we are the guests of those who brought us, and that he cannot interfere." We were not prepared for this, but, having heard so much about Toorkmun hospitality, I thought that an appeal to it might be effective, and accordingly addressed a speech to the company, which the Syud rendered in Turkish, saying, that we had come among them trusting to their proverbial good faith; that having been falsely dealt with by those who had received us as guests, we threw ourselves upon their protection, and that if they refused us shelter, there was an end to their name for hospitality, &c. Whether my speech lost in the translation, or what, they but laughed at it, and our only hope then lay with the brother of our host, who had spoken for us. "Don't you see," said Bábek earnestly to him,

" that these are not every-day food?" and he whispered (probably the report of our wealth.) " Well! you may take, may kill them, if you please, but no good will come of it; I wash my hands of the matter." And thus our case was disposed of by the man of best feeling among them.

The stolen sword now became the subject of altercation, for our captors, unwilling to let so esteemed an article slip from their fingers, loudly insisted upon its being produced. " Ai! men," was Mohummud Kouli's address to his brethren, " shall it be said that the sword of a *guest* was stolen from him while in your camp?" Istakour said that the whole oubeh should be put upon their oaths. Mohummud Kouli came to the Syud for a Korân. He had not one. " That book in your bundle?"—" Is not a Koran." —" It will do as well;" and, first raising it to his forehead, then kissing it, he carried it off and swore the whole camp without success. He then came to the Syud for a tomaun, by means of which he said he might perhaps learn where the sword was; but, strange to say among such rogues, gold did no more than the oath. During this, one of the party came in and pressed us to go, declaring that, if we attempted to stay and bring reproach upon them, they would take our lives. The Syud coolly answered, that if they were in killing mood they might kill him where he sat, and then, perhaps, some good Mooselmaun would give him decent burial; that if they wished to sell us, they might make us over to the master of the tent, for whom we would find ransom A very old woman, who had frequently come into the tent (as it had appeared merely to look at us), took the opportunity of our being alone for a moment to pass close by us, and, holding up her hand with a warning gesture, she said earnestly several times, "Getmeh! getmeh!"—Don't go! Before we had time to remark to each other upon these words, the tent was again filled. The Syud, addressing the master, said, "You put us forth then? where are your words of last night?"—"You are welcome to remain if you can arrange it with *them.*"—"Will you allow force to be used against us in your tent?"—"They do not wish to use force, but you are their guests, not mine; a Toorkmun cannot deprive another of his guests." The making guests of us per force, enabled them to put their own interpretation upon the law; and though they would hardly have allowed hands to be laid on us, we saw little use in remaining where so little sympathy was felt for us, so told Mohummud Kouli he might load the camels.

Meanwhile our servant had spoken apart with Istakour, who swore that for ten tomauns he would take a letter to our friends, setting out at nightfall. It seemed of little consequence who got our money, and there was a chance of Istakour's keeping his word in this instance, as we promised him further reward if he did; so the Syud hastily wrote a few words to our Astrabad friends, explaining our situation, and begging them to stir in our behalf. Istakour had but just gone out with the money and letter when Mohummud Kouli entered, and warned us, on peril of our lives, not to attempt to send a letter by other hands than theirs. It struck us that Istakour had betrayed us, but nothing more was said. The old woman stood in the doorway of the tent as we went out, and twice gave me her benediction. I never felt kindness so much, and hope the blessing may return a hundred-fold upon her own head. Abdoollah said that she was an enfranchised slave; perhaps she had not quite forgotten her home.

None of the men vouchsafed an Allah Yárin; they remained at a distance from the camels, sulky at having been made to swear that they were not thieves. When clear of the encampment, Mohummud Kouli rode close up, and affecting to be deeply hurt at our distrusting them, bade us fear nothing. The Syud answered with much discretion, that to threaten men's lives, and then bid them not fear, was acting very inconsistently, but that we did not fear; first, because our lives could only be taken by the will of Him that gave them; secondly, that we both could and would defend them; and that for every injury done to us, our friends would return ten-fold upon Orauz Kouli's family. This was the only language we could hold after what had passed, and though they put on a very affectionate demeanour, it sat but awkwardly upon them. In the evening, they came for money to purchase a lamb, saying, "Though we're your hosts, we must trust to you for food till we get home, for we rode in haste to serve you with only our swords; these are at your service, and we are your slaves. "Then escort us to Astrabad." "You must go to Bábek's oubeh." The lastnamed worthy went off, as he said, in search of this oubeh, and we saw no more of him that day.

Early in the morning of the 6th, we came to an extensive burying-ground, where there were several large stuccoed Goombuz* in tolerable repair. Round one of these, which was built upon a hillock, the old man led us to Ziarut,† and, not to be out of fashion, we also tramped three times round it. Outside, near the door, was fixed in the wall a small black slab, about the size of a pane of glass. This, the old Toorkmun said, was one of three which fell from heaven; that Abraham, on receiving command to build Mecca, had commenced it here, but that subsequently ordered to found the city in Arabia, he had left this stone to console the people of Toorkmania. The second stone he said was at Meshed the Holy in Khorassaun; and the third all the world knew to be in the Caaba at Mecca. The interior of this temple was a well-sized apartment. There was a stone in a niche, on which were cut sentences in

* Domed mausoleums.

† The ceremony of walking round a sanctified place, which is supposed to balance many sins. My friend feared that they were compounding for that of killing us, and had come thither to make the dead "*hallal*," as the Wahabee pirates thought they did, by exclaiming "Allah Ho Acber!" when they cut their victims' throats.

large "Kufi" character; the Syud deciphered the first word, "Bismillah," and guessed the verse to be the opening one of the Korân. From the centre of the roof hung an iron lamp, and in one corner was an old chest, containing a few leaves of the Korân and slips of manuscript, and also many coloured rags, left there by votaries. These last are evidences of a custom which prevails all over the East, and which, though degenerated into a superstition, may perhaps be traced back to the early vows of the Hebrews. A man who has set his heart on any thing, (among the Toorkmuns generally an increase of camels or mares,) a woman who has a sick infant, or who is childless, goes to a spot reputed holy, and ties a piece of string or leaves a rag there. If the wishes of the votaries come to pass, they repair with joy to the spot, and remove their marks, making a feast according to the extent of their means, or setting aside a trifle to be given in charity. If nothing results from the vow, (and, to judge from the number of rags which are to be seen in such places, such is generally the case,) the tatters are suffered to remain, to the shame of the saint at whose shrine they were offered. The Sheahs have a custom of writing small notes, describing their needs and wishes, which they address to their twelfth Imaum, *Mehdee*, who is invisibly roving the earth, and who is to become apparent when Mohummudism declines, and the world becomes very wicked. The notes are either deposited at the shrine of a holy man, or thrown into water (running water is the best), and the Imaum comes to a knowledge of their contents.

Meshed-e-Misreaun was plainly visible about five miles to the west; and, on Bábek's rejoining us, after (as he said) a vain search for his oubeh, we marched on, and passed close under the south wall of the ruined city. It was four-square, each face of somewhat more than three quarters of a mile. I think we counted twenty-five bastions in the south face; they were chiefly of burnt brick, and some were double, like two nuts of one shell. Being on a camel, we could see over the broken wall, before which was a nearly filled up ditch. In the centre of the ruined houses were two very high broken minarets, with a stuccoed mosque in good keeping; and on two sides were remains of high-arched gates, such as now front royal residences in Persia. In advance of the south wall was a watch-tower, and fronting the eastern entrance was a large white mosque in excellent repair. Outside the city had evidently been mixed houses and gardens, and at some miles' distance we passed a broken mosque, round which we thought we could distinguish where the beds and walks of a garden had been, from the rain resting in the former.

Of Meshed-e-Misreaun we could obtain no satisfactory accounts. From what the Toorkmuns said, it was evident that they knew nothing about it. They do not pretend to know when the city was founded, but they ascribe its ruin to an invasion of Kalmuck Tartars. "Formerly," said the old Toorkmun, who acted as our cicerone, "the river Attruk flowed past Meshed-e-Misreaun, and the city was defended against the overflow of its waters by a high dam made of lead. When the Kalmucks came, the city held out against them, and seeing that they could not ride up walls, they were for returning to their own place, when a hero mounted on a gray lame horse, rode up to the dam, and proposed destroying it by fire. His advice was attended to; large fires were lighted, and the lead melting, the waters of the Attruk rushed upon the city and levelled the walls." Some Astrabadees told us that the name of the city formerly was Meshed-e-Mustaun, so called by reason of the temperament of its inhabitants, who were remarkably *must* or swaggering fellows; moreover one of these, seeing that we were keen upon etymology, deduced the word Gôklan from the above-described hero of the gray (Goog) lame (lung) horse. Those who had been within the walls of Meshed-e-Misreaun, said that there were many Kúfi inscriptions; and we learned that coins impressed with the same character had been found there by Toorkmuns, who, unfortunately, not being antiquaries, had sold them to Persian money-changers for a trifle under their weight. No doubt coins could be procured from the ruins in this desert, by means of the Astrabad merchants who are on terms of intimacy with the Toorkmuns. I can scarcely believe, from the fresh appearance of many of the buildings about Meshed-e-Misreaun, that so many as five hundred years have elapsed since it was deserted. There are many other large ruined towns in advance of the present Persian frontier, which probably only fell to ruin when the founder of the Karazmian dynasty invaded Khorassaun at the death of Shah Ismael Sôfi, not three hundred years ago; for Ilbars Sultaun, or his kinsmen acting under his orders, fought with the Toorkmuns as far west as Abulkhan and Mangishlauk.

We kept on towards the sea, a little south of west, meeting no one; but during the whole of this day we viewed marks of buildings and canauts,* which proved that the plain had once been populously tenanted. The remains were evidently Persian, showing that the latter people had yielded to the encroachments of the Tartars, till they had been brought up by the hilly country, which it would not suit the Toorkmuns to occupy.

In the afternoon we halted at a pool of water, in a patch of coarse grass from which our captors started a young antelope; they were immediately off in pursuit, screaming with delight, and firing and reloading their guns at speed; then, taking up points, they drove the animal from one to another till it was tired when one of the horses kicked it down. Old Peerwullee, in his eagerness for the sport, was making off with my carbine, and I had a struggle with him to recover it: he looked very black at this, but any thing was better than parting with our fire-arms.

There were signs of rain, and the Syud reminded

* Water courses.

Mohummud Kouli that he had promised to shelter us in an oubeh that evening. The man answered sulkily that we seemed determined to misunderstand them, and muttering something which sounded like a threat, he ordered the camels to be loaded again. There were two ruined buildings in the distance, but we avoided them, and rode on S.W. till after sunset, when we halted in the plain. By this time the rain had set in, and by their heaping up the baggage so as better to cover it, we saw that we were to remain out all night.

During the last march, our servant had requested us with much earnestness to listen to his advice. "You have had the direction of affairs," said he, "since setting out, and a pretty business you have made of it: now let me direct." We gave him a half promise, and he proceeded to disclose his plan. "You've seen how they have treated us, and how, avoiding all camps, they have brought us to this desert place; I've overheard their words here and there, and their intention is to murder us: now when they have lain themselves down to sleep, let us fall upon them, then seize their horses, and make the best of our way to Astrabad." We at once rejected this murderous and wild proposal, but bethought us of administering a strong dose of laudanum to them in tea; yet again we thought that some might drink too much and be poisoned, and others not take enough to make them sleep; besides, Astrabad was forty fursukhs distant, and we could hardly hope to make our way through the many camps on the road. The sea-coast was near, but there was little chance of our finding a Russian vessel, so we finally resolved upon what proved the best course, to trust in Providence, and keep on our guard.

Mohummud Kouli this evening assisted Abdoollah from off his camel, taking him round the waist, and calling him by the affectionate epithet of "Abdoollah brother." There was, perhaps, never a better subject for a Hogarth than Abdoollah presented when hugged in the embrace of Mohummud Kouli, anxious to appear flattered, yet horror-struck at finding himself in the grasp of one whose every motion he distrusted. The head of the deer which they had caught was turned towards Mecca, and his throat cut with the ceremonies; but they had difficulty in keeping alive in the rain a fire by which to cook their meat. We lay in our kajavahs near the baggage, on which was seated Abdoollah. He had taken it into his head to be offended, because we would not commit cold-blooded murder, and from time to time he vented his ill humour in such expressions as the following:—"Ai Khoda! What asses we were to thrust ourselves among a nation of dogs!"—"Yah Ali! get us out of their hands."—"Didn't Moollâ Nusr Oollah warn you? Didn't I, didn't all the town, warn you? and yet you would come. Aiwah!" —"Dust on your head, ye son of a burned father!" exclaimed the Syud, roused into fury; "is your life more worth than our lives, that you make such a cry about it? If you're killed, you're killed, and there will be one ass the less in the world—Barikullah!" Then Abdoollah would sigh and recite a scrap of Hâfiz, or drop his beads for a "*fall*" (a mode of casting an event, less romantic, but much in the manner of Margaret's decision by the "Forget me not!").

The Toorkmuns ate the deer themselves, and sent us a little rice: when they had finished their meal, they put their guns under the kajavahs, and asked for ours, that they might also cover them from the rain. As it would have been an open declaration of war to have altogether refused, and as I had pistols in my kajavah, I gave up my carbine; but Abdoollah would not be induced to part with his gun; his cloak he insisted upon it would keep it dry, and at last they let him retain it. Contrary to their usual custom, they slept close round us, covering themselves from the rain with such things of ours as they could use for the purpose. Just before we lay back in our kajavahs, Abdoollah put his head between ours, and said with a heavy sigh, "Aiwah! we'll be murdered this night, and then you'll regret that you did not follow my advice." There was something so Irish in the expression, that it was impossible not to smile at it, though there was nothing else very pleasurable in its import. I indeed lay down in the fear that they would attempt our lives: there was something alarming in the alteration of their manner towards us since Bábek's return, and not understanding a word of their language, I was obliged to trust to Abdoollah's interpretation of it; and then the old woman's warning came to mind. Whatever were the Syud's thoughts, he slept upon them; I did not venture to close an eye. Abdoollah, who wished to be on the alert, was overpowered with fatigue; but on the slightest stir he would throw off the cloth that covered him, and start to his feet. They were thus often roused, and abused him for disturbing them; he said that he was dreaming. A drizzling rain was drifting upon us, and, what with wet and feverish uncertainty, I don't think I could pass a more comfortless night.

With the earliest light of day we were all glad to rise. They held a consultation apart, and then coming to us, said that as Bábek's oubeh did not appear to have marched up from Goorgaun, as they had expected, we should but lose time in seeking for it; and that, the threatened danger being past, our best course would be to make a fresh start for Khiva, under their escort. First, however, they said, they must examine our baggage, to see how far the reports concerning us were true; and, as our provisions had been nearly consumed, they would go to Astrabad and buy more for us. The Syud affected to fall in heartily with this plan, for assured that they would not take us to Astrabad, he thought our best chance of relief would lie in a letter of his writing; and with a view to induce them to carry this, he spoke as though we had deposited much money in the hands of our Astrabad friends.

Our effects were regularly inspected, the Syud standing in the midst of them, and explaining the nature of each article produced, with the grace of a lecturer. "In this bag, I beg leave to state for your excellent selves' information, is pepper; in that, ginger and other spices. These are Kerman shawls, and those silk scarfs; and in that bundle are furs—furs for the Khiva market;" and thus our heavy baggage was passed. They appeared disappointed at finding pepper where they looked for ducats; but, said Mohummud Kouli, "now for your private property." The old man was sent to bring in the camels, that he might not view the wealth which they thought would now see the light, and they crowded eagerly round the Syud as he produced two or three small boxes from the luggage-bags. One was a small medicine-chest: they took out vials, held them to the light, smelt, and slowly returned them, evidently not without a suspicion that we were conjurers or alchymists. "And that box?"—"Also contains medicines;"—and under that head we passed our thermometers, (which they took for bottles) and a few small parcels. There remained but one box, in which were some papers and books, and a brass astrolabe. The papers they could not read, so took the Syud's word for their being scraps of poetry, &c.

The books, English and Persian, they raised to their foreheads, and kissed, deeming them sacred ones; and it was farcical enough to see rascals who were robbing us, handing round a volume of "Elphinstone's Caubul," and kissing it reverentially.

Bábek weighed the heavy brass astrolabe in his hand, and, shutting one eye, nodded significantly to his opposite neighbour, as if to say, *so* much weight: we hardly satisfied him that it was not gold. "Where then is your money?" said they. "We have one hundred and forty tomauns in our girdles." These were produced, and the gold pieces were shaken out on a cloth. Their countenances brightened at the sight, and as for Peerwullee, he was so delighted, that he could not help expressing his satisfaction in a sort of hysterical chuckle. "You'll pay Bábek for the horse he killed on your account?"—"You see what little money we have to take us all the way to Hindostan."—"We'll be considerate; say twenty-five tomauns,—he was worth a hundred!—and now for my own trouble," said Mohummud Kouli.—"You best know what your exertions deserve," replied the Syud, resignedly.—"I'll take five tomauns; and, counting out thirty for the deceased horse and himself, he made way for the others. Bábek valued his labours at eight tomauns. "Give Daoud Nuzzer seven,—he came all the way; and Kourban Kouli,—give him six. A tomaun will do for the old man, and then there are the other two. Money was taken for two men who *were* to have joined us, and we were relieved altogether of about half our cash.

The price of the dead horse was sociably divided on the spot, and our bundles of clothes were next looked into. Bábek wanted an alkhaulik, and the red-flowered one would just suit him. Kourban Kouli had no jubba; we could have no possible occasion for three, so he took the best, and borrowed the Syud's green sash to keep it tight to his body. I don't know how far their fancies would have reminded them of wants, had not one of them stumbled upon a chess-board: seizing it with a shout, they called to the Syud to explain the pieces to them, and were presently stretched on the ground, earnestly engaged in a game of chess.—"We must now write for money as well as provisions," said the Syud.—"Good," answered Mohummud Kouli, looking up from his game, "write for what you please, but a word against us, and '*yaik shumsheer!*'—*one* blow of a sword for you." My friend wondered how he could be supposed capable of acting in an underhand manner, and then composed a letter which he hoped would cause the bearer of it to be secured. It was addressed to Ali Khan, Hossein Kouli Aga, and Hâjee Motallib, and it requested them 'to send us three hundred tomauns of *our money in their hands*, and also provisions, since *our friends who had ridden after us*, had had occasion to eat all our stores.' To Ali Khan, my friend added a postscript which he looked upon as the very essence of *double entendre ;* it was founded upon the Khan's parting caution to me, and ran thus: "My companion is sick, send a little *shraub,* for all the *arrack* that we had has fallen to the ground." "Arrack (explained the Syud) signifies perspiration as well as strong spirit; and if Ali Khan has any understanding, he will comprehend that we have been so worked, that all the perspiration has, as it were, gone out of us." I could hardly conceive that the Khan would have perception enough to gather from the words written that we were so completely dried up by sorrow; but knowing that they would have the letter read before delivering it, we could only write guardedly, and if our friend but guessed our situation, there was chance of relief.

We parted with a thousand courtesies; they commending us to the care of Peerwullee, and promising to return in five days with money and provision, and then to escort us to Khiva. Mohummud Kouli followed us some distance, under pretence of paying parting compliments, but in reality with the hope of getting my pistols;—if it was only on a *loan,* he said; but the Syud took an oath against parting with them, and said, "I've sworn it," so he rode off. We had now leisure to reflect upon their past treatment of us, and to compare opinions as to their probable intentions. Abdoollah was of opinion that they had intended to murder us, but that he had twice thwarted their plans; first by forcibly leading the camels up to the oubeh which Peerwullee wished to avoid, and the night before, by sneezing when he saw them conferring together,—a sure mode of causing people to defer what they have on their minds; but when we asked his advice for the future, he could think of no less desperate course than shooting Peerwullee and running away with the camels. It was next to a certainty that if the party returned they would sell us, or take us to Khiva and give us up there as spies; but we were as little able to free ourselves from the half-captivity in which we were held in the desert by one man, as if we had been in the custody of twenty, and our only comfort (if comfort it was) was the Syud's philosophical motto, which may be translated, "Che sara sara."

For the next two days Peerwullee led us about the desert in every direction, flattering himself that we did not know which way we were going, and marching and halting just when it pleased him. The sight of a camel in the distance was sufficient to make him alter his course, and his object evidently was to keep us out of sight till his allies should return. We only saw one solitary individual, who, attracted by our appearance, came within hail, and shouted out, "I must share in that."—"Oh no," returned Peerwullee, "these are guests." This old villain grew positively impudent, talked about requiring a brace of slaves, and a matter of two hundred tomauns, and hinted that we had better make him our friend. We were obliged to assist in loading the camels, no easy work, for the spice-bags were very heavy, and the beasts having dreadful wounds on their backs, would twist their long necks round and gnash their teeth at us when we essayed to tighten the loads on them; the effluvia from these animals was most offensive, and I confess that I began to despond at the idea of slavery among such people.

The whole of the second day we got no water, and the sun being hot, we began to suffer the misery of thirst; we found indeed a well in the afternoon, but the water stank. I could only conceive that Peerwullee had a bladder in his stomach, like a camel, for he did not look at all thirsty, but walked doggedly on with the leading-string under his arm, scarcely vouchsafing a reply to our requests that he would seek for an oubeh. At last the choler of my friend was roused, as we were being led up and down some steep sandhills: preserving with difficulty the equilibrium of our panniers, and rising in his seat, he launched a torrent of invective at Peerwullee that perfectly astounded him. "Hear me, old faithless!" were his words; "are we dogs, or Jews, or Armenians, that you should lead us about like asses over your cursed desert, where there is neither herb nor water? Answer me, dog of hell and accursed! is this your faith? Was it for this I held you by the beard? and do you think to come off free? No, by Allah! if there's a curse in the world: toof!—I spit upon you, you old beast." Just then we got sight of some far-off camels, and told Peerwullee to make for them. He assured us that they belonged to Jaffer

Bïs, who were *enemies*, and would rob us; but being curious to see the contrast between their enmity and his friendship, we insisted upon his going to them, and by using the only argument that prevailed with him (threatening to shoot him), we induced him to obey us. We found two tents, belonging to a party who were on their march, but they told us of an oubeh ten miles off, and by nine at night we reached a Jaffer Bï camp of forty-five tents, pitched in the form of a long horseshoe, under a high ridge of sandhills. The space between was nearly filled with camels, old and young, and the whole looked very picturesque in the moonlight. The camp was called the *Cazee's* oubeh. There was a sound of justice in the name Cazee, and we desired to be taken to his tent; but Peerwullee had ascertained that one of his own (Otaboi) tribe had married into this one, and he had sent on a messenger, he said, to announce that we were coming to be guests in his tent. This was a young man, Ai Doguedi by name; he came out and gave us the Khosh Geldin, and at his order some rice-milk was sent before us, a young negro slave-girl officiating for her mistress, who was sick. Having been in a great measure without meat or drink for two days, even this sour mess tasted very good (so true is the proverb), and as soon as the many who came to look at us had satisfied their curiosity and retired, we lay down to sleep outside the tent.

9th.—Our servant went to try and seduce the

Cazee, but he sang the old song, that we were Peerwullee's guests. Ai Doguedi, our new host, was next sounded; but though he seemed willing to serve us, he said that he could not do so in opposition to Peerwullee. The latter was anxious to get us away again, but hearing that two Astrabad merchants were expected in camp, we determined to remain at all events, and said (what indeed was the truth) that we were unwell from broken rest and want of food, and that we would remain some days as Ai Doguedi's guests to recruit. To the latter we offered a *carte blanche* for his assistance, and soon had the satisfaction of seeing that he was rogue enough to deceive his friend. We told him that if he wished for the merit of serving us, he must send away Peerwullee, and detain us a few days; and this he effected by persuading our guide to go in search of Bábek's oubeh (where he hinted we should be more safely lodged), while he would take us with him to the station they were about to march to.

CHAPTER VI.

Sojourn in the Cazee's oubeh—A march with this camp—Arrival of Persian merchants, through whom a return to Astrabad effected.

MAY 10th.—Peerwullee went off early, and we were accommodated in the tent of Ai Doguedi. The whole day we were subject to the gaze of the idle of this oubeh, who would examine every thing we had about us: a vest of flannel, which I had retained under my Asiatic garb, called forth a shout of surprise, and went far to convict me of being a Russian. One old man who seemed to be considered an oracle, sat for about ten minutes with his chin upon his hand, fixedly staring at us, and at last decided that I was talking *Roos*. We assured him that it was Hindoostanee, but like Hans Van Pelt, he only shook his head;—"and there was a general shaking of heads throughout the assembly." Still we were not treated with any particular incivility; and my friend, with the great ability which he possesses of accommodating himself to the dispositions of those among whom he chances to be thrown, set himself quietly to create a counter-feeling by working on their superstition.

He assumed the air of a punctilious theologian, talked about Mecca Shereef, and took the heads of the company to task for their inattention to certain prescribed ordinances of the Soonnee creed; hinting that out of such negligences arose the evils which enabled infidels (on whom God's curse!) to strike at the root of the true faith. The good effect of this conduct was immediately apparent, for when he produced a large black book upon the orthodox forms of devotion, and began gravely to peruse it, the whole assembly remained respectfully silent until he deigned to look up, and then an old man of the party modestly begged a charm for a sick camel.

The women also, when they could spare a moment from their many labours, came to satisfy their curiosity, bringing with them their unweaned children, and performing for them, *sans cérémonie*, all those little affectionate offices of which mothers are prodigal to their offspring. Many of them were like any thing but women; but whatever case you put a woman's heart into, it is always the same, full of goodness and charity. The mother of our host, seeing that I relished but indifferently the sour rice-milk offered us in the morning, baked bread, and set it before me with fresh milk, and the little negro slave-girl was continually endeavouring to show us kindness.

This evening, rather to our astonishment, we discovered that the whole oubeh were very regular in their devotions. The women said their prayers at their tents, and most of the men ranged themselves in a long file behind the Cazee.* My friend took care to be prominent among them, and, when the prayer was ended, endeavoured to gain the good opinion of the leader, by addressing a few words of compliment to him; but he was interrupted in consequence of the arrival of the two expected merchants from Astrabad, whom the Cazee went to welcome as his guests. The Syud got a few words with one of these after dark, and learned that we were reported murdered, and that the sons of Odekka were said to be still ranging the desert.

This proved what we had suspected to be these men's intentions; they had given out a report of our murder, to try the effect of the announcement, in order that they might sell us if our friends appeared resigned to our loss, being prepared at the same time to produce us as saved from the attack of the pretended Jaffer Bï party, in case it should appear that we had patrons influential enough to cause annoyance to their relations on Goorgaun. The certainty of this made us determine to risk any thing rather than put ourselves in their hands again, and one of the least romantic of our schemes was purchasing a tent and a few camels, and becoming denizens of the

* The way in which all Mooselmauns pray together. A leader stands out in front of a file of men, and goes through the motions like a fugleman. This is a post of honour, and many and bitter are the jealousies that mingle with the more devout feelings of two rival doctors of divinity. "Whom do you pray behind? is a question often asked.

Jaffer Bï, until our friends should take measures altogether to release us.

11th.—The tents had been partly stripped the night before, and with the earliest dawn the whole camp was in motion. The tents were struck and packed on the roaring camels, the women performing nearly all the labour, abusing their beasts and screaming to each other; very old women and young children were stowed away between large felts, and balanced by various articles of domestic furniture; and after half-an-hour of bustle and noise that no description could give an idea of, we fell in and marched away. There were (old and young) six hundred camels to the forty-five tents, and two thousand sheep and goats. We took one line of march, and the sheep were driven ahead by themselves. The women led the camels on foot, and the men, on horses, patrolled on all sides at a great distance.

Nothing could well be conceived more wild or picturesque than this scene; the gipsy-like, elfish-looking creatures called women, stepping resolutely out, leading their strangely-laden camels, by the side of which the young ones trotted. We brought our camel alongside of the two Persians, who were on horseback, and had a most comforting confab with them. They desired us to enlarge our hearts, and eat no sorrow, for that, confident in the virtue of our eminent fortune, they would engage by the oath of our esteemed heads and the life of the Shah, to get us out of the hands of these "dogs without religion."

We thought they promised too much, but the voice of a friend was cheering, and though they were most raggedly attired, we conceived that it might be discretion not to wear good clothes among such a people.

Aga Mohummud Caussim, or as his name was shortly pronounced, A' Mo'mud Caussim, the worst dressed, but still the most respectable-looking of the two, assured us that his "House" had used many arguments to induce him to defer his trip to the desert, but that he had felt an irresistible impulse urging him from home, and that, "Inshallah," it was not for nothing. They were guests they said of the Cazee, who for their sakes would serve us as far as lay in his power; and there was something so hearty in the spirit of freemasonry (if I may dignify Sheahism with the term) with which they set about procuring the Syud's release, that we could not help feeling sanguine about the result. Abdoollah, or (as he now insisted upon being called among ourselves) Meshedee-Norouz, was a changed man: his spirits had been broken by hard labour and sorrow, but now his joy knew no bounds. "Hei Kaufir!" was his continual exclamation, "murdered, they declared us!! but please God we'll burn the fathers of them yet;" "Ai! broder, Jan-e-mun!" "O brother! my life! *but* get us back to the Hummaum* of Astrabad, and if I put foot among your Toorkmuns again, say, 'His father was a dog.'"

* Bath.

We marched about twelve miles north, but did not pitch tents at our ground, merely setting up two pieces of the stickwork, and throwing a cloth over them, to avoid the hot rays of the sun. Videttes were set early in the evening, and except by the occasional bark of a dog, the deep silence of the camp was not broken till dawn, when the tumult of the day before drove away every idea of sleep.

12th.—This day we marched somewhat more than twelve miles to between two high ridges of sand, where the tents were pitched. With the exception of one heavy piece of wood forming the top, that required to be held in the air awhile by four persons, the tent was put together by the little negro girl; and as for neatness and comfort these tents surpass all others, I may here give a description of them.

Four pieces of framework (made of light sticks loosely pivoted on each other, so that they may be drawn out, or together, at pleasure*) are set up in a circle of twelve feet diameter, place being left for the lintels of a wooden door. To the top of this frame are tied the ends of many long pliant sticks, which bend up in the shape of a dome, and are fixed in a circular hoop of wood, which forms the top and the chimney of the tent. Over this skeleton work are laid large cloths of thick black felt: they are raised on forked sticks, tied round the dome, and kept close by a broad band which goes round the centre of the whole. Not a pin or a pole is required for these

* Like the toy of moveable soldiers, or ladies' "lazy scissors."

tents, they are roomy, and a defence against all weathers, and one is no more than a load for a camel.

I certainly think that a hint might be taken from the Toorkmuns in this particular, and that tents something after this fashion might be contrived, better adapted for military purposes than those which we use. A large camp could be pitched in a small space, be better defended, and not so easily set on fire; felts will burn to tinder rather than blaze, and they are in a great degree waterproof. In India especially, where troops frequently arrive at stations at which there are no quarters for them, these tents would be invaluable; soldiers might be out at all seasons under such covering.

This evening the Syud went in the company of our Persian friends to see the Cazee: he appealed to this elder in the name of their common religion, desiring him not to forget that a Cazee was a man selected, for his superior knowledge and sanctity, to see justice done; assuring him that we had not been taken in a chuppao, but that we had come to Goorgaun as guests, and consequently that none of Orauz Kouli's connexions were justified in constraining our inclinations.

The Persians not only corroborated these assertions, but declared that our friends, hearing that we had been prevented from going to Khiva, were anxious for our return to Astrabad, and had solicited them to leave their homes some days sooner than had been their intention, in order to find us and escort us back. The Cazee was perhaps aware that his guests were stretching a point, but still they were his guests, and he felt bound to attend to their wishes. Perhaps too the Syud's speech roused a dignified feeling in him. He expressed a willingness to see justice done us, and after the Syud had talked our case over with the Persians and him, it was resolved that one of our new allies should set out for Astrabad on the morrow, and apprize our friends there of our situation; but, to our great disappointment, early next morning came Peerwullee, bringing with him a boy, the son (he said) of Bábek. This he thought would show that he had found the oubeh, but he was much disconcerted when we told him that we felt ourselves so comfortable where we were, that we would remain. He protested loudly against the breach of Toorkmun honour in those who would escort our messenger, and his departure was accordingly stayed. Still Peerwullee could not force us away, so he sent off the boy with intelligence, and remained to keep watch over us.

We had gained considerably upon the good opinion of this oubeh, a circumstance of which our Persian friends apprized us operating greatly in our favour. We learned that ill-blood existed between the Otabois and Jaffer Bïs, in consequence of a quarrel of which I shall presently speak; and the Syud, with a spirit worthy of Machiavel, set himself to increase this feeling. Whenever a party assembled round us (and it was not often that we were alone), he commenced an attack upon Peerwullee, lamenting that a Mooselmaun, and a Toorkmun, should behave so villanously, shaming his religion, and bringing the hospitality of his countrymen into reproach. "If," he used to say, "you had not yourselves known the cowardly spirit of the Otabois, you might not believe that they named you Jaffer Bïs as those who wished to rob and murder us! Ullah! that such men should call themselves Mooselmauns!"—He talked much of the dignity of the Prophet, (upon whom God's peace!) as violated in the person of his descendant, and of the sure vengeance that would follow; at other times, he uttered hard Arabic sentences, calculated to increase his hearers' veneration for his character as a holy and learned man; and with such effect did he play the latter part, that he had to use an entire deer-skin in writing charms for the prosperous increase of man and beast. To the Persians the Syud addressed the epithet of "broder-e-deen-ee" (brother in religion), grieving for every hour spent in the society of dogs who worshipped the three first caliphs, upon whom might all due curses remain!

Abdoollah and I, not to be idle, practised a little physic, and affected an interest in the health of the children. One lucky cure of inflamed eyes caused my fame to spread so rapidly through the camp, that from every tent sick were produced. We were astonished at the great prevalence of disease: in the whole oubeh there were few whose eyes were not partially affected; there were some bad cases of ophthalmia, a stone-blind old woman, and a raving madman. Cutaneous disorders and rheumatism seemed to be common, and we saw cases of leprosy and elephantiasis. One child was brought to us who was a most extraordinary object: on his legs and arms large excrescences of bone had formed; they were covered like the other bones with flesh, and the veins were carried over them: the child's health and spirits did not seem to be affected, and he had the use of his limbs. The mother of this hobgoblin wished me to work an immediate cure upon him, but I made him over to the Syud, who gave him a promissory charm at two months' date; and Abdoollah, calculating that we should be free or disposed of before then, promised the old blind woman a recovery at the same period. We gained over all the women, who, to do them justice, were grateful for the apparent interest we took in their offspring. Some brought presents of *Koussouk*, a root like a radish, but very sweet, which is found in the desert, and which the Toorkmuns dry in the sun, and eat as a dainty. The mother of our host, whose heart I had won with an embrocation of hot vinegar for her lumbago, begged me to remain her guest for any period, rather than go with Peerwullee, of whom she expressed her bad opinion by a very significant gesture. This old lady and I conversed after the manner of Inkle and Yarico, and managed to understand each other admirably, as our signs were chiefly used to express civilities. The little negro-girl, who having lately been bought in

Persia, understood the language of that country, used to listen to Peerwullee's conversations and translate them to us; and little as the Tartar ladies are said to guide their husbands' actions, we found that they were not without a share of that indirect influence which the soft sex every where exercise over the lords of the creation.

The great thing in our favour was, that it was more to the advantage of these men to serve us than to injure us; and as no people are more keenly alive to their interests, they suffered themselves to be persuaded that we were ill-used persons. The Cazee was completely brought round to our side. He was at first scrupulous about receiving any favour, but it was thought expedient to get the better of his delicacy, and we were able to persuade him to accept a turban for himself, scarfs for his two wives, a sash for his son, and one or two other articles, worth in all about fifteen tomauns. As he could read and write, he had acquired that consequence which the ignorant generally give to a man of extra learning, and he had beside a strong party of relations, who were disposed, for kindred-sake, to suit their own wishes to his. He was the best Toorkmun specimen we met with, a mild kind-hearted old man, and in spite of their unwillingness to allow an authority above their own, looked up to by the majority of the camp. Every spring, he said, a party went to the Attruk river to sow *jowgan** and melon-seed on the alluvial banks; a set were then about to

* Holcus sorghum (jawarree).

go, but he would delay their departure, and do his best to send us with them: if not, the Persians should go and work our release at Astrabad.

Peerwullee had a hard time of it, for he had only one stanch ally in the camp (another Otaboi who lived next tent to us, and who, to render him justice, proved his clanship by showing us particular enmity); he felt that the Jaffer Bïs did not like him, and not knowing how we became acquainted with his conversations, he superstitiously thought that the Syud could read his thoughts. A dozen times was he frightened into consenting to our return to Astrabad, but as often did he retract again, and unravel the webs which he caused our friends to weave with so much industry, by starting a fresh difficulty. His object was to gain time, but the sowing party, who were anxious to be gone, became angry at his inconsistency, and frankly said that if he did not make up his mind they would depart, and take the Persians with them, since the latter at least were free to come and go, and they could not prevent their telling what story they pleased at Astrabad. Peerwullee was alarmed, but still not quite persuaded. Seeing what a favourable effect our presents had produced, we determined to establish our character by getting the Cazee to give us the honour of his company at dinner. There were difficulties in the way of this, for it was the part of our host to give the feast; and though he was inclined to assist us from motives of personal interest, he wished to do it in his own way, and was rather impatient of the Cazee's interference. His jealousies however were happily got the better of, and we persuaded him to kill a sheep, and provide a bag of rice, the merchants engaging to bring him a a plentiful supply if he did not himself accompany us to Astrabad, where, they hinted, there would be better things than rice for him. We took care to have it known what guest we expected, and, after sunset prayers, to receive the Cazee and some of his most intimate friends with as much ceremony as we could throw into our manner; for the more honour we showed him, the greater of course was the reflection of it upon ourselves. I say we, because I was a party concerned, not that I took by any means a prominent part in the ceremonies. The Cazee hardly noticed the very humble salute that I made him by crossing my hands upon my breast and bowing, and I was glad to take a low seat, and leave the labour of entertaining him to one so well versed as the Syud in all the minutiæ of etiquette. Little is needed among Toorkmuns, but the Cazee had travelled into Mawara-oon-nuhr, and studied three years at Bokhara Shereef, and was not to be treated *à l'ordinaire*.

We were in all a party of eighteen. A little preliminary conversation was carried on before the pilau was brought, in which the Syud displayed his own learning, without detracting from that of the Cazee. He produced his book upon the Soonnee forms of devotion, and in remarking upon one ordinance, gave a long Arabic quotation that absolutely struck the party dumb. The Cazee turned the book all ways, dipped into parts of it with pretended intimacy, and then, returning it with reverence, said with a modest sigh, that *he* was a poor Cazee, but his *father!*—his father had corrected a book from beginning to end! The Syud with great skill drew out the old man's small stock of knowledge, leading off with one of those scraps of poetry with which every one who has been where Persian is spoken is familiar, and leaving him to finish it, so that the old man at last conceived that he really had studied to some purpose, and his little eyes brightening up, he began to look most kindly on my friend. *Nous autres,* we sat upon our heels in a circle, wonder-struck at the discourse of two such wits, but longing for the introduction of less intellectual food, the savoury steams of which were occasionally blown in upon us. There was little ceremony about the meal; pilau was brought in large wooden bowls, into which hands were thrust as soon as the Cazee had said Bismillah! and there was nothing left in them to show that the food was not approved of. A large bicker of sour camels' milk went round, from which all drank, and then the Cazee said an Arabic grace, all raising their palms the while, and stroking down their beards at the conclusion of it. The Cazee retired as he had come, and the Persians, who accompanied him to his tent, assured us that he had formed a most favourable opinion of the Syud.

16th.—This morning, what with promises and threats, Peerwullee was persuaded to consent to our return to Astrabad. The Syud took him in the mood before the Cazee, but there he jilted us again, saying doggedly, that we were the guests of his friends as well, and that he must hear from them before he consented to our departure. The Cazee reasoned with him, but to very little purpose, and he appeared likely to get the better of us, when the Syud exclaimed with a solemn but impassioned manner, "Well then, it is evident that this is a man without faith or religion, and therefore I'll bare my head, and hold up my hands, and curse him, and his family, camels, mares, and sheep, and all that does, or ever will belong to him. Cazee—do you say Ameen!" Peerwullee's superstition was not proof against this; he hastened to deprecate such a horrible list of calamities, and, kissing the Syud's hands, declared himself willing to act as he wished. They gave him no time to recover himself, but wrote a paper, which he signed in presence of the Cazee and the number of witnesses required by the Mohummudan law. It acknowledged that we were free agents, and in it Peerwullee agreed to accompany us to Astrabad, and in no respect to thwart our wishes. For this we wrote that, out of our esteem for Peerwullee, we would not demand back any part of the money which we had paid him to take us to Khiva, and that we would not detain him or his camels at Astrabad. There was no lack of distrust on either side, but we took each other's professions for no more than they were worth; and our object of getting away was accomplished. We at once hired three horses from Ai Doguedi, and engaged him to accompany Peerwullee, lest he should make off with our baggage. It was arranged that we should set out that very night, as soon as the moon rose, and the Cazee invited us to a farewell dinner. To give colour to the story of their having been sent for us, the Persians left such of their wares as they had not disposed of under their host's charge, and prepared to accompany us, we agreeing to indemnify them for all loss. Peerwullee and Ai Doguedi were sent off at once with the heavy baggage, and we made small packages of our silks and shawls, which we fastened behind our saddles.

The Cazee's party was a small one, composed of ourselves, the Persians, and two of his own relations, whom he said he had selected, with three other trustworthy persons, to be of the sowing party. It was probable, he said, that a party was on the look-out for us, but that if they attempted to take us, those whom he had mentioned would resist them. The Jaffer Bïs being so much more powerful a tribe than the Otaboïs, he thought that the latter would be cautious of commencing a feud; but he frankly told us, that if, in the event of a dispute, we struck the first blow, the consequences would rest with us, for that a feud between tribes was not a thing lightly to be engaged in. We assured him that we were most peaceably disposed, and desired nothing more than a safe return to Astrabad, at which he begged us to fall to, and eat our fill before the moon rose upon us. We tasted *cooppook* (whipped camels' milk), a thick and pleasantly acid drink; the pilau was very good, and our host most anxious that we should do justice to it, but the idea of getting away almost deprived me of appetite. We took a most friendly leave of our kind patron, and then bidding grateful farewell to the family of Ai Doguedi (not forgetting the negro slave-girl), we mounted our horses, and rode out a short distance from the camp, when we halted till the escort party assembled.

There was just light enough to distinguish the figures of those who rode up from different parts of the camp: as during our stay we had become familiar with most of the men's faces, we were anxious to know who accompanied us; presently the moon shone out, and we thought we had reason to be satisfied with the selection. Some carried implements for breaking the ground, the largest of which was a long thick piece of wood, to which was afterwards fastened a wooden share. We distinguished the three men mentioned by the Cazee, in consequence of their being well mounted and armed, as were his two relations. Our Persian allies looked most valiant, with their long matchlocks and innumerable cartouch-boxes, and Abdoollah declared that we might snap our fingers at any Otaboï party. We rode at a brisk pace till daybreak, when we halted for prayers, and slept for two hours. We found a puddle of rain-water some miles beyond, and about two in the afternoon halted for three hours at a ruined mud fort. What had been the ditch was cut into separate reservoirs for rain-water, and there was a well close by, the water of which lay so near to the surface, that, lying on my face, I was able to take some up in the palm of my hand. It was not till the Toorkmuns asked us for food that we found ourselves to be unprovided with any, and we were obliged not only to disappoint them, but to beg some oil-cake which they had. Continuing our march till dark, we halted where there was plenty of grass and a pool of water, and lay down to sleep; but our rest was broken after two hours, and we marched on till dawn the next morning, halted half an hour to graze our horses, and then rode on again till eight, when we arrived at the bank of the river Attruk.

The Caspian was not within view, but we were told that the coast of it was eight miles or so to our right. For nearly twelve miles before we came to the Attruk, the ground which we rode over was sprinkled with little white shells, such as are commonly found on a sea-shore. The Toorkmuns said these shells had been deposited eight years before by an inundation of the sea, of which there were marks two or three miles still further inland. The sky was clear, and the sun very hot, but thirsty as we were, we could not drink the slimy water of the Attruk; therefore setting up a cloth on guns and spears, we made shade enough for our heads, and lay down. The Toorkmuns, I think, have the faculty of sleeping and waking when they choose: those who accompanied us were like dead men the moment their heads touched the ground, and, awaking after two hours' sleep that would have given any body else a brain-fever, exposed as we were to a hot sun, they shook themselves, and, yoking a camel to their rude plough, began to break ground, and to throw in seed as the furrows were opened. Peerwullee, whom we had passed on the road, came up after noon; he thought that we should only travel as far as Attruk under escort of the sowing party, and was at his wit's end when he saw that five of them were about to go on with us. "What have I done," he exclaimed, "that five Jaffer Bïs should step in between me and my guests?" lamenting as if he had been engaged in the most laudable work possible. Ai Doguedi too, who was not aware of the extent of the Cazee's plan, was out of humour because he had not been let into the secret, so that we did not expect that he would take great pains to bring Peerwullee to the Jaffer Bï camp on Goorgaun, to which our Persian friends proposed taking us; however our great object was to get back to Astrabad; so saying a few promising words to Ai Doguedi, and taking civil leave of the sowers, we forded the Attruk, and rode on south.

It was four in the afternoon when we left the Attruk: we slept for two hours in the early part of the night, but rain coming on, we continued our journey. Our road now lay for the most part over fine grass land: it rained incessantly all night, and we were thoroughly soaked, but the sight of the Elborz mountains, Meshedee-Norouz said, made him feel quite comfortable. The camp we looked for had changed ground, and we kept along the Goorgaun some distance in search of it. This gave us an opportunity of observing how thickly the Toorkmuns were encamped upon its banks. Our Persian friends seemed to be known by every body, and from several of the oubehs which we passed, acquaintances came out to speak to them. They seemed surprised to see us, and congratulated us on our safety, for the report of our murder was very general, and on asking the news from Astrabad, my companion had the satisfaction of learning that the Vuzeer had declared the killing a Syud to be an atrocious act.

When we this time forded the Goorgaun, the water was deep: half our saddles were under water, and not only were our great boots filled, but our merchandise was wetted and damaged. The name of our friend's friend was Wullee: he was out, but we were kindly received by his wife, a large good-natured looking woman, who was superintending a dozen girls, most of them with marriage caps on, who were seated carding wool. A large fire was made on the hearth, and we sat down by it to dry ourselves, while a caldron of rice-milk was being boiled. Meshedee-Norouz, in a fit of extravagant happiness, produced two cakes of sugar (all that remained of our store) and threw them into the boiling mess; upon which the Syud heard one of our escort say to his companion, "He *is* an Elchee."* This is a trifling incident, but it shows how watchful a traveller should be in these countries, where his every action is commented upon. Two cakes of sugar were actually of no great value, but to Toorkmuns, who seldom thought of tasting such a refined sweet, the throwing them unconcernedly into a mess of rice-milk, appeared to argue great wealth on our part.

When Wullee came in, we hired three horses from him, for Ai Doguedi had stipulated that his were to be taken no further, doubtless not without good reason. When a Toorkmun sells a horse to one of his own people, he specifies (if necessary) the places it is *not* to be taken to, and if the buyer neglects the caution, and the animal is claimed at any one of them, the loss is his own. But if the seller does not warn a purchaser against any place, and the horse is there proved a stolen one, he must refund the purchase-money. This is very like Yorkshire.

Having refreshed, and partly dried ourselves, we gave presents to our Jaffer Bï guards, and started for Astrabad, under escort of our host Wullee and our two Persian friends. The distance from where this camp was pitched to the town was about fifteen miles; but owing to the badness and narrowness of the paths that we followed through the wood, the ride occupied

* Ambassador.

us nearly five hours and a half. Our short rest had only served to tighten our muscles, and make us sensible of our fatigue; we were all so stiff and wearied that we could with difficulty keep our saddles, and when we reached the house of A' Mo'mud Caussim, we threw ourselves upon the floor, and slept till noon the next day.

Hossein Kouli Aga, we learned, and Hâjee Motallib, were out in the desert searching for us. On the evening of the day after our return they came in, both looking very much the worse for their journey, having been (they declared) six days in the saddle, half the time in rain. Poor old Hâjee Motallib looked quite hideous; for not having had an opportunity of dyeing his beard for some days, it had become piebald—deep orange upon grey stumps. His eyes were bloodshot, water was dropping from every part of him, and the fatigue had caused his old bones to ache so, that when he sat down to have his wet boots taken off, every pull called forth a deep groan. Both our friends were at first much in the humour in which Juliet's nurse returned, after her fatigue in her charge's service: they said we had been precipitate in leaving the party that Orauz Kouli sent to serve us, flinging away our money to relieve ourselves from an imaginary danger, bringing a bad name on our friends, and causing them to fatigue themselves to death for us. We coaxed them a little, and when they had dried and refreshed themselves, succeeded in restoring them to good humour, and convinced them that we had been very fortunate to escape from such rascally hands upon any terms.

Istakour, we learned, had actually brought our letter. On the receipt of it, Hossein Kouli Aga and the old Hâjee had ridden out to Goorgaun, and interrogated Orauz Kouli, who assured them that his kinsmen had gone to our rescue. Not satisfied with this (they said), they took two or three Toorkmuns as a guard, and rode to Istakour's oubeh; but unable to gain further intelligence of us, they returned to Orauz Kouli's camp, and there met Mohummud Kouli, who gave them our letter requesting that money and provisions might be sent to us. The pith of the postscript was lost upon them, but suspecting something wrong from the whole tenour of our epistle, they were about to set out again in search of us, when they learned that we were coming to Astrabad with a party of Jaffer Bïs. They still seemed inclined to believe Orauz Kouli's professions, and stated their conviction that the man's kinsmen had blackened his face by acting entirely against the spirit of his orders; but Ali Khan would not allow them to express a good opinion of their friend. "The Toorkmuns," he said, "were all unbelievers and rascals, and no doubt Orauz Kouli was at the bottom of the plot, if it did not originate on this side of the border, and the only way to recover our property, would be to seize that arch-deceiver and sell him for what we had been robbed of." This advice, we saw, was very displeasing to Hossein Kouli Aga, so we begged that the matter might rest till Ai Doguedi should arrive with what remained of our merchandise; and as the Khan's zeal was grounded on the vanity of his great foresight, his tone moderated when he had obtained a sufficiency of credit for it, and we all dined very sociably together.

Inaction, after the great labour of the last few days, threw us all upon our backs: Meshedee-Norouz and I took fevers, and the Syud complained of a general indisposition, that had turned his liver into water, drawn his intestines tight to his back, and otherwise caused an unprecedented revolution in his system. But the hot bath recovered us all. On the second morning after our return, my friends made the hummaum private for me, and to this kindness I owed my recovery. The bath however into which I had been admitted, was shut up for a week, in consequence of the defilement it had undergone, and even the kindness of my friends was not altogether proof against their prejudice. I was strictly enjoined, when in the bath, not to touch the doors with my hand, but to call the scrubber when I would be let out, &c., and the barber came to me for an extraordinary gratuity, for having shaved my head in direct violation of his religious principles.

On a second occasion when I made use of this luxury, a regular turmoil was excited; for the wife of one of the little great men at the place protested against Ali Khan's right to introduce an infidel into the public bath, and threatened to withdraw her patronage altogether from it. Several lady friends added their protests to hers, and some of the most scrupulous men took the advice of their head Moollâ, as to what degree of impurity the hummaum had contracted in consequence of my visit, and how many days might be considered sufficient for its purification. The Moollâ, though a bigoted man, knew the law in this instance, and decided that as there was much more than the requisite length, breadth, and depth of water in the cistern, I could not defile it; and that with regard to the walls, such parts as I had touched, might be made clean by dashing water on them. Our kind friend the Khan was very indignant at the fuss made, and, protesting that his townsmen were unlearned asses, declared that I should bathe whenever I had a mind to do so; but though the Moollâ's verdict exculpated me, I thought it best to avoid offending any body, and did not go again.

Moollâ Nusr Oollah, who propounded the law in my favour, had a special care for his own conscience; for coming to visit his old friend the Syud a few days after, he expressed a wish to see a thermometer. I took down one and gave it him, and he regarded it with much interest; but on returning it, he went to a small reservoir, and washed his hands, lest, as he told the Syud, any moisture might have been on mine when I gave him the instrument. The eldest son of the heir-apparent to the throne of Persia is so bigoted a man, that on his receiving as presents a gold chronometer and a velvet chair, he ordered them to be purified by immersion in water. But before I say more about Persian manners, I would devote a chapter to a few remarks on the inhabitants of the desert, the many accounts which we received regarding whom, we were able to correct by what we ourselves observed among them.

CHAPTER VII.

Descriptive and Political Remarks concerning the Tribes of the Caspian Desert.

THE Toorkmuns are like other wandering tribes, fond of the name of some virtues, but little inclined to follow the spirit of them at a sacrifice of their own interests. They profess the Soonnee Mohummudan religion, but if they ever had a real regard for any feeling other than superstition, avarice has superseded it. They are in many cases guided more by old custom than by the ordinances of the Mohummudan law, though they are glad of a text which they can turn to their own purposes, and they give great latitude to the one which authorizes them to make war upon Kaufirs. This has by degrees become so common a term with them, that they apply it to every body but themselves: according to the "Soonna," they may make slaves of unbelievers: they look upon a Sheah in a worse light than a Jew or a Christian; but in times when admitted infidels are scarce, they will not scruple to lay hands on foreigners of their own sect. By the law of Bokhara, the chief slave-mart, a man brought there as a captive, who professes himself a Soonnee, must prove himself such by four known Soonnee vouchers, whom he is little likely to find at no warning and far from his home. Some of the most scrupulous Bokharians are averse to purchasing a man who declares himself to be of the true faith, and Soonnees of other nations tell you, that the Toorkmuns, when they capture a stout man who persists in declaring himself orthodox, will prick his tongue so that he cannot articulate, and sell him in that state in the bazaar; or beat him dreadfully, till he is inclined, as the least of evils, to deny his faith, and suffer himself to be sold as an infidel. Such men never can become truly religious, for the greater the heresy of their neighbours, the greater must be their profit.

One Nufsauli Shah, a Soonnee Derveish, related to us how he was once taken prisoner by a party of Toorkmuns, when travelling in company with two Affghauns. His companions made instant declaration of their faith, but this so little satisfied their captors, that they nearly beat them to death, cursing them for impostors, and the Derveish considered that he saved his life by professing himself a Sheah. He was taken to Bokhara, and, not being robust, was sold cheap to a Jew there. Shortly after, he obtained his release in a manner which is sufficiently illustrative of Eastern modesty to deserve relation. Ameer Hyder (Toora), was then king at Bokhara, and the Derveish, following him to the mosque one

Friday, took an opportunity, after prayers, of mounting the pulpit from which the Moollâs lecture, and of haranguing the congregation to the following purpose:—" There are two qualities required for the good of men in this world; when you find them united in one person, reverence and serve that person as God has commanded.—What are those two qualities? —the first is, the faculty of perfectly understanding the Korân; the second, the ability rightly to expound its ordinances, and to cause them to be obeyed. I have travelled into many countries, but have only found one such man: that man is—Ameer Hyder." Palpable as was this flattery, it did not disgust the king, for on returning to his palace, he sent for the Derveish, who, on being led to the presence, told his story so well, that the Shah exclaimed, " Let my friends come forward to ransom this man of God." The obsequious courtiers, eager to merit such a title, on the spot made a subscription, which not only purchased the holy man's liberty, but left him a handsome surplus, and the king was very gracious to him so long as he remained at Bokhara.

The introduction of the Mooselmaun religion among the Toorkmuns has caused some of them to belie their ancestors. There are those among them who (I know not, nor could they well explain, how) call themselves descendants of Abu Bukr, and assume the honorary title of *Mukhdoom.* Others, who trace their descent from Omar, call themselves *Shaikhs*, and those who conceive themselves to be descended from the third Caliph, Oosman, take the surname of *Atta* (the Turkish for father). These holy men are all called Syuds, for the Toorkmuns do not discriminate between the descendants of the Prophet and those of their great Caliphs; they are not expected to fight, except in religious war, their duty being to make up quarrels between individuals and tribes. One who says his prayers often, and who does not smoke, they call a Sooffee. They are all very fond of smoking, but those who affect peculiar sanctity refrain.

My friend the Syud, at the time when we were in the Cazee's oubeh, was whiffing away, with great zest, from an old wooden bowl topped by an earthen cup, when the women of the tent inquired wonderingly how a man who had been to Mecca could smoke. He assured them that, on the contrary, all smoked at Mecca, and then, to do away with any bad impression that might have remained on their minds, he produced a piece of old cloth, which he gave out in shreds, with great solemnity, as part of the tapestry of the Caaba:* this, he afterwards told me with much glee, was a piece of a coat given him by an Armenian friend at Tabreez.

I do not know with whom originated a law that is in existence at Bokhara to prevent smoking. The penalty is a disgraceful one, the offender of whom it is judged proper to make an example, being seated

* The hangings of the Caaba are changed annually, and the old cloths are cut up and given to the pilgrims.

on an ass, and led through the city with his pipe tied about his neck. In points of Mohummudan law, the Oosbegs profess to be guided by the opinions of the Oolema of Constantinople, but a year or two ago, when a Moollâ of that capital came to Bokhara with his pipe, and set himself to reason his Soonnee brethren out of what appeared to him an absurd prejudice, bordering upon the dogma of the Wahabees,* there was talk of opening his mouth from ear to ear, and he was glad to take himself off. The Affghauns have partly borrowed this conceit from their northern neighbours, and the scrupulous among them will only use the weed in the form of snuff, of which they take immoderate quantities. Few of them know why there is a restriction on the indulgence; they can hardly apprehend any intoxicating effects from using it, as an Asiatic would smoke for a week without feeling dizzy, and the only thing at all like a reason for disapproving of it we afterwards heard from an Affghaun Moollâ, who travelled with us from Heraut to Kandahar. "It is written in the traditions," he argued, "that the blessed Prophet (on whom be God's peace!) said, 'He who makes himself like to those of another tribe, becomes as one of that tribe." Now, as Sheahs, Hindoos, and Jews, all smoke, we by smoking should assimilate ourselves to them,—which God forbid!" The Toorkmuns

* The followers of Abd-el-Wahab, the John Knox of the East, who strictly forbad the reformed Mooselmauns either to smoke tobacco or to wear silk.

have got hold of this text, and use it as an apology for selling Affghauns and Hazaurehs, because they are like the Persians.

The Toorkmuns capture many beautiful women in Persia, but prefer making money by selling them in the markets of Khiva and Bokhara, to taking them to wife. The women of pure Tartar blood are proud of it, and ill-disposed to share their lords with strangers, so that, for the sake of peace, a man will content himself with a wife or two of his own race. "*Women!*" said a Toorkmun female, in allusion to the Persian girls; "do you call those thin-skinned daughters of the devil—*women?*"

The condition of these poor captives must be very wretched, torn from their homes, and taken under every indignity and suffering through the desert, to be sold in the Oosbeg markets. The following anecdote, though told *à la Persan*, I believe to be true: the relater was a young man of respectable family, who lived at Meshed, and I give the story in his words. "When Ameer Hyder died, I was sent, I beg to state, with the Elchee who went to carry Hussan Ali Meerza's condolement to the royal family at Bokhara. The day after our arrival at the city, I strolled out into the bazaar with a man of the Mehmaundar's,* and passing down the street, saw that it was lined on either side with groups of men and women. It did not at first strike me that they were prisoners, for every thing

* Host.

was new to me; but on a remark of my companion's, I stayed to observe them, and then my heart turned within me, for they were of my own country and religion, and lotted like beasts, to be sold to worse than infidels. I could do nothing,—nothing but curse their oppressors,—so I very sorrowfully took my way home again. At the head of the bazaar I once more stopped, to watch a bargain that an Oosbeg was driving for a very beautiful Persian girl; *so* beautiful, I beg leave to state, that I have not seen her like. A neck a cubit long;—eyes, large as—this cup (taking up from the table one which helped him to a simile): her tears fell like the rain in spring, and she was altogether so lost in grief, that she appeared bereft of her senses. Her master treated her with the grossest brutality, making her rise and uncover herself, that her intended purchaser might see the beauties of her person. Once he rudely snatched the veil from off her, and God is witness! that when from shame she crossed her arms over her bosom, he cut her on the back with a whip to make her withdraw them: further, what shall I say?—my heart burned, and I became as nothing; but I was powerless, a stranger, and without the means to ransom her.—'Inshallah,' a day will come!"

Sometimes a Toorkmun allows the power of beauty to prevail over his love for lucre, and he takes a foreign prisoner to wife, but there are objections again to this, in the very arbitrary laws that they have in regard to their progeny. A Toorkmun may free his captive, but his issue by her, and their descendants, bear for ever the name of *Koul* (literally slave), though they live among, and on general terms of equality with, the *Eegs*, or free-born. Among the Kouls again there are gentle and simple: the son of a foreign woman by a Toorkmun father is merely a Koul, but for the child of a slave married to a slave, there is an inferior designation, *Dôgmah*. As there is no outward difference between Eegs and Kouls, a stranger would not know one from the other, except perhaps that he might guess, from the thicker beard or handsomer features of a man, that he had not the honour to come altogether of a beardless and noseless race.

In speaking of a Koul, a man will say, Koul-e Otaboï, Koul-e Eelghï, &c.; the term is not one of more reproach than peasant is with us, but the Toorkmuns of unmixed descent do not from old prejudice intermarry with them, and retain certain privileges, the greatest of which extends even to the life of a Koul, which an Eeg may take without entailing on himself the blood feud which would be the consequence of his killing a freeman. On this account it is not considered safe to travel with a Koul, because he cannot defend you against an Eeg who may wish to injure you. By a strange Chinese-like idea of retaliation, though an Eeg may kill a Koul with personal impunity, the clan to whom the murdered man belonged, consider themselves warranted in slaying a Koul from the aggressor's tribe in lieu; but this privilege has its limits, for the freemen esteeming their honour concerned in the protection of the Kouls who live with them, resent an abuse of it, and wedded as the Toorkmuns are to old customs, this one will probably become yearly less influential, as the Kouls already form a large majority among the tribes.

An instance occurred while we were in the desert, which shows the force of the custom: it was the circumstance to which I alluded as causing ill blood between the Jaffer Bïs and Peerwullee's clan. There were two half-brothers of the Jaffer Bï tribe, the one an Eeg, and the second a Koul. The first, speaking rudely to his brother's wife, was taken to task for it, upon which he drew his sword upon his reprover: the Koul fled, but, perceiving himself to be pursued, he stopped, and desired the aggressor to be satisfied with the submission he had rendered him, saying that he fled before him because he was an Eeg, and his elder, not from fear. Some others coming up, mediated the quarrel for the moment, but at night the Koul struck his tent, and took his wife to a tribe of Doogoonchee Yimoots (a branch from the Otaboï tribe), among whom he settled. The Jaffer Bïs, hurt that a family should have forsaken them for a Chooni clan, sent to demand that the woman should be sent back to live with her relations; the Doogoonchees refused to give up those who had sought their protection, and then a body of Jaffer Bïs, coming unawares upon their camp, forcibly carried away a bride, a free-born girl. Still the Doogoonchees would not give up the fugitive, and the quarrel became very bitter: the Jaffer Bïs were the strongest party, and the others, not being able to recover their woman by force, called in the Cazees, who patched up the business by reconciling the brothers. The women were restored, but an ill feeling remained between the tribes, to which we were in a great measure indebted for our release.

The Toorkmuns marry at a very early age, according to the ability of their parents; for as, among these people, a man is influential less on account of his wealth, than from the number of his kindred, it is an object with them all to strengthen themselves by extending their family connexions. There is no betrothing, but children so young even as of six or seven years of age are ceremoniously married, and they live together after a proper interval. The girl brings her clothes, carpets, and the lighter articles of domestic furniture; the lad's father gives him a tent, some camels and sheep, and perhaps a mare, according to his means. It sometimes happens that a man cannot afford to give his son a separate establishment, and he then takes the young man's wife into his own tent, until he is able to provide for him, or till he himself dies and bequeaths his establishment to him. When a son goes out from his father's tent with his portion, he cannot claim further inheritance, which is generally left to those living in the paternal tent. This is rather in accordance with old custom than with Mohummudan law.

It is known when two families are about to form an alliance, and some days before that fixed for the ceremony, friends of the parties ride to the out-campments, and bid guests to the wedding. They assemble, and ride in by twenties and thirties, and when a party come within a little distance of the camp, they put their horses to the gallop, and riding with joyous shouts thrice round the tent of the bridegroom's father, they rein up at his door, and are welcomed with the usual compliments. Their horses are picketed outside the tents, and for that day they are guests of the whole camp, a party in each tent. The next day by noon all the guests have arrived, and from the tent of the bridegroom's father, a camel bearing kajavahs gaily tricked out, is sent with a party of men to the bride's tent. The damsel awaits them, reclining on a carpet outside the tent-door; in her hand is a cord, one end of which is fastened to a horse-pin driven into the ground: she affects to sleep, and over her is thrown a cloth, in pretended concealment of her person. The bridegroom's men advance to carry her off, but she is defended by her male friends, who, armed with sticks, are very liberal of their blows to the opposite party. After having been tolerably well beaten in five or six attacks, the bridegroom's men exclaim against the rough treatment, and they are no longer resisted: they run with shouts to the girl, snatch her up, and, carrying her off to the camel, seat her in the kajavah, and convey her in triumph to a tent pitched next to the host's. The women are all busy preparing food; the men get together and amuse themselves, sitting in circles and listening to the melody of a pipe, or a two-wired guitar; or they converse and tell stories, or play at odd or even, push each other about and halloo, or get up and wrestle in parties, and no small part of their amusement lies in endeavouring to steal from each other as they sit. Spartan-like, they keep what they steal, and pride themselves on their dexterity. At evenfall they seat themselves round the bridal tent, and a Cazee coming, calls for the two sponsors of the parties, and addresses them with some mock words, which mean "Prove your vakeel's commissions." This raises a shout of merriment, and the vakeels, going away to a little distance, return and answer in like mock words—"We are proven." When the mirth excited by this mummery has subsided, a bowl is brought covered with a kerchief, on which is a piece of money; at the same time trays of raisins or sweet rolls are produced, and distributed among the guests as bride-cake. The kerchief and the piece of money are the Cazee's fee. The marriage words being read, and the hands of the couple joined by the Cazee, the nuptial cap is put on the girl's head, and the ceremony being completed, the company wish the pair all sorts of happinesses, when they walk together into the tent, to show that they are "one." Then the rough sports are resumed, and a crier goes about on the part of the bridegroom's father, proclaiming races for the morrow, and inviting all to send their horses to the starting-ground. The best horses have been previously trained, and those that are four years old are sent out a distance of twenty or more miles. Many of our informants seemed angry when we doubted their horses running from the Attruck to the Goorgaun river, which is twenty-seven miles and a half, in the hour; but the same men would not believe me when I told them that a horse from "Yengee doonia" had trotted sixteen miles and a half in an hour; they said it was *impossible*.

The horses are ridden by boys. Starting at dawn of day, they keep up a long trot for two-thirds of the distance, when they change their pace to a canter. Long before they near the goal, they are met by those interested in the race: the latter station themselves at intervals, and shout to encourage the horses, which, now pressed into a gallop, come in to the winning-post amid the acclamations of the assembled crowd. To the owner of the winning horse a prize is awarded, which consists of mares, camels, or sheep, and sometimes money. This donation is proportionate to the wealth of the host; we heard instances of prizes to the value of one hundred tillas (£65) having been given on such occasions by wealthy parents. Then there are races of less distances for younger horses, and a general plate for all untrained nags, for a distance of eight miles or so, the winners of which get smaller prizes. Private races and bets are made; promising horses are sold or exchanged; and, as a Newmarket man would say, "business is done."

On this day, all are guests of the bridegroom's father. He provides meat, rice, flour, &c., and the women of the oubeh assist to cook the same. The work of eating goes on during the best part of the day, flaps of bread, and bowls of soup, or pilau, being served up continually at the master's tent; the guests partake of the good cheer in relief parties, and then, saddling their horses, make their parting compliments to the host, and return to their homes as they came.

These "gatherings" take place in the spring of the year, and the Toorkmuns look forward with much delight to the pleasures of this season. They did not appear to me to have any great taste for either music or poetry, but to the few simple airs that they sing are set words descriptive of the charms of such meetings, and the manly pleasure of war. The inhabitants of Karazm formerly had the fame of being great proficients in the art of music, and it is said that on the occasion of an ambassador's arriving at Petersburg from Karazm, in the year 1714, to treat of an alliance with Peter the Great, the Tzar expressed a liking for the Toorkmun music. What we heard inclined me not to think much of it. I once heard a young man sing through his nose for half an hour, occasionally striking the two wire strings of his guitar: I could not make out any tune, but was told that he was rather an "artiste," and that he had been extemporising the history of a famed horse.

The Toorkmuns differ from other Mohummudan pastoral nations in some of their marriage customs: very few take the authorized complement of wives; I do not think that we saw a tent in which there were more than two. Most commonly, virgins are given to unmarried lads; if a widower desires to wed a maiden, he must pay largely for her, which is a distinction that does not accord with Mohummudan law. For a man to marry a widow is a still more difficult matter; for unlike the Arabs, who consider marriage with a widow ill-omened, the Toorkmuns prefer them, on account of their superior knowledge of the *ménage*, they being of course better acquainted with household duties than unmarried girls. In Arabia but half-price is given for a widow, but the Toorkmun relicts are generally at a considerable premium. It was related as an instance of a man's great generosity, that he gave his daughter, a widow, to the brother of his deceased son-in-law, when he might have gotten to the value of—I am afraid to say how many tomauns for her. Of the passion of love as civilized mortals imagine it, these barbarians have in general but a faint idea; and indeed, if they valued personal beyond other charms, they would soon be disappointed in their wives; for the hard labour that the latter perform, soon causes them to appear wrinkled and aged. A really old Toorkmun woman looks as if she were made of leather, and as much like a witch as any creature that can be imagined; yet the old poets have written very pretty verses on Tartar women, and the ancient kings of Persia used to send into Toorkestaun for beauties for their Harems.

Putting a woman away is a thing hardly known among Toorkmuns, and in this respect again they differ from the Arabs; for, according to Burckhardt, an Arab separates himself from his wife by the easy method of saying, "Thou art divorced," and giving her a she-camel with which to return to the tents of her family: thus, whenever he will be at the expense of a camel, a man may change his wife: the Toorkmuns either are fonder of their women, or they set greater store by their camels, for they have no such law, and would think it bad economy to part with so useful a portion of a domestic establishment. Our friend the Cazee, indeed, had dismissed a wife, but then he had travelled to Bokhara Shereef, and learned the usages of good society. For adultery, either party may be killed by a freeman witness to the guilt; but secret intercourse must be rare among all desert societies who live in small open camps, while dread of summary law, or bloody feuds, probably operates to check advances to the crime. Some Isphahanees, who had seen more of Tartar life than they wished, gave us light accounts of female character to the northward; but the chastity of the Toorkmun women who are settled near the Persian border is a proverb.

The usual food of Toorkmuns is unleavened wheaten or barley bread. They knead the dough in a wooden trough or upon a dried skin, and bake it on the hearth, by covering it up in wood embers. They also prepare meal with oil or clarified butter—the widow of Zareptha's cake!—The loaf being laid upon a cloth, is broken into four pieces; the master says "Bismillah!" as a signal to commence the meal, and a stranger who happened to be present, but not inclined to eat, would break off a morsel and put it in his bosom, not to slight the invitation. As a better food, they eat rice, or *yarma* (bruised wheat), with sour milk, and on great occasions a sheep is killed, and soup or pilau made. Camels are too valuable to be killed for food, but when an animal breaks its leg incurably, or appears likely to die, they cut its throat with the usual ceremonies, and eat it. Their common drink is buttermilk, and, in season, the wealthiest are said to get tipsy on *kimmiz*, or fermented mare's milk, but we did not taste any. To judge from the accounts of former writers, the Toorkmuns are less carnivorous than they were. Mr. Anthony Jenkinson, who travelled across the Caspian desert to Oorgunge in the year 1558, makes no mention of bread, but says that he was "very gently entertained with mare's milk and the flesh of a wild horse;" and Abulghazi Khan relates that

Kian Khan, son of Oguz Khan the great Tartar, gave a feast which lasted ten days and nights, in which time were consumed nine hundred horses, nine thousand sheep, and ninety skinsful of *kimmiz*.

The Toorkmuns pride themselves much on their hospitality, and they feel affronted if a traveller passes their camp without stopping. When a stranger comes to an oubeh, he is invited into the first tent, the master of which welcomes him by taking his hands within his own, and, holding the bridle of his horse, orders his wife to prepare refreshment for their guest. There can hardly be a livelier illustration of the manners of the Patriarchs than this;—instance Abraham's running from his tent-door in the plains of Mamre to meet and welcome the angels, praying them to rest themselves, and comfort their hearts with a morsel of bread; and then his desiring Sarah his wife to make ready quickly three measures of fine meal, knead it, and make cakes upon the hearth. The manners in particular of the pastoral nations in Asia have undergone so little change, that you may see among them illustrations of nearly all the customs that are described in scripture; and a traveller in any part of the East will meet with the most satisfactory evidences of the unaffected veracity of the sacred writers. To an European, the description of many simple oriental customs appears a romance; and connected as they are with so much miraculous anecdote, it is very assuring to find that those who described the lives and actions of the people of antiquity, did it not in any spirit of exaggeration, and that relations which appear to us highly coloured, are told in the simple and natural idiom of the countries and days the writers lived in.

As far as giving to eat and drink, the Toorkmuns are hospitable; but the very man who gives you bread in his tent, will not scruple to fall upon you when you are beyond its precincts. This same hospitality of wandering tribes has been so lauded by poets and others, that it has become a fashion to talk as if the virtue existed only among demi-savages; and a man who exercises it, shall be excused though he be a thief and a cut-throat. Your person is sacred, and your life is to be dearer to him than his own while you are under the shadow of his tent;—but you cannot remain there for ever. Perhaps at the very moment you are eating his salt, your host is thinking how at a future occasion he may best transfer part of your wealth to himself, and when you do meet him on his plain, the odds are very much against you.

We are taken with the poetically expressive idiom of the Arab, who, as a hint to a stranger to surrender his property, says, "Cousin, undress thyself; thy aunt is without a garment;"—but we think it expedient to hang a man who translates and applies the saying in our own country. The fact is that, in our love for the romantic, we judge these wild people nearly by the same standard with which they measure themselves. The Arabs for instance,—we only think of them as a nation of freemen, whose deeds have been chivalrous, and whose annals are told in high-sounding verse, and we overlook their vices; but the Bedouins are perhaps the greatest rogues who wander (read Burckhardt's summary of their character, and ask any one who has gone the land route to Mecca about them). The virtues and vices of all Nomade people are much the same; they entertain exaggerated notions of hospitality and bravery, but they are generally greedy, mean, and thievish; and though they may keep good faith with their own race, they will find means to evade the spirit of a pledge given to a stranger, if it be much to their interest to do so. Their hospitality appears greater than that of settled people, because when travelling they rely upon each other for food and shelter; but they must of necessity do so. Perhaps in earlier times the feeling was exercised more as a virtue, but now there is to the full as much pride as generosity in it, for you will anger a man to the extent of making him your enemy if you pass his tent, though he may not have wherewithal to feed you; and even allowing that a generous feeling prompts his courtesy, it is not so strong a one but that avarice will get the better of it if you have that which tempts him.

An excellent illustration of desert hospitality was given me at Meshed by a Mooselmaun of Lahore, who related how when he went on pilgrimage to Kerbolah, he was robbed on the road by some Bedouins. They took all his money, and the very clothes from his back; "but," said he, "they've the fear of God before them; they are an *hospitable* people: when they had stripped me, and were going away, one of them, seeing me nearly naked, turned back, and drawing an abba from off his own shoulders, bade me take it in the name of God; and afterwards, having nothing, at whatever tent I stayed I got food and a welcome."

One is apt to wonder that men with so few apparent wants should be so very avaricious; but the inhabitants of deserts seem to have no less a desire than more civilized people to possess greater wealth than they have occasion for, and the burden of their prayers is,—more mares, more camels.

In no people is the pride of birth stronger than in the Toorkmuns: these ugly little savages have the most sovereign contempt for their good-looking neighbours the Persians, and believe that they are the only people of any real consequence in the world: the Syud once saying to Peerwullee that he had some thoughts of settling in the desert, and asking for his daughter to wife, was answered gravely by this dirty and ragged old villain,—"Nay, nay, Thyud Aga, a jest's a jest, but nothing of *that*, if you please." Among themselves (excepting the distinction of Eeg and Koul aforementioned), the Toorkmuns possess the French revolutionary motto, "Liberté, Egalité." Some respect is paid to old age, and a man of marked courage or military skill exercises an acknowledged influence over his associates; but, as our rascally guide poetically expressed himself, "Each Toorkmun is lord of his own tent, and a slave to the beck of no man."

I expected to find these Tartars the very Parthians of old, and to witness prodigies done with the bow and arrow, but we hardly saw this weapon: the sword and light lance were in general use, and all who could afford it had a gun of some sort or other. It is, I imagine, chiefly to the cowardice of the Persians that the Toorkmuns owe their great reputation for bravery, for when they exchange blows with the border Koords, who are good soldiers, they are generally worsted; but they are unceasing in their harassing skirmishes, and considering the immense fatigue that both they and their horses can undergo upon the scantiest fare, it must be admitted that few irregular troops are equal to them.

In every tent we observed one or two cast-iron pots, which are brought from Russia; these were placed over the fire on tripods, and every thing was cooked in them. The luxuries of the Toorkmuns are, articles of gayer clothing than they can manufacture themselves, a few spices, coarse sugar, and tobacco. These things they get chiefly from petty merchants who come among them with a "sauf conduit" from Persia. The produce of their flocks, and the felts and carpets which their women make, they barter with these "jaggers," or take across the border themselves and sell in Persia.

In Persia they also sell the camels and horses

which they breed for the purpose. Camels able to carry a load of eighty Tabreez *muns*, or 570 lbs. English, are sold for five tomauns each, 3*l.* 5*s.* The Astrabad merchants purchase yearly for the markets in the interior about two hundred horses, which they obtain at the average price of from twenty-five to thirty-five tomauns. They generally pay the Toorkmuns in merchandise, which they themselves purchase wholesale at Tehraun or elsewhere, and retail at their own prices. Hossein Kouli Aga told me that the Toorkmuns would put extravagant prices upon their well-bred horses, and that as they felt affronted if less were offered, he humoured their pride by affixing a proportionate value upon his goods when he dealt with them. At Khiva, good horses are sold at the rate of from fifteen to twenty tillas each—10*l.* to 13*l.*

The national dress of the Toorkmuns is very similar to that of the Oosbegs: the men wear a shirt and loose trousers, a vest, and a camel-hair cloak, which belts round the waist over all. They cover their heads with a large sheepskin cap, and when on horseback they generally wear hessian boots with pointed iron-tipped heels; but the two first-named articles frequently suffice them, and they are not always dressed in character, for accustomed to relieve travellers of their wardrobes, they find it good economy to wear them. Sometimes, on a journey, instead of boots, they roll folds of cloth round their legs: when at home they go barefooted, or wear a sandal, which is fastened on by a string round the big toe.

The women dress in a long chemise, open down the bosom, which reaches to the naked heels, and covers a pair of trousers. They wear the hair in two long plaited tails, with a bunch and ornament at the end: young girls part theirs *à la Madonna*, but it is the privilege of a married woman to put upon her head a heavy and ugly cap, something like an hussar's: from the back of this drops a red silk scarf, and in front are strung as many gold coins as the husband can afford.

The men, who have an overweening idea of the consequence of their sex, and of their part of it in particular, do little but lounge about and sleep, and the women perform all the labour. Early in the morning they milk the camels, bring water, make buttermilk, and gather bushes to bake bread. After noon they milk the sheep and goats, make curds, or prepare the milk for butter and kooroot, and provide the evening meal. In their leisure hours they occupy themselves in sewing and knitting, or in carding wool. Then they weave carpets, and make felt cloths and horse-clothing, and prepare camel's hair for making jubbas. Many of them are assisted in their labours by slaves, who for the most part live very much like dogs. When men are seated conversing near them, the women draw up a small piece of cloth from their bosoms over their mouths, to signify that they take concern only in their own occupation. It is a wild scene, a Toorkmun camp: all its tenants are astir at daybreak, and the women, after a short busy period, retire to work within their tents: towards evening the men get together, and sit in circles discoursing; the mistress of a tent is seen seated outside knitting; near her is "an old negro-woman, dry and withered as the deserts of Libya," who is churning in a skin hung upon three sticks, or dandling the last born; and the young fry, dirty and naked, except perhaps a small jacket, or skullcap, fantastically covered with coins, bits of metal, or beads and charms, run about in glee like so many imps, screaming and flinging dust on each other, the great game of these unsophisticated children of nature. As the day declines, the camels are driven in, and folded within the camp; soon after the sun has sunk, a few watchers are set; here and there perhaps in a tent, remain for a short time "the light of the candle and the sound of the mill-stones," but soon the whole camp is in still repose.

There certainly is a charm about this mode of life, and I can understand the dislike that a Toorkmun has to living in a city. It has been thought that inhabitants of mountainous countries have the strongest feelings of love for their homes, because they retain the most vivid recollection of the bold scenery that they were born in; but the Swiss or Highlanders scarcely sigh more for their mountains, than do the Arabs and the Toorkmuns for the desert:—home is home all the world over!

When a Toorkmun dies, a Cazee or Moollâ is called in to superintend the last offices. The deceased is washed, sown up in a sack, and put into a shallow grave, over which the earth is heaped in a conical form. The tent in which the person died is struck, and over the ground that it covered is raised a mound of earth, on which is planted a pole with a small flag. Those who are killed in fight with infidels, are honoured with the name of "Shiheed," that is witness (to the true faith); when they can, they bury their dead in holy ground, such as that near Meshed-e-Misreaun. On the third, seventh, and fortieth days after the death, they distribute victuals in alms; and, after a year, they close the obsequies with a feast to the memory of the deceased.

On our way towards Khiva, we advanced about 210 miles beyond Astrabad. From the circumstance of our being taken so far north at first, we were induced to suspect that our guide was not following the usual route, but subsequent inquiries from merchants who had travelled from Astrabad to Khiva, went to prove that he did not mislead us. These travellers stated that they passed Meshed-e-Misreaun and Cheen Mohummud: to the latter place, they said, they made eight days' journey; beyond, to Khiva, twelve days. At Cheen Mohummud they laid in a supply of water for three days, and they found the country beyond more sandy than that from Astrabad. Some said that they went in fewer days: twenty, by al accounts, are the greatest number necessary. The country being plain, a more direct road might doubtless be taken from Astrabad, but the Yimoots are at enmity with the Gôklans, and choose as much as possible a road through the country inhabited by their own tribe. We marched day and night, halting as we found fit spots to graze the camels on. Of the 127 hours that we were on the road from Goorgaun to Cheen Mohummud, we marched 84 hours, and halted 43. The Syud and I both noted the time carefully by watches, and I think we were justified in laying it down as a rule, that caravans march nearly two hours for one that they halt: laden camels advance at the rate of about 2½ miles an hour, so that, if the number of days' march can be ascertained, the distance may be very nearly guessed.

The ordinary communication between the Caspian sea and Karazm is interrupted in summer by the great heats, which render passage across the desert a serious undertaking, and the road may be said to be only open for 9½ months in the year, that is, from the middle of August till the commencement of June.* In winter these plains are travelled, and the snow that lies on them obviates the necessity of carrying water.

The Caspian desert is generally of a light soil,

* From the 26th of April to the 19th of May, the thermometer (in the shade at noon) ranged from 76° to 80° Fahrenheit: one day it rose to 84°, but there was usually a light wind stirring, and the nights were cool.

white, and inclined to be sandy, yet so firm, that in dry weather camels barely leave the print of their feet upon it. This soil produces light thorns and weedy bushes, much of the juicy camel-thorn, a root like the stem of a vine called *Taukh,* and stunted tamarisk-bushes; and in parts spring patches of coarse grass, probably where fresh water is near the surface. Much of the ground is hard, and quite bare, showing occasionally patches of salt, doubtless the cause of the sterility. A third feature is the sand:—this is either spread loosely over the plain, or gathered in broad ridges, which assume some consistency. Near such spots the Toorkmuns prefer to pitch their tents: their camps are more private and sheltered, and good water is found at no great depth.

The Toorkmuns have, I think, obtained credit for more independent strength than they actually enjoy, in consequence of their having been supposed to command unrestrained range over wide plains containing many resources for Nomade life. Now, seeing how scanty is the vegetation of this desert, and how many cattle the roving clans in their several strict divisions possess, it may be concluded, that as many inhabit the interior as it can well support. Unable to raise grain in a dry waste, these errant tent-abiders are dependent either upon Khiva or the Persian frontier for their very bread, unless it suits the Russians to send it to them through ports of the Caspian sea.

We satisfied ourselves that it would not be difficult

for the Toorkmuns, or for a power stronger than them, to reclaim a considerable portion of cultivable land that now lies waste a little way in from the sea. Much of the soil (that especially between the rivers Goorgaun and Attruk) is good, and water is to be had for little labour. The Persians might do this, but they want union and direction. The Russians seem to have established a good understanding with the Toorkmuns settled along the eastern coast of the Caspian, who profiting by the navigators that visit their shore, have not that jealous hatred of them which the inland tribes entertain for strangers who they think would deprive them of their much prized liberty, and whether directly through these coast clans, or through means of the Persians, I confess it would not greatly astonish me to hear of the Russians causing Meshed-e-Misreaun to be reoccupied, or some other conveniently-situated spot near the coast to be inhabited.*

Ever since Peter the Great's expedition in search of the gold dust which was supposed to lie on the banks of the ancient Oxus, when poor Prince Bekowitch's skin was made into a drum by these Tartars, the Russians have been supposed to have an eye upon the eastern coast of the Caspian, with a view to the invasion of Kharazm; and a few years ago, their

* Since the publication of these speculations, a map has been printed (see "Progress and Present Position of Russia in the East") which professing to be compiled from the latest and best authorities, gives the Russians two forts at Mangushlak, besides a land station named *Krasnovodsk* outside the bay of Balkan.—Note to second Edition.

political delegate to the capital of this province, wrote sanguinely about marching to capture Khiva, and revolutionise Tartary, with 3000 of the Czar's regular soldiers; his plan being, to transport this force across the desert through the co-operation of some of the coast Toorkmuns, and to establish himself at Khiva by the additional assistance of those whom he would there liberate from captivity, the long oppressed aborigines, and several other parties unwillingly subject to the Oosbeg masters of this oasis. I do not anticipate that entire revolution in the trade of Asia, and the "shaking to its very centre the enormous commercial superiority of the dominators of the sea," which Colonel Moravieff predicts as consequent upon the taking of Khiva by his countrymen, still, as there can be little doubt that the Russians would gain great political and commercial advantages if they should succeed in establishing their authority at the said place, it may be worth while to examine the idea thrown out, especially as we may be sure that the envoy quoted would never have expressed his conquering zeal so warmly, unless satisfied that his words would be approved by the "Emperor of all the Russias."

It appears from Moravieff's estimate, (and as far as we could learn it is a correct one,) that the Khan of Khiva's authority is owned by about 300,000 souls. Of these, 30,000 are Oosbegs, lords of the soil by right of conquest: 100,000 are Sarts, the inhabitants of the country before the Oosbegs took it: the Kara Kalpacks (who are found chiefly to the south of lake Aral) number as many; and the remainder are Toorkmuns, a few Kirghiz, and some Taujicks, or domesticated people of foreign extract. The Oosbegs, pluming themselves only upon their warlike propensities, behave in an overbearing manner to the other inhabitants of the country. Between them and the Toorkmuns there appears always to have existed great jealousy: Abulghazi Khan,—the fourteenth Oosbeg Sooltaun after Ilbars Khan,—who reigned twenty years over the Kharazm Toorkmuns, details many attempts on their part to free themselves from the obligation of tribute, and the later accounts of Moravieff and Meyendorff, show that time has not much amended their dislike of their conquerors. The other subjects are by all accounts much oppressed, and they might not be sorry to change masters.

Khivah itself is certainly not at present a place of any strength: the people who possess it, though superior irregular cavalry, are not an enemy who could offer effectual opposition to disciplined troops, and I see no reason to doubt the Russians being able, at the favourable season, to march a sufficient force across the desert to beat any Tartar enemies who might muster to oppose them on the banks of the Oxus; but I question whether Colonel Moravieff's 3000 regulars would anything like suffice to lay the ground of his great purposes, and whether, in spite of any battles that they might gain, the

Russians could permanently sustain themselves in Kharazm through the partial aid of Toorkmun tribes. These vagabonds being greatly divided against each other, some of them might be induced to assist the invaders, for interest is a first principle with their race; but they are generally as treacherous as greedy, and any who might help infidel foreigners as long as they plainly had the best of it, would readily find excuse for turning upon them on the first symptom of their being in difficulty. Besides, the very internal disunion upon which the Russians count for auxiliaries, would probably induce all clans opposed to their allies to support the Oosbegs, and increase the difficulty of making lasting terms with any party. Colonel Moravieff was a prisoner during his stay at Khiva, therefore his information could not well be certain. All accounts that we could obtain, lead me to think that there are not so many hundreds of Russian slaves at Khiva as he was told thousands,*

* His information was gained from Russian slaves, who, anxious that he should work their deliverance, would naturally represent their case strongly. David, he says, a Russian slave, at the risk of his life, came at midnight to see him, and stated that there were 3000 Russian and 30,000 Persian slaves at Khiva. Again, when he was leaving Khiva, he found this affecting note rolled up in the barrel of his gun:—"Very noble Sir!—We take the liberty of announcing to you, that in this country there are 3000 Russian slaves, who have to suffer hunger, cold, and the insupportable labours with which they are oppressed, as well as all kinds of insults. Take pity upon our wretched situation, and place it under the eyes of his majesty the emperor. Act so that a poor prisoner may eternally pray to God for you!"

Moravieff was also led to believe that there were as many more Russian slaves in Bokhara. Now Baron Meyendorff, a year afterwards, wrote that there were only between *five and six hundred* in the latter country, which is six times as densely populated as the Khanat of Khiva.

and these, at any rate, could all be taken out of the way. The slaves of other nations who might be left, would for the most part be desirous rather to return to their homes than to remain under Russian rule; but they would find it difficult to get away, and some of these, and the original cultivators of the fine oasis which surrounds Khiva, might doubtless be of service to the conquerors. Still, if in spite of every obstacle the Russians succeeded in thus sustaining themselves at Khiva, their communications with the Caspian would be very uncertain, and it is difficult to imagine of what use such an insulated and distant post would be to them.

Baron Meyendorff, who, in 1820, went on a mission from Orenburg to Bokhara, assists Moravieff's plan, by showing how Khiva could be brought considerably more within reach of the Russians than it at present is, from another quarter. According to his itinerary, two-thirds of the distance from Orenburg to the Aral sea, are through easy hills of clay, in which there is plenty of water. Grain and forage can be raised in the valleys of these hills; they appear to form a stronger frontier than the present one upon the Oural river; and, at the expense of a few slight fortifications, they might be made impervious to the nomade tribes at their foot. To the end of these hills, to "Monts Moughodar," it is a distance of about 434 verstes; it appears that the Russians could extend their frontier thus far, and a glance at a map will explain, better than I in many words could, the advantages of such a position.

Hence, according to the same authority, it would be very practicable to march to Khiva. The Baron points out a land route by which Khiva might be best approached—" A l'ouest, l'Aral est bordée par la chaine des monts Karaghoumbet, dont la pente est roide vers la mer, et douce de l'autre côté, où elle donne naissance à des ruisseaux; ce serait en longeant ces montagnes, à une distance de cinq, dix, et quinze verstes de la mer d'Aral, que des troupes Russes pourraient approcher le plus facilement de Khiva;" and, on the other hand, he shows that they might carry boats or rafts to the Aral sea, and coast it to the mouth of the Oxus, which they might ascend to Khiva. " Cette communication par eau entre le Sir et Khiva est frequentée par de pauvres Kirghiz, et c'est un simple cabotage."

As far as the river Sir (*Jaxartes*), or even beyond, it appears that the Russians might count upon assistance from the Kirghiz, who are partly tributary to them, and nearly all enemies to the Khivians. Meyendorff relates that when the Russian mission went to Bokhara, on the fine banks of the river Ilek they joined the camp of—" le puissant Sooltaun Kirghiz, Haroon-Ghazi, Aboul-Ghazi," who, pursuant to an offer made to the military governor of Orenburg, waited with some hundreds of devoted Kirghiz, to escort them to the Sir:—" pour témoigner, par cet acte de bienveillance, tout l'attachement qu'il portait au gouvernement Russe, dont, à la vérité, il avait grand besoin, à cause de ses querelles avec le Khan de Khiva." And Meyendorff not only dilates upon the influence which the Russians have already acquired over this people, but anticipates the period when they will be generally tributary to Russia. He writes—"Dans les deux autres hordes, les Khans doivent être confirmés dans leur dignité par la Russie, qui exerce même une grande influence sur leur nomination, et qui leur fait prêter serment de fidélité. De même que les hordes nomades des Turkomans paient un tribut aux Khans de Khiva et de Boukharie, de même les Kirghiz pourront un jour devenir tributaires de l'Empereur de Russie; mais il faut préalablement les défendre contre les Khiviens, et leur prouver ainsi l'efficacité d'une protection dont ils sentiront bientôt tout le prix."

If it is rightly said that the Kara Kalpacks, on the south of the Aral sea, are oppressed, poor, and discontented, they might rise to assist, or refrain from attempts to oppose* the invaders, and thus the

* This large, but unwarlike tribe, has shown a disposition to submit to any power for the sake of peace and plenty. According to Meyendorff, in 1740, the Kara Kalpacks inhabited fertile plains immediately south of the Jaxartes, but finding themselves unable to resist frequent invasions by the Kirghiz, they begged protection from the government of *Russia*, as well as from Bokhara and Khiva. Their prayers were unheeded, and their descendants struggled on till 1807, when, in hope of a quieter life, they deserted the good lands of their inheritance, and divided into two hordes, one of which emigrated to a location west of Samarkand, and sat down under the rule of Bokhara, while the other (now in question) settled under the Khan of Khiva, to the south of the Aral sea.

whole road would be open to them; but be this as it may, by throwing on their frontier from Orenburg to Monts Moughodar, the Russians would be able immediately to influence the desert tribes nearest to them, and always having it in their power to force a passage to Khiva, they would greatly support any of their countrymen stationed there according to Mr. Moravieff's plan.

The latter officer seems to imagine, that as the object of his countrymen when established at Khiva, would be to increase the fertility and trade of Kharazm, the different tribes attached to that province who are now held in subjection by Oosbeg masters, might be induced by views of interest, as well as by dread, to settle down under the rule of the "White Emperor;" while the roving Toorkmuns, finding themselves left in possession of their beloved desert, and more advantageously supplied with the necessaries and luxuries of their life than before (Russian slaves excepted), would soon compound with the conquerors of conquerors so far as to yield them passage to and from their new capital, and after a while be glad, for trifling pay, fairly to serve the Czar, whose military power they would as barbarians admire; so that, commencing with the most influential tribes on the roads which they would require to be kept safely open, the Russians might gradually enrol, and more or less discipline, bodies of superior irregular cavalry, who could be used for the still further extension of what Baron Meyendorff terms "*The salutary influence of Russia upon Western Asia.*" These are speculations to which nothing can be confidently replied; I have expressed my belief that the Toorkmuns would in most cases be chiefly influenced by what they thought their immediate interests, and when I look at what we have done in Hindoostan, or, to speak nearer to the point, at what the Russians have done in Persia and in Turkey,* I cannot pronounce that our European rivals may not subdue and manage these Tartars by steadily combining the means suggested by their officers quoted; but at best methinks they would have a troublesome and expensive bargain of Kharazm thus acquired, and in what period of time they could make either this country or its people available for their ulterior purposes, I will not attempt to determine.†

* At Tiflis I saw Persians of the provinces ceded to the Russians, belonging to an irregular corps of, I was told, three thousand men, who, under their commandant, Prince Galitzin, had fought gallantly against the Turks. Nay, there was a troop of Turks who, having taken part with the Russians, had fought boldly against their brethren. Many of these horsemen were decorated with medals and crosses. The great Count of Eriwan, who took pride in showing his troops, remarked,—"We have taken a hint from you in India: those fellows, who as enemies ran before us, when backed by our cannon, fought like heroes."

† Baron Meyendorff is hardly less positive than Colonel Moravieff about the ease of this conquest, or about the necessity of it, for the sake of Russia in particular, and of the Asiatic world in general. Speaking of the trade between Bokhara and Russia, he says, "Ce commerce prendrait de nouveaux accroissements, sans les dangers auquels on est exposé sur la route qui mène de la Boukharie aux possessions russes. Cette route serait parfaitement sûre, si le Khanat de Khiva était soumis à la Russie. Indépendamment d'un grand avantage commercial, l'acquisition de ce khanat aurait celui de diminuer de beaucoup l'affreux

I see a much likelier way of the Russians attaining all their ends on the Oxus, through means of the Persians, whom they may push on in more directions than one, to advance their own purposes. Kharazm was a Persian province in the time of Shah Ismael Sôfi* (I may say so late as in the time of Nadir Shah), and if any energy were introduced into Persian councils, it might again become so. The same difference of religion which led to Shah

commerce d'hommes et de sujets russes que font les Turcomans et les Kirghiz; elle augmenterait aussi l'influence salutaire de la Russie sur l'Asie occidentale; enfin, elle procurerait peu à peu à la Russie le moyen de faire germer et d'étendre, dans cette partie de l'Asie, les bienfaits de la civilization Européenne."

* An early account of Kharazm tells the reason of its name. Kai Khoosroo, the third Persian king of the Kaianian dynasty, crossing the Oxus, took Sarmarcand and Bokhara from Afrasiab, King of Tooran, and next marching to engage that monarch's son Sheidah, he slew him in single combat, and called the province in which he had fought *Khowarezm* (easy victory).

The Arabian conquest extended over this country. When the power of the Caliphs had declined, Mahmood of Ghuzni annexed Kharazm to his empire, and it passed from the hands of his successors into the possession of the Seljook kings of Persia. At the death of Malek Shah, the Hâkim who had been placed over the province declared himself independent, and founded a power which destroyed that of the Seljooks. Chengis Khan caused the Kharazmian power to merge in his immense empire. The province remained with his descendants 120 years, and then fell to petty Oosbeg princes. It is next remarkable as becoming subject to Timour Lung, A.D. 1379. The famous Shah Bukht Sooltaun took it from Timour's descendants in 1498, but he being defeated and slain twelve years afterwards, at Merve, by Shah Ismael, Sôfi, the province reverted to Persia. Again, two years afterwards, the people preferring the Soonnee creed to that of the Sheahs, which Shah Ismael desired to force upon them, revolted, and invited Ilbars Sooltaun, Oosbeg, to come from Toorkestaun and rule over them. They proclaimed him king in 1512, and his descendants have since kept the country.

Ismael's losing Kharazm, still exists as an objection to the Persians recovering the province, but it would not avail against them if they were organized and well backed.

The Persians, I need hardly say I think, are, and long will be, a cat's paw in the hands of the Russians, and if the two agree to destroy the state of Kharazm, they may cause great changes in the political condition of the neighbouring countries. Of the actual superiority of Persian means to his own for the conquest of Khiva, the Czar himself seems to be sufficiently aware, for, since the last war, he has proposed to Abbas Meerza to join with him in an expedition to crush a horde so especially obnoxious to Irân, to liberate the captives of both nations, and to secure Persia against future irruptions.

Abbas Meerza* may send five thousand disciplined troops, half of them Russian deserters in his pay; and through his influence can be obtained light cavalry suited to the service, as well as every supply requisite for the march. The Gôklan Toorkmuns, being subservient to Persia, and having a long standing and bitter feud with the Khivians, would lend their assistance; Abbas Meerza could also command the services of his Koord subjects on the border, who are old enemies of the Tekkah Toorkmuns, and quite a match for them. The whole force would ren-

* Any Persian ruler filling this deceased prince's place, can lend sufficient aid to ensure the success of a Russian expedition against Khiva.—Note to 2d Ed.

dezvous at Astrabad, where supplies, and camels to carry them, could be got together.

In spring, or winter, with such assistance, I conceive that the Russians would make light of a march across the desert to Khiva. The enemy might harass them with skirmishing attacks, but they would probably only attempt regular battle to be convinced of the danger and inutility of it. It is hardly to be imagined that the fine country round Khiva could be entirely laid waste, or that all the people inhabiting the town and its neighbourhood would leave it. If they withdrew into the desert, they could not keep together there long, because they would not find sufficient forage for their cattle; the invaders would command their supplies both at Khiva and in Persia, therefore they would have no choice between submission or abandonment of their country.

The only near place of retreat for those who continued obstinate would be Bokhara. The ruler of this kingdom is in point of religion the "Commander of the Faithful,"* to the Soonnee Mohummudan states east and south of the Oxus, so that on his example would probably depend the conduct of all the latter principalities, in the event of their desiring to form a holy alliance, to repel such a doubly abominable invasion as that presented by a Russian and Persian league would at first appear to them. Between Bokhara and Khiva there has long subsisted

* "Ameer-ool-Moomineen" is the hereditary title of the ruler at "Bokhara the Holy."

hostility; for the people of the smaller state, being better soldiers from their more warlike habits, and rather an intangible enemy from their half nomade life, are enabled, with comparative impunity to annoy the more settled inhabitants of the rich province of Bokhara, and their freebooting ruler (Mohummud Raheem Khan) gives them encouragement to any robbery on which he reaps a per-centage. Meyendorff relates that, some years before his mission, this chief had seduced away from the Trans-Oxanian king a whole tribe of Toorkmuns, who had ever since been proving their new allegiance, by pillaging the country of their old masters. The Bokharians were calling out for decided reprisals upon Mohummud Raheem Khan, but the Ameer could not be moved to put out all his force against this troublesome member of the Oosbeg body politic, whom he could only subdue by taking from him the whole unsettled province of Kharazm—a measure which he deemed inexpedient as well as difficult.* The Khokan chief has for many years maintained a friendly understanding with the Khiva Khan, and displayed enmity against the Ameer, while the rulers of smaller Oosbeg states, that ought to show nothing but submission to the head of their race, have asserted pretensions to independence, which he has been very imperfectly able to curb. These are not circumstances strong enough to make the Ameer wish his

* In 1808 the Ameer of Bokhara took Khiva from the brother of the present Khan, but restored it again.

western neighbours supplanted by Russians or by Persians, but they might operate as inducements to him to fall in with an evil which he would feel he could not avoid, and dispose him to court the friendship of the Russians, rather than to bring their vengeance upon himself by heading against them parties of whose adherence to his standard he could hardly feel sure. It is but twelve days' march, through an easy country, from Khiva to Bokhara, so that the monarch of the latter capital would have his immediate interests to look to. It may be doubted how far his prudence would allow him to join with the Khiva Khan, or any way to enter into hostilities with two such powers as Persia and Russia; but if pride or fanaticism impelled him to a struggle, I conceive that a few trials would convince him of his inability to cope with such a combined enemy in the field, and his keeping up a desultory war would be to little purpose, as Bokhara is a place where an army could well sustain itself,*

* "In all the regions of the earth, (says the Arabian traveller Ibn Haukal,) there is not a more delightful and flourishing country than Ma-war-al-nuhr, especially the district of Bokhara. If a person stand on its ancient citadel and cast his eyes around, nothing is visible on any side but beautiful green and luxuriant herbage, so that he might imagine the green of the earth and the azure of the skies to be blended with each other."—"The vales and buildings and cultivated plains of Bokhara extend above thirteen farsangs by twelve!" &c.

"L'extrême fécondité de cette terre, et l'art avec lequel elle est cultivée, me frappèrent d'admiration.

"Des espaces qui s'étendent à perte de vue, sont tenus avec un soin admirable; on n'y voit pas un pied carré de terre laissé in culte."—*Meyendorff.*

and the invaders could follow up their advantage, if necessary, with fresh troops.

The great shortening of the distance between the present frontier of Russia and that of Bokhara, suggested by Baron Meyendorff, if effected before the invasion, would probably have the effect of checking the Commander of the Faithful's disposition to attack the new comers, and induce him to agree more readily to any proposition that came from their government; and once convinced of their superiority in arms, and means of reaching his territory through Persia, he might perhaps be made submissive by a threat of the Czar's helping his Kuzzilbash ally to regain, and to keep, *all* the country conquered in Toorkestaun by former kings of Iran.

From these considerations I venture to draw the conclusion, that although the allied invaders might at first be resisted, they could keep their ground; and that after a while all parties would look to their interests and come to terms. What arrangement would then be made is perhaps uncertain. It need not be doubted that the Russians would at once assume the government at Khiva, with Persian assistance to sustain them there, if they could conveniently do so; but should such a plan not appear immediately expedient, with the concurrence of the Persians, they might perhaps establish there an Asiatic state directly tributary to the Emperor of Russia; or, transplanting to Khiva, and strengthening there, a colony of Persian subjects, — Koords, or Goklan

Toorkmuns,—they could make Kharazm a Persian province, leave Khiva in the hands of their allies, and support the latter in every way until it suited them to take the place into their own possession. Russian influence must be great wherever Persian rule is established, and while Russia can effectually serve or menace Persia, she can order such arrangements as best answer her own views; but until the Russians are themselves established at Khiva, they will not be able to advance their projects so vigorously as they wish to do, and therefore, although they may not consider the country to be yet in a proper state to receive them, their eventual aim, I conceive, will be to make it fit, and to occupy it.

There is, however, yet a third view which suggests itself. Russia, though she could actually conquer at pleasure here, might find it too expensive and troublesome either to sustain herself, or to uphold Persian authority, in Kharazm; or, desiring to attach Bokhara completely to her interests, she might deem it advisable to remove the galling appearance of her constraining force, and the root of sectarian bitterness which must be planted with any Sheah power established through her direction at Khiva; then she might make a great merit of building up the Tooran monarchy, throw Khiva into Bokhara, and help the Ameer not only to settle the country which is now but nominally his own, but gradually to extend his dominions in the direction of the Indus. The conditions of this friendly aid would of course be, that the Bokharian king should put an entire stop to the capture of Persian as well as Russian subjects, and keep trade roads securely open between both countries: it would be well worth the Ameer's while to make such agreements, and it would be hard if the three powers together could not enforce them upon all the intermediate nomade tribes. All three parties would benefit by this new order of things; most of all Russia, as is fitting. Persia would gain for her people security of life and limb, with a peaceful extension of commerce, and means of forming a cheaper internal government. The Czar would give the Ameer the outward show, and large advantage, of an extensive rule from which Russia would derive unmixed profit, and making himself perfectly at home in the continually-improving territories of his trusty and well-beloved ally, while strengthening his own frontier, he might establish over Tooran a control similar to that which he now exercises over Irân, and use both these empires as levers to his other weighty projects in Asia.

I have ventured to shape out a series of events from what appear to me the most probable of several possible accidents. The complexion of oriental politics is ever varying, but when European diplomacy is opposed to them, the result may be pretty nearly calculated. Russia may fall to pieces, as many expect, and if so, my theories will of course fall with her; but this consummation so devoutly wished may not happen for many a day yet, and it behoves us, at least, in the interim, to guard against injuries that may result to us from our rival's ambition in the East.

The last of my remarks upon the Toorkmuns is that they are a very dirty people. Water is but sparingly used by them, and they wear the same clothes for a shockingly long time. To this cause much of the disease which prevails among them may be attributed, and taking into consideration all things connected with their mode of life, their exposure to the extremes of climate, their bad food, and their total ignorance of medicine, I think a conjecture may be hazarded, that the population of these nomade tribes is not on the increase.

I will not conclude my notice of these barbarians quite in the spirit of Meshedee-Norouz, who prayed that both they, their ancestors, and their posterity might be accursed; but, for humanity's sake, I will express a hope that their power may be broken, even though by the Russians, who as a consequent are, they think, to cause such a change in the political condition of the nations of central Asia, as will eject us from Hindoostan, ruin our commerce, and establish their authority as lords paramount of the universe.

CHAPTER VIII.

Detention at Astrabad—Arrangements for a journey to Meshed with Persian friends.

I BROUGHT up my journal to the 22nd of May, when we were settled at Astrabad, in the house of our new Persian friend Agha Mohummud Caussim. On the 23rd, Ai Doguedi came in to report that he had with great difficulty succeeded in lodging our baggage in a Jaffer Bï oubeh, Peerwullee having refused to come into Astrabad, and gone off with his camels. We paid the hire of horses to bring the things in, but when they came, we remarked a considerable diminution in the size of the spice-bags, and I will be bound Peerwullee has had well-seasoned broth ever since. We sold, at a great loss, what remained of our unlucky venture, and when we had indemnified the Persians for the loss they had sustained in their trade, and rewarded them for their services, we found ourselves without a "sous." Hossein Kouli Agha had bought horses for the Tehraun market with his money, and Hajee Motallib declared that he had not got any; but we were so fortunate as to meet a merchant going to Tehraun, who gave me fifty-five tomauns for a bill upon the British Envoy, and writing to our friends requesting that money might be sent to us at Meshed, we used what we had obtained in equipping ourselves for a journey to that place.

Our intention of immediately starting was however opposed by the one-eyed Vuzeer. This gentleman seemed quite perplexed at our return, and took the Syud to task for not having delivered the letter of introduction that we had on our first coming to Astrabad, in which case, he said, all that had happened might have been prevented. It was explained, that we merely carried the letter as a protection; that having travelled through *his* province, it was needless to observe that we had had no occasion to use it; that the honour of a presentation to the Prince would have caused the eyes of all men to be turned upon us, and have made the Toorkmuns unwilling to believe us mere travellers to India by the route of Khiva and Bokhara. "Had not this reason, which your wisdom will at once see the force of, intervened," said the Syud, "nothing would have prevented our hastening to render our homage to a prince who owes his widely-spread fame to the sagacity, learning, ability, and goodness of his minister." Then the Vuzeer talked very big about the Shazadeh's honour being concerned in the recovery of our property, and requested us to remain a few days until proper measures could be taken. The days passed without bringing us any of the stolen goods, and having from the first set no store upon the minister's promises, we were anxious to be gone; but he was always urgent for a little more time, declaring that the prince would not give us congé till something had been done for us.

We did not spend the time very pleasantly; the weather was rainy, and our house consisted of one confined room and a loft. To say that fleas swarmed, would be but half-describing our misery; they came out at sunset with flights of bloodthirsty mosquitoes, and I used to lie in torture the night long, till the Muezzin sang out the first call to prayer, when surprised by the dawn, these real enemies of our rest, like the fabled powers of darkness, used all suddenly to depart. Then in the day time, when I would have slept, we were broken in upon by the townsmen, who considering that a Feringee, and men who had escaped from the Toorkmuns, were sights not to be seen every day, would intrude themselves upon our privacy, and thinking a salaam alekoom introduction enough, would seat themselves, and pester us with all sorts of questions. It may serve to show how gratuitously Persians will lie, and yet how easily they will believe each other, and also what exaggerated notions they entertain of the wealth of Europeans, when I state that a man who professed to have seen 80,000 tomauns in our cell at the caravansera before we started, was believed;—when it appeared that the Toorkmuns had not found much money among our effects, our good friend Hossein

Kouli Agha was said to have taken charge of our wealth for us; and another party, improving upon this version, hinted that he had ordered us to be made away with, in order that he might appropriate our treasure.

Hossein Kouli Agha was wellnigh frantic at these reports, which he said would bring ruin upon him and his, and it was only his civility that prevented him from openly cursing the day on which he had made our acquaintance. Before we went, however, we were able, from information that we received from various quarters, to guess the party to whom we owed our ill-treatment. When we were at Tehraun, reports were prevalent that Abbas Meerza, aided by the Russians, intended to march into Khorassaun, and thence to proceed to invade Kharazm. When we left Astrabad it was known that I was a Feringee, and some one connecting me with the reports in circulation, I was reported to be a Russian agent of Abbas Meerza's, going into Kharazm, with much money, to spy the land, and seduce tribes on the road, or some such story. The young Shazadeh was silly enough to believe this, and instructed his master of horse (Orauz Kouli) to prevent our journey.

The Vuzeer, who, we were told, was against our being interfered with, not rightly understanding who I was, suffered himself to be persuaded against his better judgment. I am inclined to believe this, because Orauz Kouli had too much at stake to injure us, unless he had been backed by the highest authority at the place: he was servant to the prince, and on terms of great friendship with Hussein Kouli Agha, by whom he profited much in a mercantile way; moreover, Peerwullee told Ai Doguedi in confidence, that the party sent after us had orders to report what wealth we had, and to send our *books* and *instruments* to Astrabad. It is a likely story, because there are few men in authority in Persia who would not order an act of violence and folly if they saw a chance of getting any thing by it.

I should not, however, omit to say that I brought much of the misfortune on myself; for, not thinking it safe to visit Khiva as a mere traveller, I determined, against the opinion of the Syud, to assume the character of a merchant; but as, from the shortness of our stay, we were obliged to buy our merchandise at once, and not in the usual way of traders, the curiosity and suspicion of those with whom we dealt was aroused. My friend's advice was, just to travel to Khiva, and make out any story that circumstances might appear to dictate when we arrived there. I do not know how this would have succeeded, but I am inclined to think, not well. It is indeed safer for a man to be thought a liar than rich in these countries, and if tact could have brought us through, the Syud did not want it; but, considering the character of the Oosbegs, and their jealousy of foreigners, I question whether the consequences of my friend's plan would have been on the whole better for us than those which resulted from mine. It is easy to detect an error when you have suffered from it, and the one which I would particularly notice in my plan is, my having hastily adopted a character, and purchased goods at the prices asked for them.

If I were to travel again in such countries in the disguise of a native, I would take the character of a poor one, but I think that a European can hardly hope to escape detection; for, though he may be conversant with the idioms of the language, his mode of delivery, his manner even of sitting, walking, or riding, in short, his *tout ensemble*, is different from that of an Asiatic, and the very care that he takes not to betray himself, gives him an air that causes him to be noticed. A man may, I think, get on best in the character of a French or Italian doctor. These itinerant gentry are sometimes met with, and, as their country is supposed to be somewhere about the antipodes, they are not viewed with distrust. Among people so ignorant, a Sangrado may pass for a great hakeem, the simplest medicines will cure most of their ailments, and you may tell those who are beyond your skill, that it is not their fate to be cured just then. No character will gain you such good treatment, and it has this great advantage, that it does not oblige you to conceal your religion, or what is worse, to affect the Mohummudan. You may freely use the names of their most esteemed hakeems,—Sokrat and Bokrat, Lokman and Aboo Allee Seina; few will question you, but if you should happen to meet a man of as great pretensions as yourself, and he should begin to try you with queries, ask him whether a shivering fever is a cold or hot disease.

You need not be harassed with apprehensions of putting a patient to death in an unusual manner, such as running a lancet through a vein into an artery, for if you deem phlebotomy requisite, you order a barber to come and operate; and though it may startle you to see him open a seam halfway up the patient's arm, you may rest assured he will not draw too much blood. Then for physic, the stronger you can venture to administer it, the greater your reputation. "On peut tuer deux ou trois dans une année," as Signor Turconi observed, "mais ça arrive toujours!" My friend the doctor was a romancer, and he threw out so many hints about bright eyes that had flashed upon him, and soft tongues that had spoken to him, in the course of his professional career, that my mind was engrossed with thoughts of high-heeled little slippers, and silken skreens, gazelle-like eyes, and henna-tipped fingers, till I became quite anxious to see the mines of dazzling beauty that the Signor described as buried in the depths of the infidels' harems, and to get an insight into the interior economy of Persian houses.

After our return from the desert to Astrabad, I was often applied to for medicine and advice, and did not reject the honourable title of *hakeem*, which was thrust upon me by several of our acquaintances. At first, indeed, I was diffident on the score of my abilities, but after protesting that my knowledge of the noble art of healing was so very slight that it ought not to be called knowledge, I was always overwhelmed with compliments on my modesty, so calling to mind the good success of my Italian acquaintance, I resolved also to have *beaucoup de courage*, and to put the best face upon the business.

The first man who called me in to see his "house" was our friend Hossein Kouli Agha, and I promised myself matter for a good chapter upon Persian harems, knowing that my friend had three wedded wives. I had given his child a lucky dose from a packet I had, labelled "*for children*," and the head lady of the establishment had been seized with a desire to consult me upon a complaint of long standing.

I breakfasted at Hossein Kouli Agha's house, and afterwards, when I expected to be led, like Baba Mustapha in the Arabian Nights, up stairs, down stairs, to my lady's chamber, I found that I was not to go beyond that in which we were seated. At the end of it was a common skreen hung before a low door, and from behind this was slowly thrust the wrinkled hand of an elderly woman, by feeling which I was to decide what ailment possessed the body that it belonged to. In a moment vanished the romance of many days:—henna there was no lack of, for the palm as well as each finger-nail was dyed with it, but the hand looked old enough to belong to a grandmother; a touch was sufficient to convince me that the owner of it laboured under a cold complaint, and

I therefore ordered a hot remedy,—a pill of ginger to be taken twice a week until the patient felt a disinclination to continue it.

After this, my patients were chiefly of two classes,—thin men who wished to become fat, or old men who wanted to be made young again, and as I found more annoyance than amusement in such difficult cases, I gave up practice as far as I was able.

We dismissed Ai Doguedi with what he thought a handsome reward, and a messenger arriving at this time from the desert, with many civil messages from our friend the Cazee, we bought a good quantity of brown sugar, and sent it a present to him, with a letter of fine verses; anxious also to prove ourselves grateful for the kindnesses we had received in his camp, we sent some of our acquaintances there parcels of tobacco, to the slave-girl a gay blanket, and to Ai Doguedi's mother a pair of party-coloured trousers.

Orauz Kouli came to see us, and swore *Wallah! Billah! Tillah!** and by a host of Toorkish oaths, that he was innocent of any ill-intention towards us. His kinsmen, he said, of whom he was very much ashamed, had deceived him, and he had been trying to recover our money, but unfortunately they had spent it all. We did not believe him in this, any more than we did when he promised to lay hands upon their property, and sell it on our account, but we could do nothing; he was servant to the prince, who affected to be exerting his authority on our be-

* Three solemn oaths by the name of the Deity.

half; it would have been slighting that authority to have laid hands upon Orauz Kouli, and in any case we could have done nothing with him. Indeed, as spring was closing, we felt content to bear the loss and say no more about it, so they would let us depart; we therefore intimated to the Vuzeer, that it was positively necessary we should continue our journey, and after a little demur, he fixed the second morning for an audience with the prince.

The usual skirmish about rank and place was carried on between the Vuzeer and the Syud, which ended when the Vuzeer conceded points which he fought about only for etiquette's sake, and early in the morning we repaired to the palace. We were kept waiting in a court of the interior, until the prince's dignity had been wellnigh compromised by his impoliteness. When he condescended to be ready to receive us, we were ushered into a small room, the walls of which were covered with little pieces of mirror-glass, set close together so as to multiply objects without end. On a small carpet at the upper end, near to a large open window of stained glass, sat the young scion of royalty, handsome in appearance and dress, and leaning in a studied attitude upon a jewelled mace. The effect of the mirrored walls was pretty though gaudy; however, seeing that he expected it, we were wonder-struck at the magnificence of the apartment; the Syud expressed unqualified admiration, and the young Shazadeh very complacently said in answer, that in no palace in

Irân, with the exception of that of "the father of the world," was there such a room. The Vuzeer stood leaning on a stick close beneath the window, in a small court wherein a fountain was playing, and from the back of which beautiful green swelling hills ran up to the foot of the wooded mountains.

The prince, after welcoming us, and graciously inquiring about the state of our health, condescended to congratulate us on our good fortune in escaping from the desert, and expressed a hope that his Vuzeer had done all that was requisite for us. The Syud made a suitable, indeed a most elegant reply, complimented the Vuzeer on his having a "Noorshewan" for a master, and the prince on his having an "Aristoo"* for a minister; quoted a couplet significative of the blessings that were enjoyed by a people governed by a beneficent prince, and said that if we had been ill used in the desert, we had been more than indemnified in the days of rest that we had enjoyed under the shadow of the Shazadeh's authority; that by his favour we had all things, and that "Alhumdoolillah" having now to travel through the Shah's dominions, what was there to fear! Considering that our road onward lay through a country which a Persian travels "Tewokul be Khoda" (specially trusting in Providence), this was pretty well; it was suited however to the capacity of the person to whom it was addressed, and was taken in such excellent part by him, that he dismissed us with many civil

* Aristotle.

expressions, and our friend Ali Khan, who was witness to the introduction from a distance, said when we had regained our slippers and were walking home, "Mashallah! but the Shazadeh was gracious to you!"

This kind nobleman was a constant and most amusing guest, and helped to pass many that would otherwise have been weary hours. He would drop in of an evening, and fight a battle at chess, or, when more sentimentally inclined, he would chant affecting passages of the Shah-nameh. His voice was like that of a bull, and as he rocked his great body and sang, he would sometimes identify himself with the hero of a tragedy, till the tears ran down his rough cheeks into his black beard. Then being an old soldier, he could tell a good story about the Jung-e-Oroos, the war of the Russians, and he introduced a half-brother of his own, whom he begged us to notice as a regular man-eater in battle, a sort of fellow who dyed his whiskers with the blood of his enemies, and who in the last war, not content with cleaving the head of a Russian footman, dismounted during the fight, and hacked it off with his dagger, then hanging the trophy to his saddlebow, brought it off a present to the heir-apparent.

There was another Khan who used to make one in our assemblies; a very gentlemanlike man, but a thorough Persian: he was very curious about the world of the Franks, but had imbibed such strange notions about us, that he would hardly believe what I told him. He would not be persuaded that their matrimonial law was not reversed in Europe, and that every woman might not take unto herself four husbands: he had read it in a book, and would not be gainsayed. I was able, I hope, to correct some very erroneous impressions that he had formed with regard to the laxity of our moral system, but there was no making him understand the nature of the power exercised by European women. "I see your drift," he said, "and I admire it; you are right to put the thing in its best light, but you will not deny that the *hookum** rests with your women; have you not women kings? and do you not wait on women like slaves, and do whatever they order?—The world call you men of understanding; do your women excel you in this respect, that you bow to them?" A dissertation upon moral female excellence, and its consequent influence over enlightened minds, would have been lost upon the Khan, but I referred him to the days of Alexander the Great, when it was thought no shame to be gallant as well as warlike;— "*Oh! Oonha kaufir boodund,*" was the reply, "they were infidels."

The Khan was a country gentleman, whose world was comprehended within the circle of his horizon, and his notions were contracted accordingly; but we may still hope that the natural gallantry of the Persians will be turned into its proper channel, for the Kuzzilbâshes are quick at imbibing foreign ideas,

* Authority.

and the reaction of their present unworthy system should be sudden and romantic. At Tabreez I had the honour to visit one of the Princes Royal, who in the course of conversation said, with a very good accent, which he had acquired from an intriguing old French lady who had settled herself in Persia with a view to enlighten the natives,—"Nos pauvres femmes sont emprisonnées!" We may yet see the *French of the East* breaking lances for their Lylees and Zuleikhas, and the light of a harem seated in all the pride of her displayed beauty, as the presiding divinity at some Ashby-de-la-Zouch—!

It was in this society that, talking about the Tartar tribes beyond the Oxus, I first heard mention of a very remarkable Eastern ruler of modern times, Shah Moraud Beg, familiarly and *par excellence* called Beggee Jân; a king whose equal has not been known since the days of the Caliph Omar, whose character indeed he appears to have closely imitated, like him, affecting to despise the honours of sovereignty, and descending to undignified and affected actions to display his humility. He surrounded himself with a court of devout and learned doctors, to whose opinion he professed to bow, and assisted by whom he used to sit in open durbar, to judge the people according to the principles of the Mohummudan law. In such assemblies, the party sat on goat-skins which were ranged round the room, and the Shah took any seat, to show that he did not esteem himself above his fellow men in the faith.

He performed the most menial offices; his kitchen establishment consisted of a wooden bowl, an iron caldron, and some earthen pots; he made his own market, cooked his own *pot au feu*, and when he had guests, went round himself to pour water on their hands, and ate from the same bowl with them. He had a donkey of no price, which he would ride without a saddle through the streets of Bokhara, and the common people, charmed by this show of humility, thought that there never had been so single-hearted a man; but many stories which are related of him show that much worldly sagacity lay under his assumed simplicity. He was the Louis XI. of his day; cold-blooded and hypocritical, but superstitious, and covering much craftiness and knowledge of mankind with a quiet and smooth exterior. Not of "Shah Abbas the Great" are more good stories told than of "Beggee Jân;" in hearing them related, you cannot but be struck with the recurrence of phrases and idioms that appeared so singular and amusing in the "Arabian Nights," and it is to be regretted that an Omar al Siftee does not exist to imbody the tales that are related of these two monarchs in another series of a thousand and one evenings.

The following striking anecdote was told my friend by an old Cujjer nobleman, who being governor at Merve when it was taken by Shah Moraud, was carried away prisoner to Bokhara. One day as the Shah was riding through the city on his ass, followed by a cortège of Oosbeg, Affghaun, and Kuzzilbash nobles, he led the way to the coppersmith's bazaar, and stopped at the shop of an artisan, to whom he addressed the following singular conversation: "Salaam alekoom." — "Alekoom salaam." — "Your health is good?"—"By your condescension and favour."—"I am concerned to see you, born a gentleman, toiling in an occupation that is beneath you: rather abandon this profession, and come live in the town as becomes a man of your birth: fear not to write to your friends all that goes on here; God be thanked, our actions are not such as we are ashamed should be known; but what you *do* write, write *truly*, and send it openly and worthily." The pretended coppersmith whom he addressed, he had discovered to be a man of some rank, sent secretly by the Affghaun court to report upon his actions, and by taking this quiet way of exposing him, he both preserved his reputation for mildness, and gained credit for knowing every thing that passed.

It was his custom to speak of himself in the third person, under the affected designation of *the Fakeer*, though he allowed himself to be addressed by the title of *Huzrut-e-Wullee-Naiamee* (His Excellency the Lord of Beneficence,) and a characteristic anecdote on this head was related to my friend by Ameer Nausir ud Deen (Toora), a brother to Ameer Hyder, who leaving Bokhara for some political reason, resided many years at Meshed.

The court sat a long time one morning in expectation of the Shah's entrance, but it was not till long after his usual hour that he came; he then walked in from the outer door, minus a considerable portion of his upper garment. When he had taken his seat, and exchanged "salaam alekoom" with the company, the eldest of the moollâs expressed a hope that nothing untoward had occurred. The king's answer was, "No,—the fakeer had a friend whom he had not seen for many days, and he went yesterday to visit him. On returning, as the night was dark and the road muddy, the fakeer turned into a mosque and slept there."—"But what food did the Lord of Beneficence eat?"—"A morsel of bread was in a beggar's wallet, and the fakeer ate that."—"And where is the skirt of Huzrut-e-Wullee Naimee's cloak?"—"The fakeer observed that the beggar's feet were cold, so considering that the skirts of his garment were superfluous, he cut them off to make stockings for the poor man."

Notwithstanding his affected meekness, Shah Moraud caused himself to be feared by all classes of men. Though he overlooked many strong personal offences, he seldom forgave one which was directed against his sovereign power; still he had such command over his passions, that he waited to execute vengeance till he could bring it within warrant of the Mohummudan law, and thus he preserved the distinction that he prized for those who feared and disliked him, were bound for their own credit's sake to praise him for his sanctity. He introduced a very strict moral code into the city of Bokhara, but was wise enough to give his orthodox brethren the full benefit of their law on points which much concerned them, so that he easily enlisted pharisaism in the support of his superstitious zeal, and five times *per diem* meritoriously whipped to prayers, the lazy of the multitude whom he licensed to rob and plunder *ad libitum.*

I think it was a day or two before our interview with the prince, that a Toorkmun of the Jaffer Bï tribe inquired our abode, and delivered a letter into my hands. It was written in Russian, but fortunately there was a translation of its contents in Persian on the envelope, and its purport was this: —the writer, the commandant of a Russian brig lying off the south-east coast of the Caspian, had heard that a Russian envoy, on his way to Khiva, had been plundered by the Toorkmuns, and obliged to return to Astrabad: he begged to offer a passage on board his ship to Astrakhan, and the bearer of the note said that he would put me in the way of getting on board. I returned a civil answer in French, saying that I was not a Russian, and that my road lay eastward.

A' Mo'mud Causim had a series of dreams which incited him to undertake a pilgrimage to the shrine of the blessed Imaum Reza; and as he knew the road to the holy city, we were not sorry when he announced his intention of accompanying us. His commercial partner also expressed so strong a desire to perform an act of devotion after his visit to the unclean dogs of the desert, that we promised him a seat on one of the baggage-mules, and we were all in spirits at the idea of a march. Meshedee-Norouz, whose intention it had been to part from us here, could not resist the general impulse, and though he did not care a fig for all the Imaums in the world, he determined to accompany us.

The Vuzeer, flattered I imagine by the Syud's eulogium, made an effort, and seized three of Babeck's camels, which he sold on our account, in the Astrabad bazaar, for twelve tomauns. The person whom he sent on this service was a tall ragged fellow, who rode a lean jade, and carried a matchlock about three times as long as himself; he trotted out to Goorgaun in the morning, and brought in the camels by the afternoon, which was alone sufficient to satisfy us that there was a good understanding between the court and camp. Orauz Kouli brought five tomauns, which he had collected, he said, in a thousand difficult ways, and we not only gave the Vuzeer an acquittance in full for all our losses, but added some extravagant compliments to himself, and sent our dutiful thanks to the prince. We spent the eve of our departure pleasantly with all our friends, and I believe that some of the expressions of regret which were used on both sides at parting were sincere.

CHAPTER IX.

Journey from Astrabad over the Elboorz mountains to Shahrood, and thence on with a caravan of pilgrims, *viâ* Subzawar and Neshapoor, to Meshed.—Observations on different routes between Astrabad and Meshed.

PILGRIMS for the holy city of Meshed, assemble at Shahrood-e-Bostam, to which place there are two roads from Astrabad. The first, called the Koos-look route, is eighteen fursukhs: it is the best and the most level road, but it runs near the Toorkmuns' haunts, and we preferred that by Ziarut. The latter is called sixteen fursukhs, but the first part of it is very hilly and bad. The two roads become one about thirty-three miles from Shahrood.

12th June, 1830.—We took a second leave of Astrabad, and rode south by a pass through the mountains, twelve miles to Ziarut, a village of fifty wood houses, romantically built upon a small hill coming out into the centre of the narrow valley. At the foot of the village, in a neat burying-ground, was the tomb of an Imaumzada; a quick clear stream ran past it, and on either side rose high and richly-wooded mountains. Our path from Astrabad was through a wood thick enough to shade us from the sun, and led us continually over a stream called Chehel-o-Chahar, from the circumstance of its being crossed forty-four times on the way to Ziarut. A' Mo'mud Causim found a friend in the village, who welcomed us with a speech that would have done honour to a courtier; he regaled us with a dish for which Tiberius would have given a reward,—a pullet stewed in conserve of wild pomegranate, and in his neatly mud-washed house we slept secure from the attacks we had suffered so much from at Astrabad.

13th.—About two miles from our resting-place, we commenced the ascent of a very steep Kotul over the main range of the Elboorz. So frequent are the windings, that the natives esteem the passage from base to base equal to ten miles. The soil is loamy, and in wet weather laden mules have difficulty in ascending this pass; in dry weather guns might be got over, but with labour. On the road are four springs of delicious water, named Sherbet, Sheah Khanee, Taloo, and Koor Cheshmah; to the left of the ascent, beyond the first spring, are two large masses of rock thirty or forty yards apart, which we were bidden to remark, as on one, called Tukht-e-Omar (the throne of Omar), the Caliph is believed to have sat and fired arrows at the other: indeed the most sceptical man may see the marks of the arrow-heads in the side of the stone. It was a poetical spot, for all the trees being "Narwand," my friend the Syud persuaded himself that it was the very spot whence Feridoon issued to lead his band of heroes into Khoraussaun, and his blood warming at the conceit, he started off with the quotation in point, and chanted aloud a page of Ferdosi's beautiful verses.

The day was lovely, and we all felt so excited, that we soon spurred our ponies up the ascent, on gaining which we saw before us another range, as high, but quite bare, and with snow in its clefts. From the summit attained, we looked back upon the rich forest we had passed through: it lay below us, partly overhung by a curtain of white clouds, into which the birds would occasionally dip, and be lost till they soared again, and beyond, like a sea, was the desert, stretching away without end to the north.

We passed the last spring near the foot of the Kotul, and descending into a valley, travelled up a brook which came through it from the north-east. On a hill, opposite to the base of the Kotul, were two villages, said to consist of three hundred houses each; three miles up the vale was a hamlet of five or six houses, called Jillen Billen, and a mile beyond it our road was joined by the other from Astrabad. The valley, which was at first stony, improved gradually, and at "Huft Cheshmah," where we halted, it was a greensward between the hills, kept fresh by seven springs which gave a name to the spot. So cold was it, that with all our clothing, and by a large fire, we could hardly sleep.

14th.—From Huft Cheshmah to Shahrood, we rode something more than thirty miles through a valley. With the exception of one steep but short hill, the road was level, and there was no lack of good water all the way. Eight miles on the road, we saw a village of fifteen houses under the hill on our left, called Taush; sixteen miles on the road was a smaller one, Nicarmun. There are but few villages in these hills, and those of not many houses each: the inhabitants pasture large flocks in the valleys, and portion out parts of the land for cultivation; their surplus produce is chiefly sold at Shahrood. In the morning we had been glad to stand round a fire, but when towards sunset we neared Bostam, the wind blew like a hot one in India. We left the town of Bostam three miles on our left, and, crossing a small line of low bare hills, looked down upon Shahrood.

Travellers who had met us, had told of many pilgrims waiting for the morrow to start for Meshed, and coming upon the town, we thought ourselves just in time. Horses were picketed the entire length of the outer wall, and there was a constant throng of men and horses accoutred for travel, between the centre gate and a pool of water at some little distance outside it. Within, the concourse was much greater: there was scarcely passage through the crowd of pilgrims horses and camels that filled the streets. Outside the houses, in the shade, sat some reading the Koran aloud, while others lay sleeping soundly after their travel. In all parts horses were neighing and fighting, their masters scrubbing or shoeing them, mending packsaddles, or higgling for corn and chopped straw; and many a sturdy fakeer, a sugar-loaf cap of colours set over his matted locks and insolently independent countenance, moved through the crowd, calling loudly upon the pilgrims to recollect the service they were upon, and bestow their alms in the name of Mohummud, Ali, and the blessed Imaum Réza. Many were the inquiries as we pushed through the crowd, whence we came: "We're for Meshed," was our answer. "Please God!" eltamas-e-dewa;"—the "ora pro nobis" of the pilgrims of the cross. "What time do the Zawars set out?" inquired we. "They go daily," was the answer. "But those who are to go to-morrow?"—"They went last night, a body of five hundred horsemen and more." This was a disappointment, but A'Mo'mud Causim had a second house and wife here, and we were well lodged. Meshedee-Norouz found a Tabreez acquaintance, who abusing the gone party for Isphahaunees and cowards, invited us to start on the morrow with his party of thirty or forty well-armed Toorks, and this we determined to do. The Tabreezees, and the Persians of the western countries, are called Toorks, on account of their talking the Toorkish language.

They are looked upon as regular Rolandos, and it is a vaunt with them, that the Tartars, when they come to attack a kafilah, call out to know if they are Toorks or Isphahaunees, that they may know whether to leave or to assault them.

15th.—It was resolved to wait the arrival of one hundred more Tabreezees, who were reported to be within two days' march, and we had leisure to see the place. Shahrood is a walled town of twelve hundred residences and storehouses, and three hundred shops. It is in the district of Bostam, and four miles south-west from the town of the same name, where the hakim resides. There are two other small towns (Moojim and Aversudge) in the district, and eight walled villages were in sight from Shahrood. The province of Bostam furnishes to the Shah's army four thousand regular footmen, who receive from eight to ten tomauns each yearly; they are esteemed among the best of the royal troops, and are known by the name of Lushkur-e-Arab'o Ajum (Arab and Persian), for there are many families of Arab extraction resident in this province, the natives of Shahrood said as many as four thousand. They are chiefly of the Ameri tribe, the remainder of twelve thousand tents brought from Arabia during the Bunnee Abbass Khalifate; now they live in houses, and, with the exception of a few of the oldest men, talk Persian.* The hâkim of Bostam

* At Tubbus, Kauin, Berjend, and Néhee, are settled many Arabs, who still retain their own dialect.

keeps a few soldiers in pay, and the inhabitants, obliged often to be on the alert against the Toorkmuns, furnish every third man for the Eeljaurree.* A fine stream, called, *par excellence*, Rood-e-Shah, comes from the mountains past Bostam to Shahrood, and enables the inhabitants to force a considerable quantity of cultivation from what would otherwise be a steril gravelly plain, for water is not to be had here for digging. The thermometer in the shade at noon, on the three days of our stay, was 81½° Fahrenheit; we were told that the heat of the next two months would be extreme.

Good fruits are grown, and much cultivation is carried on at the villages of the vicinity, and care is taken to have large supplies stored in Shahrood. Owing to the frequent forays of the Toorkmuns, few sheep are kept here, but they are to be procured at a low price from the neighbouring valleys. For eight months in every year, dating from the vernal equinox, this road to and from Meshed is travelled by sixty thousand persons, chiefly pilgrims; and it is to be remarked, that though much of the country is desert, every little station on the road furnishes supplies for this number of persons and their cattle. The calculation, I am pretty sure, is not too high: it was made by my companion, as well from the accounts we received on the road, as from his knowledge, previously acquired during fifteen years'

* Militia.

residence in various parts of Irân, of the average departure of pilgrims for Meshed from different places in Persia.

16th.—Early this morning the Syud and I rode to Bostam, to present introductory letters to the Shah-zadeh. We alighted at the house of the Vuzeer, who was asleep, and might not be disturbed; so we went to sleep also on the floor of the room into which we were shown, until it pleased the minister to be roused. He could not then, it seemed, imagine what the deuce a foreigner had to do in this part of the world: "Inglis! Inglis!" we heard him say to his servants,—"a Feringhee at Bostam!! in my room!!! What news is this?" and I hardly think he would have ventured in, had not the Syud gone out, and in some degree explained to him who I was, and what was the object of our coming. Then the old gentleman was very polite, gave us high seats, and ordered us breakfast, and went to announce our arrival to the prince. His servants were far less civil, and would scarcely give me a plate to eat from; telling the Syud, supposing me ignorant of the language, that it must be broken afterwards. I only now discovered, that during my residence at Astrabad, every plate, not china or metal, upon which I had been unwary enough to lay hands, had been broken and charged to my account. China being hard baked, the contamination of impure hands may be washed off, but into any thing soft it is supposed to sink. The clause is in favour both of conscience and economy.

The Vuzeer shortly returned, to say that the prince would exalt our heads by granting us the honour of an audience. Shortly after, entered a fat smiling Khan, to whom the Vuzeer made a sign desiring him to be civil to us; he took me for a Moollâ of degree, as I sat at the upper end in a black serge abba, and coming up to me, took my hands and reverently kissed them. The Vuzeer's black eyes expanded to double their size, and when the Khan turned, he was made aware of his mistake. He looked quite shocked at discovering what unclean hands he had pressed his lips to, and going over to the Vuzeer, begged in a loud whisper that, *for the honour of their religion*, the story might go no further; but the old gentleman's chuckle made it evident that it was too good a one to be kept secret, and, as good anecdotes must be scarce at so quiet a place, I have no doubt that the Khan's reverence for an infidel has been a standing joke ever since.

This worthy gentleman bore the title of "Nussuckshee Bâshee" to the Shahzadeh, a sort of earl marshal, and it was his part to lead us to the presence. We were conducted into a long walled square, near one end of which was a small cannon, and a long musket gun. It was evidently intended that we should observe this park of artillery, for, looking up, we perceived the prince watching our motions, seated at an open window above an archway: we bowed, and were graciously ordered up; the earl marshal led us with much affectation under the archway, and proposed that we should leave our shoes there, but we kept them to ascend a flight of dirty steps, up which we mounted to the door of the audience-chamber, and passing through a body of retainers, found ourselves in a small mud-plastered room, at the end of which sat the prince as we had observed him from the court below. With the affectation which is common to the Cujjer princes, he addressed us at first in Toorkish, telling us that we were "khosh geldin;" but he assigned us seats at an honourable distance from his person, and presently speaking to us in the Persian language, displayed more information about European affairs than we had been inclined to give him credit for, or than indeed is usual for princes of the blood. They are men of very much the same stamp; handsome, and, as regards their exterior, gentleman-like persons, who are brought up proudly and ignorantly in the harem, though in the strictest knowledge of the minutiæ of Persian etiquette. They condescend a few civil questions about yourself, and as many ignorant ones about "Yengee doonia," the New World, and Frangestan, always expressing astonishment on hearing that the latter is a term for more countries than one. Wonderful! is their expression when they are told any thing about Europe that is novel to them; wonderful men are the Feringees!!! Wonderful! repeats the Vuzeer, and the more humble persons of the assembly shake their heads at each other, and echo the word.

The Vuzeer was ordered to give us introductory letters to the prince's cousin at Subzawar, so taking this as a hint to rise, we made our bow, and accompanied the minister to his office, where he had a levee; the man who but a moment before had stood at a respectful distance from his master, leaning forward to catch the least word from his lips, now entirely changed his bearing, and sat above an assembly of obsequious inferiors, whose looks he scarcely condescended to return.

While our letters were being written, we were entertained with the notes of a vocalist, who as candidate for the part of first performer at the coming religious festival of the Mohurrum, was giving a specimen of his powers: they were quite stunning. The excellence of Persian singing consists in forcing the voice to its loudest pitch, and sustaining it there: it is rather recitative than singing, and is too strained and violent to please a European ear, yet the best singers throw great expression into their songs. They dwell long upon every sound, and frequently run down the gamut slowly trilling upon every note, sometimes unaffectedly weeping at the effect of their own music.

The man who was before us had all the air of a maniac, as, with a hand behind his ear, his body swayed to and fro, and his features distorted by the violence with which he sang, he shouted out the sorrows of the martyred Hossein. This loud fashion of singing must be owing to the distance at which performers are placed when singing before the king, or great men; when, as at the festival of the Mohurrum, they chant in the open air, they indeed require Stentorian lungs. The singer of this morning made so much noise, that the Vuzeer dismissed him with a compliment, and promised to recommend him to the Prince. On our return to Shahrood, we found that many Zawars* had come in, and "*such* Zawars" said Meshedee-Norouz, "each with his gun, and an English lock to it."—Departure fixed for the morrow.

17th. In the afternoon we rode out three miles to the village of Buddusht, where three hundred pilgrims were assembled. A third of the party were Arabs from the vicinity of Kerbolah; there were sixty horsemen from Tabreez and Karabaugh, and the rest, with the exception of a dozen men from Tehraun and Isphahaun, were Cazazees, who were headed by a Moojeteheid, or high priest, a thin old gentleman with a black cloak and pointed beard, the lower half of whom was lost in a pair of huge Russian leather boots. The Toorks were well armed and mounted; some of the Cazazees were in like trim, but the Arabs were the worst equipped and most ragged set of beings imaginable. One old man at their head, who was dignified with the name of Hâjee, had a matchlock, and was well mounted; of the rest, some rode indifferent mares, others don-

* Pilgrims.

keys, and half a dozen couples of old women, packed in kajavahs, were slung on the sides of mules; some of the men had an ass between them, ride and tie, and a dozen or so of the poorest, armed like their more fortunate brethren, with knives, axes, or sticks, went on foot, trusting to charity for an occasional lift.

Till sunset, those who had guns exercised themselves in firing at a target: very few shots took effect, but it was agreed on all hands that he must be a bold enemy who would attack us; indeed, to look at these heroes with their rolls of matches, and innumerable cartouch and flint boxes belted over their clothes, you might have supposed that they were prepared to stand a good fight, and I believe some of them almost persuaded themselves that they would.

At noon, the thermometer was 81½° in the shade, but in the evening a cutting wind blew. Cooking-pots being cleared away, and the beasts laden, the order of march was determined, and at half-past eight we made a start, the Tabreezees leading, and the Arabs bringing up the rear, the chaoushes* heading their divisions, and striving to keep them separate. The horses walked out, and the mules and donkeys ambled along surprisingly under loads some of which were immense, as there were many who did not disdain to add profit to piety. I asked an Astrabad acquaintance, who was seated upon a heavy bale of

* A chaoush is a leader of a caravan, or a party.

felts, how his mule kept up with such a load. "He *must* keep up, was the man's answer, with a thump to his beast; he *must* keep up, for there's danger in lagging."

Four miles from Buddusht we passed a ruined town called Khireabad. We were told that there was water there, and that the men of Buddusht used it to cultivate land, having built towers into which to retreat in case of the Toorkmuns coming. Our line of march was just distinguishable in the dark, by the dust raised by our horses' feet, which the wind blew to one side like a vapour: occasionally a calleoon, handed about, would light up the heads of a party, as the strong wind blew the coals up, and the front of the line was always shown by the Moojeteheid's pipeman, below the belly of whose horse swung a pot of live charcoal. We marched all night over a tolerably level and good road, and at daybreak halted a quarter of an hour for prayers.

Continuing our march till seven, we reached Meyomeh, a village of 200 houses, at which there is an excellent brick caravansera built by Shah Abbass. We got what we required for ourselves and horses, and even fruit,—plums and peaches. The only article at Meyomeh that bore a high price was firewood, which indeed was hardly to be obtained in sufficient quantities. The village is near a range of bare hills, from which is conducted a small canaut of good water: this, after daily filling two brick reservoirs, is turned upon very unpromising-looking land, but which generally returns wheat and barley enough for the wants of the pilgrims who pass: in times of scarcity supplies are brought from Shahrood. The distance between the two places is about forty miles. Thermometer at noon, 82° Fahrenheit; light, cool wind.

We slept till evening under the shade of trees. As the time for setting off again approached, the Arabs began to complain that they were knocked up: the Toorks, they said, went too fast, and would not halt for any one whose load fell, and by their uncharitable conduct were defeating the object of their pilgrimage. The Tabreezees, however, seemed to think that the one great act was meritorious enough to excuse all their peccadilloes, and knowing the esteem their fighting qualities were held in, said very cavalierly that *they* would go, those who would might accompany them, and those who would not, might choose their own time. The high priest, a timorous old man, harangued them all on brotherly concord, and the chaoushes addressed soothing words to their several parties; a Persian's ire is soon run out, and after a due quantity of noise and wrangling, they moderated their language, when it was agreed that we should keep together, the Arabs to lead.

We set out about eight o'clock, and travelled four miles to a large sycamore-tree, near to which is a village called Ibrahimabad, and a canaut of water, and where a road branches off to Dusgird.* Here there was a halt and a discussion; some were for turning back and marching by daylight, that they might at least see their enemy, this march being esteemed a dangerous one, because the road nearly all the way is flanked by swelling hillocks, behind which the Toorkmuns lie concealed. Finally, it was resolved to go on "Tewokul be Khoda," † the Arabs to return to their former station in the rear, as the horses pressed on their donkeys in the dark, and a party to precede the main body 100 yards or so. We were fortunate enough to get upon this desperate service, and so escape the dust. A call was made for those who had guns, and it was a farce to see the importance that some laid upon the act of going a few yards in front. "I'll go," said one upon an ambling donkey, carrying a long duck-gun, "*I'll go;* I thank Heaven I've no wife with me, that I should wish to spare myself;—dispose of me!" as if, a second Marcus Curtius, he was going to ride post to destruction. Continued halts for charity's sake, till the alarm was given of a horseman said to have been seen looking out from behind the hills:—horses donkeys and footmen now crowded together in a solid mass, which they kept in spite of the inequalities of

* Dusgird was stated to be a village of 350 houses, where there are many gardens and fields, walled in for fear of the Toorkmuns. By this road it is said to be twenty fursukhs from Meyomeh to Abassabad. The two routes are distinguished by the names of the Dusgird and the Alhauk roads.

† Trusting in Providence.

the road, and there was no more straggling till daylight; then every bush in the distance was magnified into a horseman. A whirlwind of dust two miles on our left, behind some low hills, was decided to be without doubt caused by a body of horse; the chaoushes galloped out to reconnoitre, and we halted for a few anxious minutes till they returned: they reported it to be "only the wind," and soon after, seeing Abassabad in the distance, the hearts of all were reassured, and they began to talk of—Mashallah! what they would have done had the enemy proved real! We had a pretty good criterion of their valour in that of our servant Meshedee, whom we knew to be an arrant coward at heart, but who talked as if he would carbonado all the Toorkmuns that dared come within reach of him, and who, what by the report (his own) of his having made a gallant escape from the desert, and his big words, got himself to be thought a very "Roostum," and was looked to as a protection in case of any alarm.

The distance from Meyomeh to Abbassababad is about forty-eight miles. Half-way we passed the ruined caravansera of Meergundusht, where there was no water: eight miles from Abbassabad was the still fine caravansera of Alhauk, where a little water oozed out from a marshy plot of ground. It was ten o'clock when we came to the end of our stage, after a march of fourteen hours, than which few exertions are more wearying; for though from sleep you feel inclined to drop from your horse, you are obliged to keep awake, for fear of breaking your leg against a load. I got a knock once against the corner of a trunk, which made me very cautious how I dozed again.

At Abbassabad there are forty houses and a spring of good water, within a high mud fort. A more wretchedly desolate country than that around it is not to be conceived; not an attempt is made to raise any thing vegetable, and supplies are procured from Subzawar, eighty miles distant. The inhabitants of this dreary place are Mohummudans, the converted descendants of an Armenian colony established here perforce by the great Shah Abbas. They have the credit of being on good terms both with the pilgrims and with the Toorkmuns; and this is probable, for the latter occasionally require a supply of food when they are out, and it is not their interest to cut off the supplies of those by catching whom they live. Seeing a crowd of half-dressed men come galloping out to meet us, hallooing and striving who should be foremost, I conceived that some disaster had befallen them, but was undeceived when the first of them came up to us, and addressed the most likely-looking men with "Lord of my life! you'll buy your corn of me; I've fresh bread, curds, and peaches, and my man keeps the two best rooms in the caravansera." We were so fortunate as to get one of these apartments, up-stairs, under the high entrance to a double-storied square of cloisters. The scene of noise and quarrelling as the main body came in and made for the different cells, can only be imagined by those who have seen Persians on a march; but they were all so thoroughly tired, that they were soon glad to put up with any accommodation, and to lie down and sleep wherever there was shade. The thermometer at noon was 87°. It was as much as we could do to get up in the evening to eat some bread and curds, and then to drop to sleep again till four o'clock the next morning, when, prayers having been said in the court, the gates of the caravansera were unbarred, and we marched twenty-two miles to Muzzeenaun.

This march was a pleasant one; the air was fresh, and the pilgrims, relieved from the fear of the two most dreaded stages, unfurled their gay pennons, and moved along with lighter hearts. The Moojeteheid's face wore a smile, and settling himself on his easy pad, he condescended to talk to those about him. The Toorks cut their jokes upon an Isphahaun dandy, the back of whose head was covered with long curls, and who, in countenance and general bearing any thing but warlike, was quite laden with arms and accoutrements. The chaoushes would dash out ahead, mimicking a fight with each other, halt a minute at the top of some rising ground to see the country clear, and then returning as they went, would call upon the faithful to raise a shout for the blessed Mohummud. Prefacing with some verses of which all chaoushes have a ready store, one would exclaim in a loud voice, "*Dum be dum bur gool-e rookhsaur-e Mohummud sulawaat.*"—"Upon the rose of the cheek of Mohummud may the blessing of God momentarily rest." To which the pilgrims would answer, "*Ullah hoomma sullé Ala Mohummudin 'va aule Mohummud.*"—"O God, bless Mohummud, and the issue of Mohummud," and then they would join in a shout. If they did not cry loud or unanimously enough, the chaoushes would exclaim angrily, "Better than that!—sweeter than that!—dust on your heads, is *this* your salawaat? Now one hearty shout that will ring to the tomb of the blessed Imaum Reza; *Ferishta bau shoomah shereek'und.*"—"*Angels* join with you—Shout!!"—and the air was rent with a fervent and inspiring cry. There is something in a shout which makes the heart's blood boil, and I felt so warm and excited, that for any one but Mohummud-e Moostapha, I could have cheered with the loudest: as it was, I left the part to Meshedee-Norouz, and fell to the rear that my lukewarmness might not be noticed.

We had a rich scene this morning between two old Arab women, who, whether from the malformation of their mule's back, or what, could not balance themselves in their kajavahs. All the big stones in the road were picked up and put into one dame's cradle, but with no effect, and she sat perched up, tightly grasping the centre, till she became angry, and rated her companion for being a heavy woman; the other,

I believe, retorted on her the term of a light one, and they had some very high words, the mule the while ambling along with them most patiently. As they could not afford a halt, all attempts to rectify the evil were vain; the heavy dame lay like a millstone in her kajavah, but after a hearty cry, the two old bodies became friends again, and joined in vilifying the men who had strapped them on, till the old hâjee, riding up, shook his gun at them, and authoritatively desired them to be silent.

Muzzeenaun is one of the nine belooks of Subzawar: it contains eight villages, four of which were in sight from the caravansera. The capital of the same name, once a considerable town, looked most desolate as we neared its ruins of mud brick. Many of the houses were yet standing, but not a living creature moved among them. A village of fifty houses, which now bears the name, is built at the back of what was the town, and there we got excellent water, besides two or three sorts of fruit. We had hardly got within the large caravansera of this place, when there was a cry from the village that the Toorkmuns were come: mothers ran shrieking to the small fort with their children, the villagers hastened to drive in their cattle, and the men of our party began to examine the state of their fire-arms. From the roof of the caravansera we saw a few horsemen pricking about twenty camels with all speed to the hills. A party of jungees* volunteered

* Warriors.

for the rescue, made much fuss, and received the benedictions of their friends, without having individually, I believe, the least intention of going within smell of powder. It was long before they were ready, and then, riding scarcely beyond the village, they discovered, or affected to do so, that the riders were not Toorkmuns, and so returned to enjoy credit for their gratuitous valour.

From our small upper room, which flanked the arched entrance, we looked down upon an amusing fight between a Persian and an Arab: each was in the middle of a crowd of his friends, bareheaded, and brandishing a dagger, and swearing to make mincemeat of his enemy, but at the same time not really endeavouring to force his way to him. They were eventually brought together, and made to kiss each other, and immediately after, they seated themselves with the greatest harmony to a basket of unripe plums.

June 21st.—This morning, after prayers, we rode twenty miles to Meyer. On either side of the road we saw villages in the distance, and there was an improvement in the soil, which all the way from Shahrood had been of mixed sand and gravel. On our way wo met a party of returned pilgrims, with whom questions and civilities were exchanged. First the Toorkmuns were inquired about—were they out? "None heard of, Agha Jân;" "that's good; that's good; you are welcome from the shrine; may your vows be accepted!"—"Inshallah! your place was empty."—"What's bread now in Meshed?"—"Twelve farthings a mun."—"Alhumdoolillah! Alhumdoolillah!—God is provident;* Alhumdoolillah!" were the ejaculations of our party. "Safe journey to ye."—"Thanks, thanks, God be with you! forget us not in your orisons."

Meyer is a neat village, through which runs a stream of delicious water. The pilgrims billeted themselves on the various houses; we were so fortunate as to get admission into the garden of a widow who had two daughters, the youngest of whom, a girl of seventeen, married to a young man who lived in the house, was so beautiful, that my companion did not know whether to call her a "Peri" or a "Houri." It is so seldom in Persian towns that you can catch a glimpse of a woman's features, that, unless favoured by some kind zephyr, you must be content to dream of the charms that are veiled from you. In remote villages the same strictness is not observed, and your eye may occasionally be blessed with a sight of a beautiful face. The Syud, by certain hints cleverly thrown out, managed to get himself invited in to tell the fortunes of the family. I made bold to follow him, and while he examined their palms, or traced mystical lines on the floor, I enjoyed the pleasure of unobservedly watching the expressions on the counte-

* The stay of many of the poorest pilgrims is regulated according to the price of bread at Meshed.

nances of these simple peasants, as they superstitiously believed the promises of good fortune and happiness which were unsparingly dealt out to them. The husband of the youngest girl was a village poet, and was so won by the Syud's converse, that he declared he would follow him to Meshed, to study under him. The mother was one of those gossiping good old bodies whom one sees in a village at home; she produced a plate of sweetmeats in return for the Syud's many promises, but said that her wishes only went the length of desiring wheaten instead of barley bread. My saying so much about this family may appear tedious, but even when in the constant habit of seeing beautiful women, one surpassing the rest makes us remember her long, and to meet with a creature of so much grace and beauty, after having been long debarred the sight of a woman, was like meeting a spring in the desert.

Travelling from about nine that night till seven the next morning, we rode thirty-five miles to Subzawar, which is a good-sized town, the capital of the province of the same name. In this province there are nine belooks (Subzawar, Muzzeenaun, Kau, Kurrao, Zummund, Tubbus, and three called Koo Meesh): they have so long been exposed to the inroads of the Toorkmuns, that many villages have been deserted, and much naturally fine land remains untilled; but still a good deal of cultivation is carried on, especially of cotton, which is exported in large quantities; and should the northern frontier be hereafter secured against the Toorkmuns, there is reason to believe that the country would greatly recover itself.

The town is fortified with a tolerably thick mud wall, in which are many bastions; a narrow parapet runs all round, and the top of the wall is pierced with loopholes for musketeers. The place was in the hands of Prince Arghoon Meerza, son to Hussan Ali Meerza, the Shah's sixth son. This youth, already notorious for several independent acts, was away engaged in some skirmish in the neighbourhood. His troops were rated at five hundred regular horse and eight hundred foot, and the province, it was said, would furnish four thousand eeljaurree;* but as the latter receive no pay, and as the aggressions of their lord are generally retaliated upon the lands they rent, they have no heart in his quarrels. The Prince's artillery, we learned, consisted of thirty zoombooruks, or camel swivels, and fifty shumkhals (large guns that are fired from rests). We heard also of a topchee bâsheet† and two cannon, gone to the wars with the Prince, but I presume that his guns were much of the same caliber as those which we saw at Bostam. The most accurate idea of the state of Persian artillery may be gathered from an anecdote in the Sketches of Persia, in which the besieged commandant of a fort requests his enemy to fire off his *other* ball, and so put their minds at rest.

* A sort of militia.

† Commandant of Artillery.

On inquiring about the population of Subzawar, the Syud was gravely assured that, by a census taken ten years before, the inhabitants were rated at forty thousand souls. We had but a cursory view of the city, but from what I saw I was not inclined to allow much more than a tenth of the number. There appeared to be much waste ground within the walls, and we did not see many people; however the bare appearance of the town was doubtless owing in a great measure to the absence of the Prince with his troops and suite. We rode through a newly constructed bazaar of arched brick, and the prices of provisions were moderate.

We got no house-room at Subzawar, but went outside the city, and there made a covering for ourselves, by laying one end of a carpet on a low mud wall, and supporting the other with our guns. The thermometer rose to 116° in the sun; the heat of our tent could not have been many degrees lower, and so much dust was blown into our beards, that we looked as though we had been powdered. "Light to your eyes," said an old pilgrim, when we acceded to his request that he might just rest his *head* in the shade of our carpet; "light to your eyes and increase to your wealth!" and putting, as he had said, just his head under cover, he left the rest of his body in a roasting sun, and slept composedly for some hours.

The Shahzadeh being away, an affectation of great military strictness was observed by those left in charge. As soon as the sun had set, the city-gates were closed, and some unlucky pilgrims of our party, who were inside at the time, were not let out till they had paid their way. We loaded at midnight, and marched twenty miles, to the very large but ruined caravansera of Zaffron, close to which was a mud fort containing a dozen houses; the inhabitants sold us grain and flour, and we got good water from a small canaut. At sunset, as we were saddling to continue our journey, a horseman arrived from Subzawar: his steed was jaded, and wishing to detain the kafilah till the morrow, he told of eighty Toorkmun horsemen who had chappaoed a village hard by, and who would assuredly set on us in the dark. Though his lie was palpable, he succeeded in alarming the most nervous of our party, and if the Moojeteheid had not had his boots on, I really believe that our march would have been deferred.

As it was we had much squabbling, and there was no appearance of its ending, until an old Tabreezee took the question up: "The man says," reasoned he, "that the Toorkmuns have chappaoed a village; then, it is likely that they have filled their bellies and gone to the desert; and if they be still near the road, please God! won't we burn the fathers of eight times eighty such dogs? If the Isphahaunees won't, the men of Tabreez will." Applause followed this sally, the beasts were laden without more ado, and we rode a fatiguing march of forty-five miles, to Neshaboore, without seeing any thing like an enemy.

We made two marches in one, to avoid the brackish water of the intermediate stage: part of the road was bad, between hills and weedy jungle. When day broke we were in the valley of Neshapoor, a plain eighteen miles in breadth, quite covered with cultivation and villages, the least with its little curtains and bastions embowered in green trees. "This is Persia!" was the vain exclamation of those who were alive to the beauty of the scene; "this is Persia! Bah! bah! what grass, what grain, what water! Bah! bah!"

> " *Ugger Ferdose bur roo-e zumeen ust,*
> *Humeen ust, 'vo humeen ust 'vo humeen ust!*"
>
> " And O if there be an Elysium on earth,
> It is this! it is this! it is this!"

"Yet ah! Lord of my soul, what was Neshapoor!" The commendations bestowed upon this valley, set some of the pilgrims upon the praises of their respective places, and after much had been said for the climate, fruit, or water, of this that or the other country, they generally came to the conclusion that their own homes were the best. There was a little sparring between some Shirauzees and the Isphahaunee, for the latter was disposed to be very loquacious in praise of his native city,—its palaces and colleges, its astrologers and men of art, its bread, fruit, baths, and the eternal river Zeinderood; while the men of the south seemed to think all praise thrown away which was not applied to Shirauz; and when the dandy quoted the far-known saying, "Isphahaun Nisf Jehaun" (Isphahaun is half the world), they answered him in the following couplet:

> Usphahaun jennut ust poor neamut,
> Usphahaunee dur oo ne mebiud!
>
> Isphahaun is Paradise! full of delights;
> But Paradise not the place for an Isphahaunee!

An Indian who should venture in such an assembly to put in a word in praise of his country, would be scouted by all parties. India! where the sun is so hot that it dries up men's brains in their heads, as is evident by the small quantity of understanding possessed by those who come thence; and where, if a man should see an apple, he would fall into a fit from sheer wonder! "Agha Jân!" I once heard an Indian say to a Shirauzee, who having come to Meshed on pilgrimage, was continually sighing for his home, and finding fault with every other place— "Agha Jân—but hear me! man of understanding, listen before you condemn! I beg leave to state for your very excellent self's information, that every where in Hindostân are trees, the like of which your fathers never saw in a dream; trees, I beg to state, and water every where." And then he went on to expatiate upon the wealth and plenty of the land of the sun, where the veriest beggar daily ate rice, &c.— to all which the Shirauzee coolly answered, "Ai Agha! don't distress yourself with much talking; what you have been pleased to say is true, but truth is not always truth. Hindostân is a very good place for you, and has, no doubt, many fine things; but Hindostan is not Persia, and you know the saying,

> "Sugar-candy comes from Egypt;
> *Saadi** from Shirauz."

The town of Neshapoor (or boor), though not handsome, is large; it appeared to be tolerably well inhabited, and in a flourishing condition: the bazaars were well filled, and provisions were cheap. There were said to be ten or eleven hundred dwelling-houses in the city: I walked through many of its quarters, and was induced to believe the statement, and to rate the population at about eight thousand souls.

The neglected, but still fine province of Neshapoor, is divided into twelve belooks (Neshapoor, Durb-e-Cauzee, Mauzoul, Revund, Teghankoo, Baur-e-madan, Durrood, Ishkabad, Belook-e-Noh, and three others). In each belook there are at least one hundred kullahs, or walled villages; not less than ten, nor more than a hundred, houses in each. There are twelve ever-running streams from the hills, and it was said that eight of the twelve thousand canauts of former days were still remaining; but then we were told that there was so little water in these, that they were not equal to a fourth as many of the ordinary fulness. When Hussan Ali Meerza was governor of Persian Khorassaun, 60,000 Irâk tomauns (39,000*l.*) were paid him annually from the province of Neshapoor: the

* The celebrated Persian poet.

turquoise mines were rented for 1000 tomauns, and the rock-salt mines* for 300. In addition to the cash assessment, the prince took yearly from the province ten thousand khurwars of grain, which (at the crown rate of composition of two tomauns per maund) gives a further sum of 20,000 tomauns.

Now from this a guess may be made at the yearly harvest. The Shah levies from a tenth to a fifth upon the produce of his country, according to the fertility of the soil in different countries, or to the degree of favour that he is inclined to show the people, it being the endeavour of every governor to return as deplorable an account as possible of the agricultural state of his district. Knowing that the Shah received ten thousand khurwars, we may make a calculation between the above-mentioned extreme rates, and suppose that the amount was, say a seventh of the gross produce, or seventy thousand khurwars. This, I imagine, is a low estimate, for the Shah's authority over Persian Khorassaun has hardly been such as to enable him to exact the highest rates, and Hussan Ali Meerza took many regular troops from the province, in which case it is usual to assess the country lightly. We were told that the actual quantity of grain annually raised in the province might be fairly calculated at one hundred thousand khurwars. I had been led to imagine that the soil of Neshapoor was much richer than it appeared to

* The salt of these mines is very fine, and is largely exported.

be; it is generally tilled for one year and left fallow for two, and some parts of the district are cultivated only every fourth year. The average return of the seed sown is tenfold.

We arrived at Neshapoor just too late to taste in its freshness the sweet syrup of a plant called *rewass*, which grows in all parts of Persia and Affghanistaun where the climate is cool, but nowhere so well as on the gravelly hills in this neighbourhood. This plant is a species of rhubarb, and seed of it should be obtained by botanists, as it appears to thrive where little else would, and, besides medical properties, to contain enough saccharine matter to merit the attention of those who seek substitutes for the sugar-cane in beet-root and pumpkins.*

* The following description of this plant is given in the "*Mukhzun-al-Adwiya*."—" Ribas, Rivas, Riwaj, or Jigari, so named from a person of Neshapoor who first discovered it, is a shrub two or three feet high, in appearance like beet (salk). In the middle are one or two short stems of little thickness; the leaves, which separate lengthwise like those of a lettuce, are downy and green, but towards the root of a violet or whitish colour. The heart is white, delicate, juicy, acidulous, and slightly astringent. Altogether the stalk is the size of a man's arm, and when the plant is large, every leaf has the size of a man's hand. 'Ardsheer' was named *Rawund Dust* from the length of his hands. The root is called rawund. The top is like the claw of a fowl. The flower is red, and the taste is subacid with a little sweetness. The seed is formed on the top of a long slender stalk, which springs up annually in the centre of the plant. It grows in places where snow lies, and in mountainous countries. The best grows in Persia. It is medicinally attenuating and astringent; gives tone to the stomach, and improves the appetite. A collyrium of the juice strengthens the eye and prevents opacity, and a poultice of it with barley-meal, is an useful application to sores and boils. The juice of the rivas is harsher than that of unripe grapes."

We halted during the day of our arrival, and on the 25th also, for we were all completely tired, and had I been, what most of the party thought me, a Mohummudan pilgrim, I should have felt inclined to agree in opinion with a wayworn neighbour, who said with a groan, as he threw himself down to rest in his boots, "If there be a road to Paradise, this is it."

We lodged outside the town, in a ruined caravansera which, strange to say, a renegado Russian had devoted himself to rebuild, as a mark of his sincerity in his new faith. The townspeople made much of him, and furnished him with the means of livelihood. We were told that within the last two years, several converted Russians had come this road, on their way to the shrine at Meshed: perhaps some of them were originally Mohummudans, though Russian subjects. I believe I may say that there are seven or eight thousand Russian deserters in all Persia: Abbas Meerza had about three thousand in his service when I was at Tabreez; but these, though for the most part nominal Mooselmauns, were not distinguished by a particular show of any religion; at least they did not think themselves debarred the privilege of stopping folks' passage from their houses by lying drunk at the doors, and few Mohummudans could have felt satisfaction at calling such brutes brothers.

It is easily to be conceived that a low Russian, once removed from the pomp of the Greek religion, by the superstitions of which he has been kept in ignorant submission, will be proud to adopt a creed which bids him consider himself so very much above other men, and which at the same time is more suited to his capacity, and I think that nothing is so calculated to give an Englishman an impression of the weakness of the Russian Government, as observing the degraded state of religious knowledge in which it is thought politic to keep the people. The Muscovites profess, and doubtless many of them enthusiastically believe, themselves to be a nation specially ordained for the propagation of the Christian religion, and (though not exactly perhaps as they in their vanity think) who shall say that they are not? We have seen the two greatest Mohummudan nations fall before their suddenly-raised power, and though they extend a creed which is only in principle better than that which they weaken, their minds must be brought to a sense of the errors which they have ingrafted upon the pure faith; a Luther will arise at the crisis, and their idolatries will cease at once, as ours did. This, if it be a vain theory, is at least a pleasing one.

Meshedee-Norouz and I sauntered about the town nearly the whole afternoon, and then turned into a bath, where a dozen men were lying on their backs like corpses, with their beards in paste: an unlucky slip that I made on coming out of the hot water, threw me into the midst of them, and they evidently thought me either drunk or mad. I hurried out, leaving Meshedee to make my apology, and dressed so hastily, that I unwittingly carried off one of the bath cloths. I sent Meshedee back with this, but he went unwillingly, declaring that the owner of the bath would think him either a fool or a thief: "Just keep it," he said, "and offer up a good wish for the man, that his prosperity may increase."

It is usual for the chaoushes, when there is a night's halt, to address an extemporaneous speech to the pilgrims, after which the hour and order of the next day's march are mentioned. This evening a chaoush, standing in the middle of the square, lifted up his voice and prayed for the blessing of God upon Mohummud, and recited some verses in honour of the prophet, to which the pilgrims shouted short sentences in answer. The effect of their voices coming from the cells on every side was very wild and pleasing, for it was quite dark, and the sounds rose and chimed in upon each other till they were blended in a full chorus. Then the chaoush prayed for the downfall of the Russian power, and the exaltation of all Mohummudan potentates; next he desired the prayers of the pilgrims for a sick person in his house, and lastly he begged them to pray for the recovery of his horse, which had fallen lame.

26th.—Twenty miles to Durrood, a village near the Elboorz mountains, beautifully situated in the midst of gardens of all fruits, through which ran abundance of sparkling water. Sixteen miles on the road, we halted at the village of Kuddumgau, for the purpose of ziarut, and passed up an avenue of magnificent cedar-trees into a fine garden, watered by a clear stream, in the centre of which was a neat little mosque, containing a stone with the imprint of the Imaum Reza's foot upon it. This was regarded with much veneration by, I believe, every body but the Syud, Meshedee, and myself. We paid our devotions more sensibly to a basket of delicious plums. The majority of our fellow-travellers thought me a Mohummudan pilgrim like themselves: the few who knew me did not appear to care about my journeying with them, though in case of misfortune they would probably have regarded me as a Jonas.

27th.—Twenty miles to Cheghir, as beautiful a village as the last. We picketed our horses on the bank of a clear brook, and rested under a spreading tree, through which the sun hardly shone from its rise until evening. Quitting Durrood, we proceeded up a stony and hilly path, eight miles to the foot of the mountains, which we ascended by a cotul so steep that few had the cruelty to ride their horses up it, and many were the groans and "Yah Imaum Rezas!" before we gained the top. Then all halted, for Meshed was in sight, and the pilgrims began *to build houses for the other world* with the loose black stones that lay about; some for fathers and mothers departed, others for friends left behind, and all for their own especial accommodation hereafter. The sight of the Holy City, dim as it was in the distance, conjured up some expressions of grief that I tried to think fictitious, but which I was forced to believe not entirely so. It is good to weep for the woes of any martyr, and as the Imaum Reza was not without his share of the sorrows of this world, the most zealous of his admirers contrived, by exercising their imaginations, to think of his griefs and weep for them.

One young Syud, who had ingratiated himself with all our party by his cheerfulness on the road, and whom we had remarked for the alacrity with which he ascended the pass, totally altered his demeanour when he reached the summit. After a period spent in passionate exclamations and addresses to the saint, he slowly descended the steep side of the mountain, frequently lying down and striking his head against the ground, and sobbing as if his heart was breaking; all for recollection of the indignities that had been heaped on the blessed Imaum, on Hossein, and on his noble sons. It was not genuine grief, but a sort of paroxysm he had worked himself into,—a spiritual penance instead of a hair shirt, and a duty that he owed the saints—for his feelings took another turn when he got to the foot of the pass, and we saw him standing quietly by the wayside, with a cloth spread before him, to receive the contributions of his fellow-travellers.

Early on the morning of the 28th, we rode eighteen miles to the city of Meshed. The first half of the way took us by hills, the dells of which are gardens watered by rills from the mountains.

Hence the city is supplied with the choicest fruits of all kinds, which are grown in such quantities, that they are within the means of the poorest. The rich inhabitants of Meshed have country-houses in the little villages which are built among the gardens, and in spring time parties come out to recite poetry and eat fruit.

Four miles from the city there was a halt near a small minaret, and, all dismounting, the chief priest said prayers before a party, while others prayed for themselves apart. The scene was a very impressive one, and it was rendered more so to me, by the appearance of a pilgrim from Tabreez, whom I had leisure to observe. This poor man had fallen very sick on the road, and it was proposed to leave him behind, but he expressed so much anxiety to reach the holy city, that his friends brought him on, and they were now affectionately congratulating him, and pointing to the golden cupola of the shrine, on which the morning sun was breaking. I cannot forget the smile that lighted up the deathlike countenance of this man, as, supported by his friends, he strained his eyes to look upon the place which he esteemed so holy: he was too weak to do more than utter ejaculations of thanksgiving, and we afterwards learned that he died that very evening. "Khoda Rahmut konud!" "God rest his soul!"

When prayers had been said, the chaoushes spread cloths on the road-side, and fixing each his banner at his post, chanted sentences best adapted to soften the hearts of the pilgrims, who threw down donations according to their ability. We then mounted and moved on in order: the Moojeteheid's wife showed her honour for the saint, by descending from her mule, and walking on foot ahead of the horsemen; the chaoushes unfurled their banners, and sang their loudest, and were answered by shouts as fervent as their hearts could have desired; and thus we approached the holy city. The arrival of pilgrims is too every-day an occurrence to bring out the townspeople, and as soon as we had passed the city-gates, we dispersed to seek lodgings. Meshedee-Norouz had made acquaintance with a resident of the city, who, inviting us to rent his house, led us to a dirty little room with a small terrace adjoining, on which we might sleep, he said. The first night disproved his words; it was a thoroughfare for all the cats in Meshed, and the abode of innumerable smaller, but not less active animals, therefore as permanent residence in such a place was not to be thought of, the Syud made search for another house, and found one in a retired situation, consisting of two rooms, a terrace, and a large courtyard, with stabling, which we rented for the monthly sum of one tomaun, or thirteen shillings.

Having described our route from Astrabad, I would here offer a few remarks upon the country between that place and Meshed. From Shahrood to "the holy city," by the road which we followed, we made the distance (at a rough calculation of four miles an hour for horses' walk) two hundred and eighty-seven miles; something less than Fraser does. The soil, which from Shahrood to near Meyer is chiefly of mixed sand and gravel, gradually betters between the latter place and Subzawar, and thence on to Neshapoor it still improves. From Neshapoor, the road goes for twenty-eight miles through a plain, well-watered, and not ill-cultivated country, to the foot of the Elboorz mountains, beyond which it has been described in the journal.

Another, and in some respects a better road, goes off from Shahrood, nearer to the mountains, *viâ* the town of Jau-jerm. Beyond the latter place it branches, and you may either, as is most frequently done, come down to Subzawar, and join the usual road, or go up to Kaboushan,* and so round to Meshed. There are two long marches, one before and the other beyond Jau-jerm, but water is in plenty at the stages, and the country which borders the road is better peopled and cultivated than that through which the lower route goes. The king's troops usually take this road, and Futteh Ali Shah marched his army into Khorassaun this way.

What was remarked about the district of Subzawar, may be repeated with regard to this country generally; namely, that if the incursions of the Toork-

* The road to Kaboushan, as precedingly noted, goes through a highly-cultivated country: water is in plenty, the roads are tolerably good, and the mountains are passed by a less difficult cotul than that of Durrood.

muns were prevented, its condition would be very much altered for the better, and consequently the difficulties of the roads through it would be greatly lessened.

The route eastward from Astrabad to Meshed, by the lands of the Yimoots, Goklans, and Koords, is one which offers plenty of water and forage, and for troops, supplies of grain, as well as cattle for slaughter, could certainly be procured. It is a road now seldom travelled, but it is represented as by no means a difficult one, and it has the advantage of avoiding the steep passes of the Elboorz.

CHAPTER X.

Sojourn at Meshed—Men and Manners in this Holy City.

MESHED the Holy has been so minutely and so well described by Fraser, that I may content myself with saying that it is a very large walled city, of irregular shape, the houses of which are chiefly built of mud brick. There is much to disappoint a traveller in its general appearance, but still it is a city desirable to see, for in the centre of it is a cluster of magnificent buildings of gold and coloured tile, sacred to the memory of the Imaum Reza; and there are some beautiful colleges, and fine caravanseras, which, if it interests a man to read about, he may take Fraser for his guide, and walk through them. It is a city full of interest, for there you meet with devotees who assemble from all parts of the eastern world, to the number of one hundred thousand yearly; and if the romance of Persian history has charms for you, where will you find a city which has been more the scene of its stratagems and bloody tragedies?

Though I shall not enter into a minute descriptior

of the town, I must, in order to render after-accounts intelligible, sketch its general appearance. A very broad boulevard, on either side of which are the principal shops, runs from the east to the west wall, interrupted only by the *sahn*, or great square of the sacred buildings, into which you pass, from either side, under a very high arched gate of exquisite architecture, faced with blue enamelled tile. The square itself deserves especial notice; it is a parallelogram of good proportions, enclosed by a double story of arched cloisters fronted with mosaic work, and paved with the gravestones of such men as were rich enough to pay for the indulgence. In the centre of the long sides of the square are two deep-arched porches, of the same height and proportions as the gates: one, of enamelled tile-work, leads into a fine mosque; the opposite one, covered with broad copper tiles heavily gilt, fronts a high gilded minaret, and the golden dome under which the Imaum sleeps. In the centre of the square is a small octagon temple, within which stands a white marble block of great size, hollowed to contain water, and through the square, and round this, Shah Abbass made a stone canal, that the faithful might have water at hand for their ablutions. A space of some hundred yards round the shrine is railed off for a sanctuary: within this are several houses and shops, and hither even a murderer may flee, and be in safety so long as he remains. Some have dwelt here for years, whose lives would have been forfeited had they put foot without the pale.

When Hussan Ali Meerza was governor, a man who had deeply offended him took refuge in the sanctuary, and lived within it for many days; the Prince not daring to infringe the rules, sent some artful persons to persuade the offender that his fault had been overlooked, and to invite him to return to his friends. The poor man suffered himself to be deceived, and venturing out, was seized and cruelly put to death by having a stake driven through his back. This is a Persian mode of torture, which sometimes dreadfully prolongs a victim's sufferings: the Syud, when he was formerly in Meshed, saw four men nailed to the ground in this manner, who had been convicted of kidnapping men for the purpose of selling them to the Toorkmuns: on the third day he told me, there were signs of life in their bodies.

The fixed population of the city may amount to forty-five thousand souls,* and the greater number of these are rogues, who only take thought how to make the most of the pilgrims that visit the shrine. From the high priest to the seller of bread, all have the same end; and, not content with the strangers' money, those in office about the saint appropriate to

* I found it very difficult to separate the residents from visiters. After some time, I came to the conclusion that fifty thousand souls was a fair calculation; but I was assured by some of the best informed inhabitants of both cities, that the fixed population of Meshed was, if any thing, less than that of Heraut, and I am inclined to prefer their opinions, because though the city-walls of Meshed embrace a great space, there are within them many gardens, large cemeteries, and much waste ground.

themselves the very dues for keeping his temple in repair. Thus some of the buildings were suffered to remain in a dilapidated state, and the stone canal leading up the main street into the great square was dry, because the head warden had turned the water on his own melon-ground.

Between knaves and fools, I suppose a man might gain as much knowledge of mankind in a month at Meshed, as he could in a year at most other places in Asia. The two chief men of the place were high priests, brothers, who both desiring popularity, were on any thing but affectionate terms with each other. The elder owned half the caravanseras in the city, and was a man of great wealth, proud and bigoted. The other, though far poorer, was more generally liked, on account of the greater amiability of his disposition; each had his party, and it was a great struggle between them who should get most persons to pray behind them in the court of the temple: you might always learn the strength of the respective forces half an hour after prayer time. The influence of the elder brother was greater than that of the governor: his eldest son had long been in the habit of coining false money, and passing it in spite of the Vuzeer, who could not, indeed, with any grace prohibit him, seeing that he himself had made a large sum a few years before, by coining many thousand bad Heraut reals, and circulating them over Khorassaun.

On entering the city, you are struck with the

number of Syuds in their green turbans and sashes, lying wait for novices to instruct them in the forms of their vows. Mixing with the pilgrims who throng the streets, are to be seen moollâs of all degrees, — hungry wolves in sheep's clothing, who cover a great many peccadilloes (to call them by no worse a name) with an assumption of sanctity, and who, though all bitterly jealous of each other, have certain common causes in which they unite.

One would suppose that a moollâ desirous of getting his bread in Meshed, need only go and take up his abode there; but not so, he would be attacked by the whole band of settlers, as a paria dog venturing into a new parish would be, and I have known instances of men who have been fairly bullied out of the city. Moollâ is a term which, like that of "wise men of the East," has lost its meaning. With a smattering of knowledge, and a few friends, any man may get bound over his cap the turban which marks him a doctor, and privileges him to write himself an A.S.S.; and if he add to this the cloak of sanctified manners, and can talk either a great deal or very little, he may make his way as well as his betters. The most fortunate of the Meshed moollâs keep fat upon their pickings from visiters to the shrine, directing their religious offices, and dealing in astrology and divination; the poorer ones cast smaller nets, eke out their means by living rent free in the college cloisters, and serve and fawn on their betters till they themselves have the luck to rise above the commonalty.

Early in the morning the din of this crowded city would be quite hushed; a few of the druggists' shops only being open, for the convenience of those who might want dye for their beards, and the slippers of such persons sounded as they hurried across the large empty quadrangle on their way to the baths. Two hours afterwards the scene had changed; the shops were all open, and the many trades being busily carried on; fruits and vegetables, brought in from the villages, were piled in baskets along the bazaar, which was crowded with purchasers, and many householders, or servants, laden with the day's provision, were repairing to their several homes; the moollâs were astir, and occasionally a doctor of high degree would sweep by with his turbaned train of satellites, on his way to lecture in a college; while often might be heard the joyous *sulawaat* of approaching pilgrims, who would press through the city-gate into the broad boulevard,—a dense troop of soiled and jaded travellers,—and presently disperse to seek lodging, in order that they might repair to the baths and perform their ablutions, so as to visit the holy shrine at the blessed hour of evening prayer.*

During the heat of the day the streets were nearly

* Of the five times of prayer, the hours of early morn and even are the most efficacious. Then the angel *Akhter* goes the rounds of "the faithful," and says Ameen to their prayers, to which all the heavens are open—up to the throne of the Most High.

deserted, but the stillness of noon was broken by the loud and solemn chant of the muezzins, calling from the high minarets in prolonged Arabic verses, to summon the faithful to prayer: "Ullaho Ukbur! Ullaho Ukbur!" etc.—"God is supreme!—God is supreme!—I bear witness that there is no god but God!—I bear witness that Mohummud is the Apostle of God: May the mercy and peace of Ullah be upon him and his family!—I bear witness that the Commander of the faithful, Ali, is the friend of God!—Come to prayers! Come to the refuge! Come to the meritorious action! (of prayer)—God is supreme!—God is supreme!—There is no god but God!"

We ascended the golden minaret one noon, the muezzin permitting us on condition that we should cry the Azân. When however we got to the balcony round the top, it was evident that our unpractised lungs would never reach the faithful pigmies below, and with an adroit compliment to the voice of the muezzin, my friend got us excused from the condition. From this height we had a complete view of the city and the country round, and looked directly into the nearest houses.

In the afternoon the boulevard would be thronged again, with natives from all parts of the East; Affghaun troopers, in their loose and slovenly yet picturesque dresses, Arabs, Koords, Toorks, and a few Oosbegs or Indians, with pilgrims from all the provinces of Irân, the staid, long-bearded Shirauzee, and the fop of Isphahaun, priests, merchants, peasants, and fakeers, without end.

The resident shopkeepers, still intent upon profit, sat busily working, or, if their occupation admitted it, chatting with those who, with a gunlock to repair, or a boot or bridle to mend, lounged at their boards. Other residents, men, or veiled women, moved through the crowd with baskets of fresh and stale bread,* or sat in convenient places to sell it; and at the corners of thoroughfares were posted cooks with portable kitchens, who sang out tempting invitations to the passers-by, to taste their kabobs and coloured pilaus.

A goldsmith who lived within the sanctuary, close to the high gate of the sahn, allowed me to sit at his window of an afternoon to watch the crowd below, and a more striking or lively scene could hardly have been looked upon. About the gate were booths, behind which sat venders of trinkets, and turquoises, of which every pilgrim at least carries away one, as a memento of the "holy city;" the women of the city, veiled from the crown of the head to the foot, and looking out from a slip of network across their eyes, offered for sale skullcaps and other articles of clothing, their manufacture; there was a constant hurry of feet to and from the sahn, under the high archway: fakeers, with their badges (goat, deer, or leopard skins,) slung on their backs, lounged about,

* Stale bread is sold at a reduced price.

calling loudly on the names of the Deity, Mohummud, and Ali, and occasionally a crowd would gather round a story-teller, to hear a tale of Haroon-al-Rasheed, or Shah Abbas the Great, or perhaps a humorous satire on the reigning tribe, the Cujjers. At sunset the nukkaur khauneh* would sound, the musicians getting on the roof of one side of the sahn, and, with drums and long trumpets, making a noise much like the confused music that is heard on approaching a fair in England. The people early repair to rest; and before three hours of night had gone, the silence of the night was scarcely interrupted, except by the wild shouts of the city watch, as they challenged each other all round the ramparts.

We saw Meshed to advantage, as we arrived during the first days of the religious festival of the Mohurrum. The evening of our arrival I went to the sahn, to see the representation of part of this tragedy. A kaufir is not licensed to put foot within the rail of the sanctuary, much less in the sahn itself, to defile the graves of the holy men who rest there, by walking over them; but I judged rightly, that the crowd would be too much taken up with the performance to notice me, and Meshedee-Norouz, (though he confessed that a Jew had been stoned to

* A state band, which plays morning and evening at all large places where there is a royal governor. Out of compliment to the saint, the nukkar khauneh at Meshed plays in the court of the temple instead of at the palace.

death for the intrusion) promised to give an answer to any body who might require one.

The performance this evening represented the setting out of Hossein and his family on that unfortunate journey to Koofa which ended in their murder, and the characters were acted by men and boys in proper dresses, who, standing upon a raised platform covered with black cloth, read their parts from slips of paper. The stage was in front of the golden porch, under which, at small arched windows, sat the Prince and a few favoured others. The crowd formed a dense semicircle about the platform, the men separate from the women, who, closely veiled, were made to seat themselves on the left, and the feroshes were not sparing of their blows to those of either sex who pressed forward. The performers on these occasions are men selected for their powers of elocution, and the parts are written by the cleverest doctors; it is not, therefore, surprising that a people so alive to the beauties of language as the Persians are, should readily receive the impressions intended to be conveyed in descriptions of the fortitude and tenderness, the noble deeds or the sorrows, of the martyrs of Islam.

The crowd came prepared to be moved, and they were so; at the affecting passages the men beat their breasts, and exclaimed or wept, while the women writhed their bodies, and sent up a low moan from under their veils. The whole circumstances of

Hossein's setting out were represented, some splendidly caparisoned camels horses and mules being introduced, upon which, after some affecting prognostications, the martyr and his family mounted and rode round the platform. On ordinary occasions animals are excluded from the sanctuary, but in such instances, it is presumed, the part they play sanctifies them. When they got to the end of their stage, the day's performance concluded, and the crowd dispersed. Growing bold at seeing ourselves unnoticed, we strolled into the court of a mosque adjoining the sanctum, and saw the Prince come out from his devotions: he was waited on by the chief dignitaries of the place, and escorted by some ragged fellows of all sizes, armed with English firelocks, with which they used to butt us into a lane, we bowing most humbly as the Prince passed before us. We afterwards made the round of the colleges, and returned to our abode by moonlight: the night was very still, and lying on the terrace of our house, I could long distinctly hear the sound of the devotees beating their breasts in the sahn, to the measured cries of "Hussan," Hossein," "Hussan," "Hossein."

June 29th.—This evening, at dusk, I made a tour of the places inside the sanctuary, with the Syud. I had resolved not to visit the shrine, Fraser having proved it to be an undertaking more dangerous than interesting, but my friend, unwilling that I should come to Meshed and not see its greatest wonder, thwarted my resolution before I was aware what was his intention. At a small door to the left of the golden porch, sat a man in the gloom, with several pairs of slippers before him; the Syud, depositing his shoes, moved on quickly, so it became requisite to shuffle off mine also, and follow him into what is called Aliverdi Khan's goombuz, a fine mosque, regarding which there is a very incredible anecdote.* We left on one side a room set apart for women to pray in, and passed into the "kishick khaneh," or guard hall, where the servants of the shrine keep watch. There were but few persons here, and those engaged in conversation, so skreening ourselves by the high doors, we sat down and took a good look into the adjoining chamber, Darul Houffaz, which was of semicircular form, domed, and of great height and size. There was a strong glare of many lights, and the place was nearly filled with turbaned Syuds and Moollâs, and pilgrims of many countries. Some were seated with their backs to the walls, reading or talking; others

* It is related that, in the time of Shah Abbas the Great, Aliverdi Khan was blind, and continually prostrate at the shrine of the saint. Shah Abbas coming to pay his vows, remarked the blind man, and asked him how long he had been there: "Four years" was the answer. "Then," said the monarch, "I fear you must be a bad man, and if you are not restored to sight when I come out from Ziarut, I'll order your head off." The unhappy man, report says, hastened to scatter much money that he had about his person, begging the bystanders to gather it and pray for him; and such was the success of their intercessions with the saint, that he on the spot recovered his sight, and subsequently built the mosque in gratitude for the miracle.

stood and conversed in groups; and friends, meeting, stayed to salute each other, and mutually wish acceptance of their vows. Before the door that led into the shrine, were seated devotees, weeping, and beating their naked breasts most extravagantly, while others stood muttering the form before entering, and in the corners sat doctors, servants of the shrine, reading the Koran aloud.

It was a scene to bewilder one, and I was thinking whether I was not dreaming, when my companion touched my hand, and rising, led me quickly across till we came beneath the centre of the dome. Stopping for a moment before the door of the shrine, we bent our heads in salute towards it, and then passed out into a smaller chamber, in which stood a magnificent gilt candelabrum, in the shape of a tree, bearing forty branch-lights. To have completed the ceremony, we should have entered the sanctum, and walked round the tomb, but the light was too broad to render that a safe proceeding, especially at such a season, for had the alarm been given of an infidel polluting the shrine, the zealots at the door would have shortly made a convert or a martyr of him. Being unprepared for the alternative, I was content to dispense with this part of the ceremony, and to pass out into a beautifully-proportioned enclosed square, traversing which, we found ourselves in the Gowher Shaud mosque, built by the wife of one of Tamerlane's sons, a prince who has left memorials of his piety and graphic skill, in many sacred sentences of broad Arabic writing, with which he embellished the walls of this and of other Mohummudan temples.

When we entered, the faces of the crowd with which we mixed were turned towards Kerbolah, and they were listening with intense interest to the words of a speaker mounted on a pulpit of steps, who, "'kerchief in hand," alternately wept and harangued, —his theme, the martyrdom of the sainted Hossein. The mosque was but partially lighted; sufficiently so to show the speaker, and the expression of some of his auditors' countenances; farther within, the mosque was dark, but we could discern by a glimmering light on the wall, that it was crowded to the extremity. Though I but imperfectly understood the orator's words, yet aided by my friend I could catch the tenour of his speech, and felt myself becoming gradually much interested. He was gifted with a deep melodious voice, and had entire sway over the feelings of those whom he addressed. When, detailing the cruelty with which Hossein's son was murdered in his very arms,* he spoke of the lamentations of the

* The substance of this part of the tragedy is truly affecting, and Persians, in their love for the martyr, lavish their choicest expressions upon the descriptions of it. Yezeed's general had cut off Hossein's small party from communication with the Euphrates, and they suffered the greatest distress from thirst. The mother of Hossein's infant boy, Ali Asghur, or Ali the Little, from extreme exhaustion, was unable to give the breast to her child. Hossein, therefore, taking the boy in his arms, galloped up to his enemies, and appealed to their humanity, saying, "On me be the consequence of my offence to you, but do not deny a drop of water to an innocent, helpless child, whose mother is dying!" The reply to this affecting address was a flight of arrows, one of which, "more fatally directed than the rest," struck through the throat of the infant into its father's arm.

mother,—all were softened, and wept; but as, after a pause, he went on to tell of the youthful courage of his sister Zeinab's two sons, their sorrow gradually gave way to admiration, which they expressed in a deep hum of applause; and when, still rising in energy, he described the noble firmness with which the martyr met death, when all his friends had fallen for him, they caught the enthusiasm of the speaker, and burst into a proud and prolonged shout of—"HOSSEIN!"

I have in vain tried to describe this scene: it was one of those which once witnessed is never forgotten, but I feel that my words scarcely give an idea of it.

Through low-arched vaults, which border this mosque, we found our way into the great square again, and then I to my alarm perceived that we were followed by a moollâ covered with an immense white turban, who, at a little distance, dodged us wherever we went. The Syud observing this, turned short into a small mosque open to the square, and commenced a form of prayer which I saw was not the usual one, so I thought my best course was to stand behind him in a reverential attitude, whereas I should have sat on my heels. Having resolved always to make an excuse for not saying prayers, rather than commit a regular mockery of any thing so sacred, I had not given myself the trouble to learn the Mooselmaun forms; but in this instance I should have found a slight knowledge of them useful, without being in the way of my scruples. The old man, who had seated himself at the entrance, seeing my posture, came up to me, and for what appeared a very long minute, peered hard into my face, and ran his eye over my person; he then asked me why, if I was a Mooselmaun, I did not also say my prayers. I do not remember ever to have felt more uncomfortable; the Syud was prostrate before me, unconscious of what was going on, and the old man was pressing his question with a pertinacity that made me very much inclined to knock him down and run for it; but I commanded myself so far as not to answer him, and fetched two or three deep sobs, that he might suppose me weeping for the sorrows of Hossein. He appeared very dissatisfied, and when he left me and went to the door, I fully expected that he would bring a crowd in upon us; but now the Syud had finished his performance, and seeing how matters stood, he, with an air of great *nonchalance*, walked up to the man with his cloak carelessly thrown back so as to disclose his green sash. This settled the suspicions of our persecutor: at least he left us, and hastily regaining our slippers,* we returned home.

Sir John Malcolm had given me introductory letters for the Prince and Vuzeer, and I had obtained others from the King's son governing at Tehraun;

* We had been all this time walking without shoes, no one being allowed to visit the interior otherwise than barefoot, or with stockings on. The men who keep the slippers are remarkable for their memory; with sometimes as many as one hundred pair of shoes before them, they seldom fail to select those belonging to a stranger, and to put them before him almost as soon as he can ask for them.

having forwarded these, I received an invitation to visit the Vuzeer, and accordingly this morning, the 30th, I went to the charbaugh, where stood his residence among the ruined gardens and palaces which Nadir Shah constructed.

Meerza Mousa received us in a large garden, sitting with a few friends on a carpet spread on the paved walk. He was a remarkably dignified and well-mannered man, with a sunken yet still piercing dark eye, and a very long beard dyed of a deep bluish black. He welcomed us with an agreeable smile and many civilities, regaled us with tea and fruit, and addressing his friends, begged them to understand that for honour, integrity, veracity, telling the truth, discretion, learning, and fighting, the English were unrivalled among the Franks; to which they were polite enough to yield unqualified assent. A few general questions and answers concerning our journey followed, and then the minister, changing his manner, said gravely that it was their religious festival time, therefore that he must beg me to excuse his rising; but he at the same time politely invited us to adjourn to a neighbouring court, to witness the performance of a sacred tragedy, and we were shown up a foul and broken staircase, into a slip of a room with a small window just over the stage, one of many in a large building occupied by his family and friends.

The rich men in Persia are accustomed to erect stages for these representations, and not only to pay the performers, but to provide refreshment for all who choose to come, always iced water, and sometimes sherbets. In Meerza Mousa's court was erected a platform hung with black cloth; a great crowd of men and women were assembled, and "sukkaus" went among them with skins full of iced water, bidding them drink and be thankful, remembering the thirst of the blessed martyr.

The performance commenced with an amateur chant by boys and old men, than which nothing more discordant could well be imagined. Next, boys mounted the lower steps of a pulpit, to recite verses composed for the occasion, and were succeeded by men, who took elevation according to their fame. The best of these speakers realize as much as 200 tomauns in the ten days of the Mohurrum, lecturing at three or four places daily. This is a large sum for Persia, but it is hardly earned, for the great exertions that the orators are obliged to make, cause them soon to lose their voices, and I should think must affect their lungs. The chief performer was unable to attend from hoarseness, and his place was taken by a speaker who, to judge from his discourse, had not found it a profitable avocation; for his lecture, like an Irish sermon, was interlarded with much personal anecdote, and he occasionally forgot the sorrows of Hossein in his own. "The eyes," he commenced, "which do not weep for Hossein, may they become sightless!—blessed are the tears shed for a martyr, they will cause the face of the believer to shine hereafter!" The waters of the heart thus poured forth, he assured his hearers, would form large pearls, which the angel Gabriel would put into their hands as passports to Paradise; and then he went on to say, "It is now thirty years that I have been shouting the saint's praises in Meshed, and I am actually in danger of wanting bread." The only, to me, interesting speaker was an Arab, apparently not a paid performer, who making his way through the crowd, ascended the steps, and struck at once into a vigorous strain of nine feet, to which all returned a chorus of the same measure, beating their breasts in accompaniment. The figure and the gestures of the speaker were singularly striking, and the chant was really melodious.

Then followed the tragedy of the murder of Ali Acber, Hossein's eldest son, who at the *finale* entered with a sword stuck into the brain of a false head, and living long enough to recite some pathetic verses, died after the approved fashion of stage heroes.

The order of the day was to be as melancholy as possible, and those who could not weep unaffectedly, at least beat their breasts and looked unhappy. We noticed one old man below us, with an orange-coloured beard, the fountain of whose sorrows being dried up, he could not for the soul of him squeeze out a tear, and the expression of his face, as shutting his eyes tight and screwing up his beard, he tried to weep, was quite comic. Hearing a stir in an adjoining chamber, I had the curiosity to look through a chink in a door, and saw about a dozen, I suppose the

Vuzeer's women unveiled, weeping and beating their bosoms at the representation. My conscience, however, told me that it was not polite to reward the minister's civility by gazing at his ladies, and the consequences might have been unpleasant had I been discovered, so I contented myself with a transient look. The performance over, a stout water-carrier came in, bending under the weight of a bull's hide filled with water, and not content with this display of strength, he took up three children on his back, and stood for a few moments under the accumulated weight. Sets of morris-dancers then came in, clapping pieces of wood together, and we were lastly entertained by some Bungushes (men of a Sheah tribe south-west of Caubul), who beat themselves with chains. We hoped also to have seen a wonderful boy, eater of glass and brass kettles, but were told that having become rich by his exhibitions, he had lately taken to eat nothing but pilau. A resident of Meshed assured us that this boy once offered to eat his auftauba* for half a real, but that feeling sure that the monster would be as good as his word, he would not sacrifice his pot.

Two evenings afterwards, I was witness to a more amusing act of the tragedy, which was performed under a tent in the main street. The Sheahs have a tradition that, when the Caliph Yezeed caused Hossein to be put to death, a Frangee Elchee†

* Copper jug.

† Frank ambassador.

(though from what part of Europe does not precisely appear), who happened to come on a mission to Damascus at the time, exclaimed against the foulness of the deed, and suffered martyrdom for his impertinence. The actor who personated the Elchee, wore a velvet foraging-cap, upon long ringlets which fell down his back and the sides of his face; one coloured handkerchief was tied round his neck, and another on his arm, and the rest of his apparel was Persian. He was altogether a strange figure, but seemed to flatter himself that he was quite *en costume*. "That is not bad," said a Shirauz friend of the road who had attached himself to me,—"not bad for Meshed, where they haven't seen Feringees; but *Shirauz* Agha! if you had seen the Frangee Elchee we had at Shirauz! by heavens I'm speaking the truth to you; when Elchee Malcoolm came from Hindoostan to go to the fortunate dust of the Shah's foot, he gave the men of my city a whole suit of red regimentals, cocks' feather cap and all, and you'd have sworn there was a real Feringee on the stage. Hei Shirauz!"

The Frangee Elchee being introduced with a discordant flourish of trumpets, presented several trays of presents, and muttering some gibberish which passed for a European language, took a seat at the foot of the throne. A son of Hossein's (Ali, commonly called "Zein-ool Aubideen," the Ornament of the Religious) addressed a spirited harangue to Yezeed, which I could not follow, but it appeared to affect the foreign ambassador very much. Presently the head of the martyr was brought in on a spear, and thrown at the foot of the throne. Transported at the sight, the Elchee rushed from his seat to the head, took it up, and with passionate expressions of grief kissed it, and then threw dust upon his own; he next began to abuse the caliph for the grievous sin that he had committed in causing the death of a descendant of his prophet; but Yezeed, enraged at the stranger's audacity, stopped his speech by ordering his immediate execution. He was led away to death, but when going out, he turned, and uttered the confession of the Mohummudan faith,—"La Illah Il Illah!" &c. The crowd who were assembled on this occasion repeated it solemnly after him, and, lifting up their hands to heaven, cried with much fervour "Ullah! Ullah!"

I was not allowed to enjoy this representation in peace, for my Shirauz acquaintance could not in his zeal help admonishing me by the good example of the Elchee (my countryman, he thought). He hinted that if the truth could but find its way into the soul, I should cause joy all over Meshed, and my clothes, he said, would be made shreds of, and shared among the devout, as had lately been those of one Ibn Oollah, who had miraculously received his sight at the tomb of the Imaum Reza. The temptation was great, but all my serious thoughts were put to flight by the extravagances of a ridiculous old peasant, who not being able to get a front place, had brought his donkey up to the post of the awning, and holding by it, stood on his pack-saddle, and looked over the heads of the circle. Every incident represented was to him a reality, and I question whether the family of the martyr suffered more mental agony, than did this votary at the representation of their sorrows. He applauded all the arguments of the speaker who represented Ali, weeping audibly at his address to the tyrant, and when the Frangee Elchee began to act, he could in nowise contain himself, but cried out energetically—"See to him! see him! hear the Frangee! Ai Khoda! an *infidel* pleads the cause of the blessed martyr, and the heart of stone is not moved! — God take away his blessing from Yezeed! Aiwah! Aiwah!—Alas! Alas!"

During the Mohurrum the Prince was not accessible. When the ceremonies were ended, we were honoured with an audience, having first had a sharp skirmish with the Vuzeer about my being permitted to sit in the presence. Meerza Mousa was so furious in enforcing this point, that I fancied he was in earnest, but the Syud quietly met his arguments by standing on the plea of not wishing to insult the "heir-apparent," in whose presence I had sat, and whose dignity was unquestionably not less than that of the Prince of Meshed.

The residence of the Prince was in the citadel, a place of no great strength, the interior of which was in a state of ruin, exhibiting fallen walls and rubbishy courts. We alighted at the archway of the inhabited part, and passed into a hall where twenty men, dressed in imitation of soldiers, lay asleep; these we afterwards learned were the Prince's artillerymen, who were to have been drawn up to show the Feringee the strength of the garrison, but the porter expecting to see a being like the one represented in the Mohurrum, let me pass in my Persian costume. Prince Ahmud Ali Meerza fully justified the accounts we had heard of him; he received us with an affectation of dignity which he had not the manners to support, and repeated the set speech about the honour and probity, &c. of the English, after the Vuzeer, who, leaning on a long stick, stood below the window at which his nominal lord was seated. The Shahzadeh wished to know whether I was a servant of the King of England or of the *Coompanee*. "Of the latter, themselves the devoted servants of 'His Majesty the King of England, and Emperor of the Seas.'"—"*Coompanee che chees ust?*" asked the Prince; "*What is the Company?*" I was about to explain the mystery of the twenty-four stools, when the Vuzeer confidently answered, that Sir John Malcolm was the Company. I would have corrected him, but no, he was quite positive. "Ask *me*," said he, with the air of a man entirely master of his subject, "ask *me*, I possess information on that score; Sir John Malcolm first came as Elchee to the King of Kings, and then went to Bombay and became *Coompanee*." It was plain that any assertions on my part would be lost, so, considering that the Honourable Court might be more unworthily represented, I suffered the Vuzeer to abide in his conceit, and bore the reproach of not knowing so much about my own country as did a man who had never left Irân.

Some days after our arrival, the Syud took me to dine with his old friend Meerza Abdool Jowaut, Moojeteheid, one of the chief dignitaries of the city, the same whom Mr. Fraser frequently mentions, and to whose friendly interference that gentleman perhaps owed his life when it was threatened by the fanatics of the city. Meerza Abdool Jowaut is esteemed a very Aflatoon* by the Meshedees. He is supposed to inherit a perfect knowledge of Euclid from a mathematical great uncle, and to be equalled by few in the science of astronomy; logic he has at his tongue's end, and his decisions according to the "Shirra" are regarded as little short of inspired ones, doubtless because the excellence of his disposition induces him to do justice to every party. He has a mania for every thing foreign, affects a little *keemia*,† not altogether doubting the philosopher's stone, and treasures up old books and European knick-knacks. As soon as my friend had visited him, and told him with whom he was travelling, Meerza Abdool Jowaut sent me a kind message, expressive of his regret that he could not exactly show me the civilities he wished, since the men of Meshed were short-sighted, and had given him some ugly names on account of his intimacy with Mr. Fraser, but saying that he had an

* Plato. † Chemistry.

esteem for my nation, and would be glad on any occasion to serve me. I owed this civility partly to the Meerza's amiable disposition, and to his wish to oblige the Syud, but in some degree to his curiosity, which he gratified shortly after sending me the complimentary message, by asking us to dinner in a quiet way.—"You were mentioning," said the Syud to me as we were walking to our host's residence, "that the Tartars did not invade England;—however that may be, don't dispute the point with Meerza Abdool Jowaut, for he has an historical work upon Frangestaun, which assures him that they *did*, and there is no need to put him out of conceit with his book."

We waited to pay our devoirs to the old man till he had said his prayers in a small mosque near the gate of his house. The Syud kissed his hands in token of extreme respect, while I made out a Persian obeisance, by placing a hand upon my heart, and bending forward; the Meerza, motioning with his long ivory-headed stick to the entrance of his house, gave us an opportunity of showing our breeding by refusing to take place of him, and then led us up a flight of steps to a broad terrace, where, on two parallel slips of carpet, were placed a pair of large silver lamps. The moment we were settled on our heels, the Meerza addressed me with—"You are welcome!—you have conferred honour!—you are very welcome!—your esteemed health is good? What is the latitude of London?" Reference to the work mentioned by my friend, which lay at his side, satisfied him that I knew the latitude of my birth-place, and he set me down for a man of information. He then talked of his astronomical observations at Meshed, which brought out its position, he said, nearly what Mr. Fraser had made it (a fudge, I thought, on the old gentleman's part). He pushed me rather hard upon some abstruse points in astronomy, but fortunately there was another guest, who prevented the conversation from becoming too scientific, a merchant of Reshdt, who having gone across the Caspian to Astrakan, considered himself warranted in telling some very marvellous anecdotes of the Oroos.

Our talk was seasonably interrupted by a delicious repast, handsomely served on silver trays, giving us a fair specimen of the style of living of the higher orders of this city. There was the long rice of Peshower, "that you may press down in the dish and it will rise again of its own elasticity, and which is so light, that you never know when you have eaten enough of it." With this were served party-coloured pilaus, omelettes, rich meats with sweet syrups, and garlic stewed in milk; and to drink, sherbets that "Tortoni" never dreamed of, made with "rewas," and the juice of the fresh grape,—nectars which are conveyed from a China bowl to the mouth in deep spoons of the pear-tree wood, so delicately carved that they tremble under the weight of the liquid. Our host most courteously encouraged us to eat, putting choice morsels of meat before us with his fingers, and sometimes helping us from his own plate (a politesse which certainly dates as far back as the time when Joseph entertained his brothers at Pharaoh's court, and which in Persia is as great a one as can well be shown a guest); and he gave zest to the repast by filling up his intervals with scraps of poetical wit, which he bandied with the Syud, than whom no one could play such a part better.

The Persians have been likened to the French, for having a constant fund of agreeable conversation, and for the politeness of their manners; but it may perhaps be doubted whether the French could say so much upon so little, and whether their manners do not suffer from the comparison. The Persians have no real learning from which to create their wit, and yet two men of this nation seldom get together without striking up a racy dialogue; and they express themselves with so much politeness and good humour, that you immediately feel at ease in their society, and can enjoy it even when but partly acquainted with their language. They appeared to me to be the politer people of the two; to have the suavity of the French, without their grimace, and to be without that "brusquerie" which is occasionally so offensive in the Gauls: they can indeed be as bearish and disagreeable as any people, but they seldom are so unless when their religious prejudices are excited. These are the mere opinions of a traveller: I did not form them only at Meerza Abdool Jowaut's table, but a recollection of his wit and politeness induces me to insert them here.

As a special instance of civility, I should mention that the host ordered my tray to be the last removed, a compliment which my ignorance prevented me from feeling grateful for at the time, but which the Syud did not fail to enlarge upon, in particularizing several little delicate attentions on the part of his friend, which I had not remarked, but which were evidences of the kindest consideration, coming as they did from a man of high religious rank, in a country where every, the slightest; shade of civility marks a man's value in society. I do not know what prevented our killing ourselves with this rich dinner, which our entertainer pressed upon us in the urgent way of old hospitality, unless it was some delicious green tea, recommended as "*usle uz Chine,*" genuine China leaf, and which was brought in little porcelain cups cased with silver.

A lively conversation followed, which the Meerza politely endeavoured occasionally to make general. In the course of conversation, he introduced the great question, whether the sun goes round the earth, or the earth round the sun; and the Syud, being acquainted with, and somewhat of a convert to, our planetary system, took the Copernican side of the argument. The Meerza made a stout dispute for the earth's stability, but I think one of the arguments he laid most stress upon was this,—that if the earth went round, there must be a pressure one way, and that one of two sticks driven at equal depth into the ground crossways, must in time be pressed farther in than the other. "If I were as some of this city," he said goodhumouredly, "I should stop your arguments by saying that your view of the question is heretical, but I like to hear both sides of every question. The Feringees are an astonishing people, and it pleases me to hear of any new grand principle being struck out; you would have the world in the heavens, but I confess that, having built all my small knowledge upon the belief that it is stationary, I should, considering my years, wish it to remain so till I am laid in it:"—"And then," interrupted the Syud, "there's little doubt of your going where we think the world to be."—"I am already in Paradise," was the polite rejoinder, and as it was not to be expected that any thing better could be said, we exchanged the compliments of the night and separated.

I did not venture to the public baths of Meshed, fearing to offend the people, and so lose the liberty which I enjoyed of walking where I would about the city; but Meshedee-Norouz, who in his love for liquor, had lost no time in making himself acquainted with those who had it, introduced us to some Jews, one of whom, the son of their Ketkhoda, gave me the *entrée* of their bath, which was heated twice a week. There are about one hundred families of

Jews in Meshed. They are chiefly engaged in petty traffic, and, though not rich, their situation is respectable compared with that of their brethren in the cities of Tehraun and Isphahan, who go about, as in European countries, selling and exchanging old garments; but they are not without a share of the indignities that are entailed on their race. They may not pass the pale of the sanctuary, neither may they put foot within the college-squares in which good men are buried; on their clothes, however new, they must wear a patch at the breast; their caps must not be of the same form as those worn by true believers, and they dare not return abuse, much less a blow given by a Mohummudan, so that even children of the faithful race throw stones and dirt at them in the streets, unchecked by their parents, who think it a very meritorious act to worry the soul of an unbeliever. I one morning saw a fakeer take an old Jew by the beard as if he would have pulled it from his face, and accuse him of having been party to selling him some years before to the Toorkmuns, nor did he release the terrified old man till he promised to pay a few reals, the crowd looking on as Englishmen do at badger-baiting, and thinking it capital sport.

We attended the Jewish synagogue one Saturday, and the Rabbis were so captivated by the Syud's unprecedentedly liberal opinions, that they made a point of showing all that they thought would interest us. The synagogue was a square room, on two sides of which was a gallery, with a lattice skreen-work for the women to sit behind. From the centre of the chamber, from the floor to the ceiling, rose four posts, and on steps within these was the altar. Their chanting was in the Persian style, and very discordant; parts of the Old Testament were read in Hebrew, and a homily was delivered in the Persian language. When praying, they turned to Jerusalem, and covered their heads in white mantles, and at one part of the service, the priest standing on the altar-steps, held up the Pentateuch, written on large rolls of parchment, while the congregation crowded eagerly round to look on it. It was an affecting sight, this "fragment of Israel" in oriental garb, adhering religiously to the ordinances of their forefathers, amid the persecutions of the most bigoted of a bigoted race. Not a man, they said, had gone out from them.

After the service we were shown into a small room, where were preserved with great care more than fifty copies of the scripture, written on rolls of parchment by devout individuals, who had presented them to the synagogue. Each roll was kept in a case like a drum, on which was a plate telling the name of the donor and the date of the gift, and one copy, we were told, was used in turn every sabbath.

From the synagogue we repaired to the Ketkhoda's house, consisting of a range of double-storied rooms on one side of a neat garden, round which vines were carried on a treillage. We sat on the walk, under the shade of a fine tree, and the Jew, though he would not drink with us, by reason of its being the sabbath-day, produced some bottles of strong arrack and thin bad wine of his own manufacture, and seeing that we would only taste it, lest, as he thought, some keen-nosed Mohummudan should scent us, he begged us to take the liquor home to comfort our hearts with at leisure. There was such an air of comfort about this man's house, that he thought it necessary to apologize for it, saying that we saw all his wealth; that formerly the Jews had money, but now, God help them, they had ceased to hoard it, since some extortionate ruler or other was sure to take it from them.

We became very intimate with this people, and in many of their houses I observed much to contradict their outward appearance of poverty. On one occasion I was invited to a wedding in their quarter. At evening I was introduced to a company, who were seated in a square, on a broad terrace, having before them trays containing burnt almonds, pistachio-nuts, and confectionary, with flasks of arrack, which they drank from small cups in such immoderate quantities, that I expected to see them lose their senses; but it merely appeared to have the effect of exciting them. The seat of honour was kept for the bridegroom, a most uninteresting youth, who, looking very much ashamed of himself, entered with a boy on either hand singing a discordant epithalamium, and when he had taken his place next to his father at the head, the company severally complimented him. Meat and broth was then brought in, and when it had been partaken of, health was wished to the bridegroom, and to his father the host; bumpers of arrack were tossed down, and some of the company getting up one after another, danced a ridiculous sort of *pas seul.* It was next proposed to sing, and some of the best performers being called upon, sang from the Psalms of David very sweetly. The audience were frequently moved to tears, and once, when a young man sang a psalm, which by Mehdee Beg's translation I knew to be that (even in our language) most beautiful one, "By the rivers of Babylon there we sat down, yea, we wept when we remembered Zion," they sobbed aloud. They were all somewhat under the influence of their potations, but men in their situation must ever be affected by the beautiful words of the Psalmist, and it was easy to believe their grief sincere. In the height of the entertainment came a loud knocking at the door. Earlier in the evening the darogha* had sent for some arrack, for medicine, but as he required a large dose, it was refused him. He therefore now sent his myrmidons to put a stop to what he called the disturbance in their quarter, as it was the night of a Mohummudan festival. A little money sent the officers away, and shortly after, the

* Police-master.—Such of the faithful as require spirituous liquor for medicine, must make their wants known to the darogha, who will procure it for them. All jolly fellows in a city are consequently on very good terms with that officer.

bride being brought to the house with music and torches, and a large attendance of female friends, the party broke up.

We received much kindness from the Jews. They could not lend us the money we now required, but they advanced us small loans, and served us in many other ways, and from them we discovered the chief reason why no one would accept bills that I offered upon the British envoy at Tehraun. A rascally Indian Syud, named Ameer Ali, who I believe had attached himself to the suite of Sir John Malcolm, on one of the occasions of that officer's coming ambassador to Persia, had induced some credulous persons at Meshed to believe him a spy in the regular pay of the British government, and by giving, in pretended confidence, what he called promissory notes on the envoy at Tehraun, had succeeded in raising several sums of cash. A money-changer brought me one of his notes, which was a mere scrawl, written in imitation of an English note of hand, and which was all the security that he had for two hundred tomauns. I told the man that it was a gross forgery, but he was dupe enough to listen rather to his roguish debtor, who assured him, as we learned from a Jew confidant, that I was an impostor,—an Armenian he believed, at any rate one who, wanting to draw a bill myself, felt it necessary to declare his invalid, because I could not write one like it.

This Ameer Ali was probably as perfect a rogue as ever practised. He commenced his career of villany by nearly succeeding in stealing a fortune from the King of Lucknow, and escaping from India, made his way overland to Irân, where he lived a life the acts of which, if they could be faithfully collected, would probably form a more extraordinary history than the author of Gil Blas could have imagined. Meshed was his den, and from it he sallied out at seasons to rob the provinces far and near, seldom failing to return with booty, though he sometimes ran great risks. He considered no one either above or beneath his skill, using every means to get money, but his never-failing resource with all classes was, pretending to know the secret of the philosopher's stone.

When we look back to the infatuation with which the alchemists of comparatively enlightened times pursued this chimera, we need not be astonished at the weakness of oriental people concerning the *ars sine arte* which was born among them. The eastern alchemists of the present day hold, I believe, nearly the conceits which possessed the philosophers of the European world; saying that of the minerals which are formed in the earth, some are matured quickly, while others require time to be perfected, and arguing thence that since by art we can at once bring certain minerals, such as salt, alum, &c. to perfection, by art we should be also able to hasten the maturity of others, such as metals; though touching the actual process, and the time requisite, they are as much in the dark as were the sages of the thirteenth century. Where there is a disposition to believe in more than the possibility of the discovery of the grand secret, artful men do not find it difficult to get dupes, and it was a fact well known by many, that this same Ameer Ali, having lived for years on terms of entire intimacy with one who knew all his tricks, was yet able to persuade him that he really had found out the secret, which he would communicate for old acquaintance sake, and obtained from him two hundred tomauns with which to commence operations.

The natives of Hindoostân are supposed to have attained a greater knowledge of the art than other people, and Ameer Ali's colour aided him in many an imposition. He might have been rich had he not been obliged to purchase the silence of some who watched him, and had he not been, as many rogues are, prodigal of other folks' money. He had a wife, whom he had perfected in villany, but she had one virtue, that of being devoted to him: in some of his worst scrapes she had given herself and children in hostage for him, or begged his release by unceasing outcries at the Prince's gate, pleading with irresistible tears for favour to a descendant from the prophet, and when she had worn out a good name in his service, she commenced his system in the female world. In a good cause such an attached couple would have made a figure. We often saw Ameer Ali; indeed too often, for he cheated me: occasionally he would let out a few of the incidents of his life, and truly the humorous turn that he gave to his exploits went some way to excuse their knavery.

July 18th.—I was sitting alone in our apartment, when the master of the house we rented came in hastily, and begged me to come to his son, who was dying; so taking a phial of smelling salts, I followed him to the room of an adjoining house, in which the patient lay. A grave-looking person sat at the head of the bed, professedly a hakeem, but who having caused the youth to faint, knew not how to bring him to again. So much anxiety existed for the lad, that the women of the house crowded round the door, and with one voice begged me to restore him; a mere application of the salts to his nostrils did this, and having learned that he had been at a neighbouring village to arrange for his nuptials, and had eaten too much fruit, I felt myself safe in prognosticating a cure in two days, which a strong dose of physic did indeed effect. The cure was noised about, and two mornings after, hearing a knocking at the outer door, I went to open it, and found a man who, having been a cripple for years, had caused himself to be put upon a mule to come to me. He desired to be cured immediately, and when assured of my inability to do him good, abused me so heartily, that I was inclined to wish his tongue in the condition of his other members.

The Calenter* of the city also, hearing of my skill,

* The magistrate next in rank to the Vuzeer, who has the surveillance of all the parishes of a city.

sent to request that I would visit him. I went with the Syud, for curiosity's sake, and was introduced to a strikingly handsome and gentlemanlike man, who was seated on a small raised wooden platform, in the centre of a nice garden. He invited us to mount upon the platform and sit beside him, and then, after the customary compliments, said that he had requested my attendance on account of his young brother, who had for some years been bedridden, and he hinted that nothing would be thought extravagant to reward a cure. The brother was brought in, carried in a servant's arms, a delicate, emaciated boy, whose case apparently would have been considered hopeless by a real physician; it was painful to be obliged to say that I could do nothing for him, and I had some difficulty in persuading the Calenter that the report of my skill had gone abroad in consequence of a slight accidental cure.

Up to this date we had received no letters from our friends; we had run into debt, and began seriously to feel the evil of being without money in a strange country. To add to our perplexity, Meshedee-Norouz all of a sudden took a wild freak, got acquainted with some jolly Topchees* in the Prince's service, married a temporary wife, and ran in debt thirty tomauns. His next step was to be insolent, but as dismissing him would have been bringing all his creditors at once upon us, we bore with his impertinences; indeed, remembering how well he had

* Artillery-men.

behaved to us in the desert, we became good friends again before we parted, though we had his debts to pay.

We anxiously watched the arrival of pilgrims from the west, but not one of them brought us news: the only intelligence that we could obtain concerning the gentlemen of the English mission, was given us by a Tabreez pilgrim, who said that when on the point of leaving Tehraun, he had received a letter from his home, mentioning that the British envoy and other English gentlemen at Tabreez, with many Persians, had fallen victims to the cholera morbus. The few merchants who had held out hopes of assistance to us, were decided by this report not to lend us any money, and in addition to the melancholy reflection that the accounts of friends from whom I had received so much kindness might be true, as indeed they in a measure proved to be, I had the misery of seeing my companion fall so dangerously ill, that for some days I despaired of his life. Constant worry at first made him unwell, and in the conceit that he was Hakeem enough to prescribe for himself, he swallowed a quantity of calomel, went to the hot bath to sweat it in, and then, by way of further assisting its operation, took so many miscals of blood from his arm, that the barber called in to operate entreated him to desist, fearing apparently lest he should be concerned in manslaughter. The consequence of this self-treatment was that he salivated himself, lost the use of his teeth, and became so weak that he could do little else than lie in a corner of our room and groan. Meerza Abdool Jowaut most kindly took him out to his country-house, and in a few days his health was restored; but he cost me some anxious hours, for I had a real friendship for him, and the prospect of being left alone and penniless at Meshed was a very melancholy one.

August 6th.—Agha Mohummud Caussim took leave of us to return home *viâ* Tehraun, and he promised to send us money from the capital, in case our friends should not have already done so. He was a good man, quiet in his zeal, but so full of it, that he took up his residence in a cell of the sahn, in order to be as near the saint as possible. The afternoon before he went, I observed him standing at the corner of a large cemetery which was before our house, intently gazing upon the sacred dome, which an idolater might have worshipped, so beautiful was the light of the declining sun upon its golden tiles. He sighed with much apparent sincerity when I accosted him to ask if he departed on the morrow, and said that he was thinking whether he would not leave Astrabad and make Meshed his home. "You do not look upon that dome as I do, Sahib," he said, "but I swear to you that the sight of it makes the heart fresh: you admire *that,* but if you had seen the Noorbaran Agha! the Noorbaran!" The "Noorbaran," or "shower of light," is the rain which falls in spring, when the sun, breaking through light clouds, causes the large drops shed from them to glitter like diamonds: the natives of Irân say that it falls most on holy places, and hold up their palms, to catch the drops and wet their beards with them. Looking through the sparkling shower at the golden dome when the sun is upon it, this poetically superstitious people are struck with the increased effect, and utter ejaculations of praise for what they deem a special mark of Heaven's favour upon their saint.

The cemetery just alluded to was the largest of several that occupy open spaces within the city, the proprietors of which reap great profits by letting out graves for the bodies of those who are brought from all parts to be deposited in holy ground. As it was in a retired quarter, I used generally to take my way through it, without fear of exciting the wrath of the Meshedees by defiling the graves of their fathers. The tombs were made of heavy slabs of black or white coarse granite, which is quarried in the neighbourhood, and on many of them, besides verses of the Korân, were sculptured devices which showed what had been the condition of the deceased. The resting-place of a moollâ might be known by a book or an astrolabe; that of a barber or a tailor by a razor or a pair of shears; and a young cedar tree carved on a tomb, was the affecting sign of one cut off in the flower of youth. Early in the morning, figures might be seen seated on the tombs; generally veiled women, who came to weep at the graves of departed friends; a custom which illustrates a verse in the eleventh chapter of St. John, when the Jews, seeing Mary rise hastily and go out, said, "She goeth unto the grave to weep there." Some sat by tombs reading the Korân, relations of deceased persons, or moollâs, their proxies; and sometimes were seen a party of the latter gentry in a small tent pitched over a grave, engaged to remain there a certain number of days to say masses for the soul of the dead. On Thursday evenings crowds would come to the burial-ground, to say a fateheh for all men departed in the faith.

CHAPTER XI.

Further stay at Meshed—Continuation of personal narrative—Commerce and politics of Persian Khorassaun.

JULY 26.—Meerza Abdool Jowaut conferred on us the honour of a visit; ashamed, as he protested, that a stranger should live in Meshed and receive no attention from its inhabitants. "A fig for men's narrow opinions!" said he to the Syud, "tell your friend I will visit him to-morrow;" and on the morrow he accordingly came, attended by two or three particular friends, and followed by a chosen tail of obsequious admirers. One of the train carried a large volume, which, after compliments had been exchanged, the Meerza held forward with some ceremony. It was a book, he said, of *kudeem kudeem Laatin*, the very oldest Latin, and had come into his possession years ago by the strangest chance. I think the title of the work was Cook's Surgery, but it would have been cruel to have destroyed so innocent an illusion, and as the anatomical plates showed it to be a work upon *kickmut*,* I

* Science.

read a few lines out sonorously, giving a slight explanation of the plates, and not only satisfied our visiter of the antiquity and value of his book, but was rewarded with a murmur of approbation at my skill in the dead languages. As I had displayed so much knowledge, it was necessary to give our visiter an opportunity of exhibiting his, and some learned nothings were discussed, on which the Meerza's opinions were bowed to as the best, encouraged by which, he spoke at length, touching slightly on all the sciences, to show his acquaintance with them, and delivering himself of sundry axioms, which gave his speech a pretension of great depth. We paid him the compliment of listening with every attention, and his followers had the air of being wrapped in wonder at the extent of his acquirements,

> "And still they gazed, and still the wonder grew,
> That one small head could carry all he knew."

The Meerza begged to see my curiosities, "penknives, mathematical instruments, or any thing European or strange." Some patent matches which ignited by pressure, excited the highest astonishment in the whole party, and the Meerza vowed he would not rest till he had made similar ones. This led us into a discourse about chemistry, in the course of which our visiter appealed to a grave person on his right, who had set up for a chemist and doctor, and, report said, had tried some unlucky experiments in the latter capacity. This gentlemen was inquisitive about a medicine which he understood I possessed, by smelling which a sick man might be greatly restored, and I then recognised him as the leech who had sat at the bed of my patient, but whom I had missed when I had been fortunate enough to restore the lad to his senses. The phial was handed to him, and he unguardedly took a sniff which nearly destroyed the composure of his countenance; but it was beneath his dignity to appear disturbed, so giving the salt to the Meerza with an assumed air of *nonchalance*, he decided that the contents were—camphor with a dash of lemon. We offered our visiters tea and sweetmeats, and when Meerza Abdool Jowaut rose to take away his presence, walked with him to the outer door of our dwelling, declaring that our heads had been raised, and we honoured by his visit, and hoping that his condescension might not diminish; and he, by way of expressing his sense of our civilities, turned round at parting, and said in the most public manner, that for learning and good breeding, neither the French, nor any other Frank nation, were worthy of comparison with the English.

Some days subsequent to this, we received notification of another intended visit; it was from his highness the Nawaub Mehdee Ali Khan (son to Saadut Ali Khan, the late King of Lucknow), who was on his travels through Mohummudan holy land. Hearing of my being in the city, he sent a very polite message, to say that it would give him pleasure to know any Englishman, and that he would call on us; but we determined that it would be proper to pay him the compliment of acknowledging his rank, and so, with a civil return to his message, sent an intimation of our intention to render the first visit.

We went the next day, and had an interview with this nobleman, who was travelling quite *en seigneur*, with a suite composed chiefly of Indians. We talked of the palaces of Lucknow and Calcutta, and of the comparatively poor appearance of Persian cities with those of India, and delighted the Nawaub's attendants, who had met with little sympathy on their travels, by sighing for the water and trees of Hindoostân, where a man might rest where he would on a journey, and travel securely with gold in his hand. It was pleasing to meet, in a strange land, people among whom some years of my life had been spent, and with whose language and manners I was familiar, and we sat with them some time. Two mornings after, when we were expecting a visit from the Nawaub, came his head attendant, accoutred for travel, to apologize for his lord's being unable to see us, as he had resolved to take advantage of the immediate departure of a large body of return pilgrims, to travel on to Tehraun. This kafilah was said to consist of near two thousand persons, and there was good prospect of safety in travelling with it, but some days after its departure, came a rumour of its having been taken by the Toorkmuns: the next party who came in from the west confirmed the report, and we learned that the Toorkmuns had fallen upon the travellers one morning at dawn near Abbassabad, killed a few, and carried off the majority into the desert, among them our friend the Nawaub. On hearing this, I caused the Syud to write to Nujuff Ali Khan, the border Koord chief, saying who the Nawaub was, and expressing my conviction that the English ambassador at Tehraun would arrange his highness's ransom. After arriving in India, I heard that the Nawaub's release had been effected, though on what terms I could not learn.

The capture of so large a kafilah put the pilgrims upon the *qui vive;* a small party of Toorks were the only travellers who left the city for many days, and all sorts of reports were current about the dangers of the road. One morning there was great congratulation in Meshed, a swollen and blackened Toorkmun's head being stuck upon a long spear, and paraded in hideous triumph through the street, escorted by the boys and idlers of the place. This was the head of an unlucky Serrux Toorkmun, who, it did not appear how, had let himself be killed; but it was a hydra head, for as many Toorkmuns were made to spring from it as would have sufficed to take the city. The next day a report was prevalent that a large body of Toorkmuns, having descended upon a party of pilgrims, had met with a complete repulse; fifty heads and as many prisoners were being brought in, and the number of dogs killed had not been counted: the report was surely true,—a royal courier, charged with letters to the Prince, had seen the bodies lying near the road, and had passed the victorious pilgrims and their prisoners.

For two days the city was kept in suspense: some varied the reports, a few experienced persons disbelieved them, at the risk of being thought herėtics, and those who feared to commit themselves by a hasty opinion, said that, please God, whatever had been done was the work of the blessed Imaum Reza. As the pilgrims neared the city, the accounts of their victory became gradually more modest, so that when they were a stage distant, they only got credit for having had a fight. At last the murder was out; no Toorkmuns had been *seen*, but at Muzzeenaun alarm of Toorkmuns had been given one night, and a man of the place had been caught in the act of stealing a horse from the caravansera, and brought on two stages, when his friends followed and begged him off. If the robber had been brought to Meshed, he surely would have been sacrificed to the manes of the story.

"It is like most Meshed tales," said our friend Meerza Abdool Jowaut; "I, from the long habit of hearing them, can always guess at their truth. There are three places in the city from whence extraordinary news is circulated, and an experienced inhabitant can tell by the smack of a story from which of the quarters it comes. The first is the cell of Moollâ Shumsheh, a Moojeteheid who resides in the sahn, where the moollâs assemble to gossip, and report what was said or hinted at the Vuzeer's levee,

&c. Moollâ Shumsheh is a prodigy; he has no teeth, yet cracks nuts and eats raw peas, and not being overburdened with riches, though a religious good man, and a deep theologist, (shame to the men of Meshed that it should be so,) he is content to have a levee of those who will bring their own tobacco, and give him a whiff of it occasionally. The Moojeteheid is very short-sighted, and sits in his cell holding a book close to his eyes, or making a commentary from it into one of many large tomes that are piled on a dusty shelf, hearing all that is said, and chiming in when there is a necessity for correcting an assertion: knowing something about what is passing, he is able to soften down the least credible parts of a story, and to send it out with a colour of probability.

"The second quarter for news, is the mosque at the foot of the golden minaret;—a cool place, where iced water is to be had for nothing, and where a calleon is always handing about. The third is a spice shop, the owner of which is such a pleasant fellow, and so liberal of his pipe, that he has always a crowd of newsmongers round his shop; and he so wins upon them by his witty conversation, that few go away without recollecting a want of 'dye for the beard,' or 'spice for the house.' The least founded, and most extravagant reports, may be generally traced to the Attar's shop."

We went occasionally of a morning to the Vuzeer's, and generally found him seated in a garden, at the head of one of two long slips of carpet, occupied by those who had the *entrée*, or who were admitted on business, and at the foot of which stood those whose rank did not entitle them to sit. The great man transacted every sort of business, dictated to the secretary who sat on his right, lent an ear to the favoured persons of the assembly, or listened to a suitor's request. One morning when we were there, he was persuading a young Khan to go on some service, who made many objections, and at last said, "I have no horse."—"We will provide you," said the minister; and sending for a merchant who was in readiness outside, he had two or three horses in, and chaffered for one, which he presented to the youth. "Now there is your horse; his like is not in Meshed; put on your shulwars, and go under God's protection; we will see you at chaust."*—"Have you such horses as that in Frang?" asked the Vuzeer. "Oh! by the by, here is Moollâ Youssuf;—Moollâ Youssuf has been to Hind, and can talk English." A fair and stout-looking man alluded to, who sat at an honourable distance from the Vuzeer, leaned forward, and said, "Good ewening, Saare;" which, considering that it was broad morning, did not speak well for his knowledge of my language, and he soon gave up his attempt to talk in it. This Moollâ Youssuf, we were assured, when at Bombay, was offered no less than 50,000 tomauns if he would marry a Feringee wife and become a

* Breakfast-time.

Christian. The story was his own, and he lived in a great measure upon it, for who could do otherwise than venerate a man who had given up so much for his faith?

The next thing that the Vuzeer did was to eat a tray of peaches, talking at intervals to those nearest to him, or dictating a few words to his scribe. After some time, a suitor, who had sat on his heels at the bottom of the carpet till his patience was exhausted, rose, and waiting till he had fixed the minister's eye, exclaimed, "Have I permission to depart, Vuzeer? I will return to my home."—"Home!!"—"Yes, I have put my case before you every day for the last seven-and-twenty, and as I see I am too humble a person to come under the shadow of your favour, I will give it up and return home."—"Impossible! this cannot be; Alhumdoolillah! justice is for all in Meshed."—"*Justice!*" interrupted the suitor, kindling at once, and with much gesture appealing to the company,—"call you it justice that keeps me from my home and occupation, wasting my money, and spending my days at your door?—Call you it justice that beggars and degrades me?"—"Agha Ján! Lord of my life! what words are these? You see the business I have to get through; by your head, I am ill from fatigue; hear me, my father! listen to me, my brother!—not to-day, but to-morrow I will bring your case before the Prince, and, Inshallah, it shall be arranged for you!" There was no resisting such sweet words from the mouth of the

Vuzeer of Khorassaun; the subdued suitor made his obeisance, and retired for as many more days as his patience would last him, while the minister turned to those nearest to him with a languid smile, which expressed, "You see the work I have,"—and they, in a loud under-tone to each other, praised him as the prince of vuzeers, so affable and impartial, and such an Aristotle in the way of business.

Meerza Mousa was at this time enjoying the credit of being about the cleverest man of his day, and he probably owed much of the success of his political negotiations to this good report; for it was no shame to be outwitted by so long-headed a person, and those who went with him got credit for taking a right view of things. He was a good specimen of the Persian courtier, gentlemanly and quiet, gracious to all classes of men, and imperturbably civil, even to those who abused him; always answering the most humble suitor, with "*Be ser o cheshm Agha!*"—"By my eyes and head, master! by my eyes and head!" His nominal lord, the Prince, was a mere pageant, who had so little the management of affairs, that, to use the strong expression of our informants, he sometimes "wanted bread that he might eat it," and the Vuzeer had the real exercise of what authority there was at Meshed. Some odd stories were told of him, but he was probably as upright as you could expect a Persian to be who had been brought up in intrigue, and who had rogues to deal with, and it is less the part of a traveller to scrutinize the past acts of his life, than to praise him for his tact in managing the turbulent chiefs of what is by courtesy called the Shah's province of Khorassaun.

The rule of the Governor of Meshed should extend N.W. by S.E. from Abbassabad to Toorbut-e Shaik Jam, and from the border of Koordistaun on the north, to Tubbus south; but the chieftains of Persian Khorassaun have ever been more studious to preserve the balance of power among themselves, than to honour the Shah's authority, and Meerza Mousa had enough to do to sustain the Prince at all at Meshed, by playing one chief against another. In 1828, Mohummud Khan Kara-e, of Toorbut-e Hyderah, ejected Hossein Khan (the Shah's sirdar) by stratagem, and kept the city of Meshed for six months, spoiling the place, and levying heavy fines upon the inhabitants; again, shortly before our arrival, Seid Mohummud Khan, chief of the strong mountain fortress of Kelat, had (though nominally a Sheah) leagued with the Toorkmuns, and kept the holy city in a state of blockade, until he was luckily killed by a swivel ball, in an encounter with some of the Koord chief's men.

The tribes of Persian Khorassaun have hitherto preserved an equality, by making common cause to weaken the power of any one who showed a desire to raise himself above his neighbours; but the Koords have of late years become so formidable, that it may be questioned whether they will not retain their ascendancy. In Fraser's interesting account of his journey from Meshed to Astrabad through the Koord country, may be read the history of this people: the greatest of their chiefs is Reza Kouli Khan, who being allied by marriage with the other lord, Nujuff Ali Khan, and on terms of great friendship with the descendants of Begler Khan, late a Koord chief of note, has rendered himself the most influential man in Khorassaun. His country is a fine one, therefore he pays sufficient homage to the Shah to prevent its being visited by a royal army, and having withdrawn himself in a great measure from the other chiefs, he generally finds it his interest to take part with the Prince of Meshed.

The country between Meshed and Heraut may be shortly described. A little eastward of the south of Meshed there is a considerable fall, and I am inclined to think a break, in the Elboorz, or, as they may now be called, Paropamisan mountains, which shortly after bend down to a point eight miles east of Heraut, and then I imagine turn easterly to meet the Hindoo Koosh.

A small branch runs down from about Shereefabad, in the main range, to the south of Heraut, which is useful in describing the political divisions of the country; for though for two-thirds of the distance to Heraut it nominally belongs to Futteh Ali Shah, that monarch is not able to control the tribes who occupy it.

To the west of the centre of the range is Toorbut-e-Hyderah, a town which, once much larger, now numbers, perhaps, from six to eight hundred houses. It is the seat of Mohummud Khan, of the Kara, or black tribe, a set of marauders who are well named. Their province extends from Shereefabad, on the north, to a place called Danial, four marches south of the capital: on the west it touches the "sirhud" of the province of Toorshish, and eastward it is bounded by the small range above mentioned. The country is naturally a fine one: in the time of Ishauk Khan (the father of the present chief), it was tolerably well cultivated, and afforded pasture to so many sheep, that it is said some fourteen hundred dogs were kept to watch the chief's own flocks;* but now, as Mohummud Khan is continually aggressing some one, who (according to the mode of retaliation in these countries) endeavours to lay waste his lands, and as, by plundering merchants and travellers, he has nearly shut the once great road through his country, his people have little inducement to raise more grain than suffices for their own consumption, and the cultivation of that is carried on near to Toorbut. The Persians, who seldom use the Khan's name without cursing it, say that he has sold fifty thousand persons to the Toorkmuns during his rule; the few tra-

* Seven hundred muns of flour, it is said, were daily made into bread for these dogs: each dog would eat half a mun daily, and tend one hundred sheep, which supposes one hundred and forty thousand of the latter animals to have belonged exclusively to the Khan. Exaggerated as the story is, it shows that very many sheep were pastured in the province.

vellers whom necessity now takes his way, go *Tewokul be Khoda*, specially trusting in Providence, and resigned to all chances. Some years since, a very large kafilah, travelling as they supposed securely under the patronage of Meerza Abdool Wahâb, Moatimud-ood-dowlah, one of the greatest ministers that has been known in the present reign, and who had been specially sent by the Shah *to put Khorassaun in order*, were resting at Toorbut on their way to Meshed, when the Khan laid hands upon them all, appropriated the goods and the beasts of burden, and either took ransom for the merchants and travellers, or sold them to the Toorkmuns. The chief's exteenuators say that he was prompted to this lawless life when his father was murdered by Prince Wullee Mohummud Meerza, the governor of Meshed in 1815; but as he has turned his spite upon unoffending persons, to his own great profit, this may be doubted.

The Shah hates the very mention of Mohummud Khan's name: when Prince Hussan Ali Meerza was ruler of Khorassaun,* his majesty wrote desiring him to seize the Toorbut chief, and either to kill or blind the robber, or send him to the capital. Hussan Ali Meerza did catch Mohummud Khan, but in one of those wild freaks for which he is famous, instead of killing his prisoner, he made mockery of him, by stripping him nearly naked, smearing his beard with curds, and

* Hussan Ali Meerza relieved his brother Mohummud Wullee Meerza.

exposing him bareheaded in the sun to the derision of the royal troops. The strangest part of the story remains yet to be told: when the Prince had heaped all these indignities upon his captive, he ordered him into his presence, and, putting the Shah's firman into his hand, desired him to decide his own fate. Mohummud Khan, by a clever appeal to Hussan Ali Meerza's generosity, not only turned away his wrath, but induced him suddenly to become as lavish of his favours as he had been of his injuries; when the Khan came out from audience, it was with a jewelled sword belted over "a dress which the Prince had worn," and the next thing that Hussan Ali Meerza did was, to go to Toorbut and marry the chief's sister. Mohummud Khan, probably thinking that the Prince's injuries and favours nearly balanced each other, was not restrained from his former courses, and he has since set the Shah, his governors, and every body else, at nought. I asked a Jew of Meshed what sort of looking man he was. "I can tell you," he said, "for when he took this city, he sent for me to make me pay money (God knows the Jews have little enough of it, least of all those at Meshed). The Khan was a thick-set man, and he sat leaning forward, with his cap drawn down his forehead close to his eyebrows, looking hard at those who were brought before him. No man could stand his gaze. The greater part of his eyes was white, like a Hubbushee's,* but the middle was black,—black, I beg

* Negro's.

to state, as his heart, and that is as black as a pot." Mohummud Khan must now be a well-aged man; when he dies, or if the long talked-of settlement of Persian Khorassaun takes place, his country will probably recover itself.

Eighty-eight miles south-east of Toorbut is Khaff, a town of five hundred houses, where is seated the chief of the Teimooree tribe; and west, between these two places, is the province of Toorshish, which is described as a perfect garden. I imagine that more fruit than grain is cultivated in the latter district. The prunes called Aloo Bokhara chiefly come from Toorshish, and raisins and other dried fruits are exported thence in large quantities. The capital of the province is the small town of Sooltanabad.

Chiefly to the east of the small branch described, between it and the great range from Khire-abad to Rosanuck, are found the Soonnee Hazaurehs, a turbulent, but not very numerous tribe, who live both in tents and houses, and who have rendered allegiance to the Persians, and to the Affghauns, as these powers have severally been able to enforce it. They possess the three small towns of Mahmood-abad, Toorbut-e Shaik Jam, and Kahreeze, each perhaps consisting of two hundred houses; and they cultivate grain along the base of the small, or, as it may be named (since it separates the two Toorbuts), the Toorbut range. Their chief is the son of Booneard Beg, a man whose name frequently occurs in the late history of Khorassaun. They are called Soonnee

Hazaurehs, in contradistinction to the Sheah Hazaurehs, who hold the mountainous country between Heraut and Caubul. They are violent professors of the Soonnee creed, and their features show them to be descended from the Tartars: these, or their thievish sympathies, have connected them closely with the Toorkmuns, to whom they sell those whom they have the fortune to kidnap. In order to have such convenient friends at hand, they allow them the range of their country, and consequently, it is depopulated to the very neighbourhood of Heraut.

At Heraut rules Shah Kamraun, son of the last Affghaun king, who keeps up his pretensions to the sovereignty of which rebels deprived his father; but I will treat of him in his own place.

From the time of our arrival at Meshed, there had been rumours of wars and changes, and something was evidently going forward, though nobody exactly knew what. Some were of opinion that it was intended to make Khorassaun independent; others, that Reza Kouli Khan, the Koord chief, was about to set himself up as king of it, and every thing that the Vuzeer did or said was made a subject of speculation. On a sudden came news that Yar Mohummud Khan, generalissimo to Shah Kamraun, was on his march from Heraut with six thousand men and some guns, and that Reza Kouli Khan, with all his men and a portion of the other Koord chief's* troops, was close to the city. This double

* Nujuff Ali Khan.

movement puzzled the deepest speculators, and they were candid enough to confess that they could not guess what was to happen. When Reza Kouli Khan came to Meshed, the Prince sent his own charger with the royal caparisons, that the chief might ride in with honour; and two days after, the Prince and the Vuzeer went guests to his camp. In the course of the week came the Affghaun army from Heraut, and the city was so filled by the additional influx of the soldiers of both forces, that sometimes there was scarcely a passage through the main street.

The good order of the city was not a little disturbed by the new comers; provisions rose greatly in price, and bakers were obliged to put up bars before their shops, to prevent their being taken by storm by the crowds who came for bread. The Affghauns waylaid the gardeners as they came in from the villages, sometimes appropriating the beasts that carried the loads; and next they began to quarrel with the citizens, who detesting them for their difference in creed, and feeling the security of cocks on their own dunghills, did not miss opportunities of contemning the belief which, on some occasions, they would themselves condescend to profess. Some Affghauns were at noon-prayer in the Gowher Shaud mosque, when an old Sheah Moollâ, shocked at a form of devotion different from his own, lamented, with a groan, that men calling themselves Mooselmauns should pray in such fashion. This produced an angry reply, and probably a retort containing no compliment to the first caliphs; a crowd of either party collected, swords were drawn, and, though no lives were lost, blood was spilt.

The scandal of this had not subsided, when another irritating circumstance occurred. A Persian lad, who had been given by his father to an Affghaun creditor as a servitor, for money owing, ran from the camp to the chief priest of the city, protesting that he would not serve a man who vilified his religion many times in a day, and requesting his interference. This was made a party business of by the Affghauns, who seeing that the feelings of the townsmen were against them, became open in their abuse, talked of helping themselves to as many slaves as they wanted; some, indeed, of killing all Meshed "*à la Timour*," to the very cats; on which the authorities took the matter up, caused the Affghaun general to summon his men to camp, and ordered such as did not go to be ejected "*vi et armis*." A tumult was expected, and all the shops were shut, but the wisest of the Herautees had withdrawn themselves upon the first summons; those who remained were roughly treated and turned out, though not without considerable caution on the part of the police, a dozen of whom seemed to think that they did wonders in mobbing one Affghaun. The master of the lad who had caused the quarrel, thinking his dignity concerned in remaining, had his arm nearly broken, and came, sadly battered, to Meerza Abdool Jowaut. The Meerza recommended his case to the

Prince, who ordering him to the palace, illustrated an old proverb, by giving him a suit of clothes and thirty tomauns.

The extreme ill-will that exists between Sheahs and Soonnees, to be properly understood, must be observed in countries where licence is given to the expression of it. A residence of four years in India had not taught me the bitter hatred which the two sects have for each other; for there an Englishman mixes too little with the natives to know much about their real feelings, and the strong arm of authority interposes to prevent them from making open war upon each other, not to say that the Indo-Mooselmauns are half Hindoos; but at Meshed, where the Sheahs, being on their own ground, were able to display the enmity which Soonnees never disguise, I saw the feeling in its full force. The chief outward difference between Soonnees and Sheahs is, that the former wash from the tips of the fingers to the elbow, and the latter from the elbow to the tips of the fingers; the Sheahs curse the three first caliphs through all their professors, and the Soonnees damn the Sheahs, *en masse*, as schismatics and heretics, nay as idolaters even, because they carry about with them small cakes of the earth of Kerbola, to which they press their foreheads when praying. But from these chief sects have sprung many others (seventy-two* were counted many years

* Mohummud predicted that seventy-two sects should branch from the root that he had planted, but that the followers of *one* of these

ago), and they are all so bitter against each other, that they are doing more to weaken their religion than its professed enemies could hope to effect. As I was much in the society of Sheahs at Meshed, I had frequent opportunities of hearing their sentiments. The Syud, having lived at Meshed some years before, had many friends; and our circle of acquaintance was agreeably increased by the arrival of Aukhoond-zadeh Moollâ Mohummud, a Sheah doctor of good repute, who had come up from Heraut "to tell his beads at Saint *Reza's* altar," and says a fâteheh over his father, whose remains lay buried in the sahn. Aukhoond may be translated "Dominie," and as Moollâ Mohummud's father was a man of some fame, he had a pride in being called Aukhoond-zadeh, or the son of the dominie. With him came several moollas of inferior degree, who in a great measure lived upon him, and whose duty it was to applaud his sayings, look after his slippers, and not speak when he had a mind to be silent.

Attracted by the Syud's learning and pleasant converse, Moollâ Mohummud was a daily visiter at our house;—a welcome guest, for he was a man of considerable information, and we benefited much by his friendship. I remember having been seated with him and a large party one day, when the conversation turned upon the martyrdom that a Sheah was obliged to endure when travelling in a Soonnee coun-

only should attain paradise. This tradition is an apple of discord among the various parties into which the Mohummudans have divided themselves.

try. "There is one comfort," said a Moollâ Hossein who had come up from Heraut with the Aukhoond-zadeh, rubbing his hands with an air of much satisfaction, "there is one comfort,—they will all go to hell." *Inshallah!*—was echoed round fervently, (*Please God!*) and they stroked their beards and applauded the sentiment, though they were not all remarkably bigoted men for Sheahs.

The enmity of the Soonnees disgusts you less, because it is open, and appears more honest; but this merely arises from the circumstance of their being the stronger party, and so able to affect a contempt for their adversaries, which is fully equalled by their hatred. "The Sheahs," said an Affghaun Syud (and he was addressing some Sheahs who were with us at Heraut, but who, for safety's sake, were professing themselves to be of the orthodox party)— "the Sheahs, God's curse be upon them! are utter dogs; but what can you expect from fellows who reject the law that they may serve their loose inclinations, and, in pretended accordance with the Huddees, marry wives for a month, a week, or a day? It would be well if God would clear the world of such men worse than Kaufirs." To explain the Affghaun's indignation, I should mention that the Sheahs have a convenient institution called "*Mootah*," by which they may marry a wife for any specified number of days; a privilege of which they avail themselves when it does not suit them to carry their establishments about with them. Moollâ Mohummud, who had left three wives at Heraut, talked seriously of taking a fourth, *pro tempore*, when he came to Meshed, and was, I know, only deterred from the act by a consideration of the expense which would attend it. Both sects agree that the Prophet sanctioned the custom, but the Soonnees say that the Caliph Omar forbad it. The Sheahs, at no time inclined to take the Caliph as authority, scoff at an injunction which militates against so pleasurable an indulgence, and ask what dog was "Omar!" that he should presume to correct the mandate of the blessed Prophet?

For my own part, I experienced no ill usage at the hands of the people of Meshed. I daily took my road through the sahn, and walked in all parts of the city, and though occasionally noticed, I never was in the slightest degree insulted. I doubt not that if any fanatic had met me within the sanctuary, he would have taken umbrage at my presumption, and have raised a cry against me; but on the other hand, I have met men there who, knowing me, turned aside and pretended not to observe me. Some few, who would have entered into religious discussions, did not press me beyond measure when I declined such argument on the plea of my being a soldier and no moollâ; the most judicious reply, I conceive, that a mere traveller can make to such prejudiced disputants, for no one not thoroughly skilled in the metaphors of their language can well hope to give them a just idea of our belief. By imperfect descriptions he would run the risk of making the most sacred things seem ridiculous; and if he gained the advantage in an argument, without opportunity to follow it up, he would but irritate, not convince, his opponent.

Our friend Moollâ Mohummud the Aukhoond-zadeh, who laboured incessantly to serve us, came one morning to say that he had been talking to a merchant, who was half disposed to take my bill for goods, which we might sell at a reduced rate for ready money in the bazaar. When the Syud went accordingly to see this trader, he said that as he had never dealt with Feringees, he must try a "*fâll*" in the Korân, a mode of divination similar to that of the "Sortes Virgilianæ," much practised by the natives of Irân. The man opened upon an unpropitious verse, and our hopes in that quarter were at an end; and this was not all our annoyance, for in some cases it was hardly disguised from the Syud that I was thought an impostor, and some had the impudence to assert on the other hand, that I was a spy, well enough provided with wealth, but affecting poverty for security's sake. "Don't you believe the Feringee," an acquaintance of ours heard a merchant say in a caravansera, "that tribe see a long way, and his poverty is a pretence; he will find means to leave Meshed when the time comes." This reasoning seemed plausible enough to many, and indeed it is quite suited to the Persian system.

We made the acquaintance of a Caubul merchant, who when the time of his departure from Meshed drew near, actually wept in our presence, lamenting his poverty, and went about openly begging small loans to help him on his journey, though he had several hundred ducats sewed up in his clothes, as we learned when, on an after occasion, he offered to lend us more than three hundred. The state of society in this part of the world renders such shifts almost necessary, and men who act uprightly, and tell the truth, if there be any such, really deserve great credit.

Commerce, under such discouraging circumstances, must necessarily be very uncertain: traders both fear the unavoidable dangers of the roads, and want confidence in each other; a few of the longest established merchants of different cities have correspondents in Meshed, but they only trust each other to a limited extent, and few traders requiring a sudden advance of money could obtain it otherwise than at a ruinously exorbitant rate of interest. Thus, for want of a regular understanding, many bring goods at a complete venture, and if they do not suit the market, send them to any place at which there is a chance of their selling. I have known tea brought from Bokhara, and some months afterwards sent back thither, because a large supply had come in from the west, from Russia; and a Yezd merchant assured me that once, after trying more markets than one, he was fain to return home with his investment, so as to dispose of it at least loss. The trade is not confined to regular merchants, for pilgrims commonly load a mule or two with the produce of the place they come from, and purchase at Meshed articles which they think likely to sell at a profit on the road or at their homes. The actual extent of a trade which is thrown into so many hands, and some of the details of which are so petty, could with difficulty be ascertained, but it appears to be by no means inconsiderable. The year that we were at Meshed, the Prince had farmed the import customs for fifteen thousand tomauns of Irâk, and the duties levied within the city upon all warehouse and shopkeepers (indeed upon every dealer, from the richest merchants to the persons who sold bread in the streets), for twenty-five thousand more. The latter tax evidences a thriving trade in the city, and from the rent of the customs an idea may be formed of the value of the imports.

Camels laden with gross commodities, such as sugar, spices, indigo, &c., are each taxed ten reals, or at the average rate of five per cent., and mules and yaboos* pay proportionately. More valuable merchandise, such as shawls, cloths, &c., is taxed at the lesser rate of one in forty, or two and a half per cent. It may be calculated that two-thirds of the import customs were levied at the rate of two and a half, and one-third at the rate of five per cent., which supposes merchandise to the value of five hundred thousand tomauns to have been sold or exchanged at

* Stout ponies.

Meshed, or to have passed through that city on its way to other places.*

At Meshed are fabricated silk velvets, silk pieces and kerchiefs of colours, satin, and checked cotton cloths. Foolad-e-khorassaun, or steel for the watered sword-blades which are in such repute, is prepared for sale, but very few swords are made; there were, I think, only five shops in the city, and their work did not appear particularly good. A little shagreen is prepare , and horse and ox hides are also cured; further, the turquoises of Neshapoor are sold in great quantities at Meshed, and it is a market for the produce of Koordistaun, lamb and sheep skins, coarse felts and carpets, and such provisions as are supplied by Elaut tribes.

From Yezd are brought fine silk velvets, plain and coloured silks (in pieces and made up), mixed silk and cotton cloths, cotton cloths of all sorts and sizes, felts of several qualities, shoes, and loaf-sugar (made from Indian brown sugar that is had from Shirauz). These articles also find their way from Isphahaun and Cashan, and from the latter places are brought gold and silver leaf, kimcob, cotton socks, pen and ink cases, metal trays and lamps, cooking-pots, and other domestic utensils, chiefly made from copper tinned over.

* All beasts laden with grain, fruit, &c., that come even from the neighbouring villages to Meshed, pay a duty at the gate; but I was told that the money taken in this way might be accounted for in the profits of those who rented the customs from the prince, and that I might calculate the fifteen thousand tomauns as I have done.

From Shirauz come dates, tobacco, lemon-juice, lacker-work, mats, and ivory heel-taps; from Kerman, shawls of all sorts, opium, caraway-seeds, henna, and bruised indigo-leaf for beard dye; and chiefly from the south come the exports of Hindoostan—sugar and sugarcandy, spices, musk, amber, cornelian and other stones, leather, kimcob, Indian and a few English chintzes, Indian fine cloths, and indigo.

The indigo that is brought from India into this country is of two qualities—that manufactured by the English, which is called "*neel-e-Feringee*" and a very inferior sort, made chiefly in Sinde, but which is most used. The price of English indigo, when we were at Meshed, was eighty Irâk reals for a Tabreez mun; we were told that it had been known to sell for a hundred and a hundred and twenty, and, on one or two occasions, even for a hundred and fifty reals the mun; there is not an extensive demand for it, and it is only used to stain glass and the enamelled tiles which are used in Persian buildings, for drawings, and perhaps to dye the best silks. The second sort, or, as it is called in India, the *cucha* indigo, finds its way into Khorassaun from Sinde *viâ* Kandahar and Heraut, and also (I presume from the Punjaub) by the way of Caubul and Bokhara. Its cost at Meshed, when we were there, was twenty reals for a Tabreez mun. At Heraut it was nearly a fifth cheaper (but indeed the market was overstocked), and we were told that it was cheaper, in proportion to the distance, at Kandahar. The quality of this indigo is very bad, its colour is dirty, and does not last long: if profit is to be made upon the drug in these countries, I should think that it would be well to manufacture a sort something between this and the English indigo, which bears so high a price that it cannot be commonly used.

Shawls, saffron, and paper, are brought to Meshed from Cashmere. From Heraut are brought carpets of all prices, assafœtida, lead (from mines near Heraut), cast-iron, saffron (from Kauin), pistachio-nuts, boorkhônge (mastich), sheer-e-khisht (manna), beerzund (a gum), ispiruck (a yellow dye), and caraway-seeds.

Kafilahs from Bokhara bring yearly 120,000 lamb-skins, camel-hair cloth, tea (from China direct or from Russia), and of the exports from Russia into Toorkestaun,—much leather (coarse and fine), shagreen, broad cloths, silks, satins, muslins, and coloured chintzes, nankeen, and other light cloths, loaf-sugar, Russian glass and china-ware, metal trays, cast-iron pots, plain and unwrought iron, copper, pewter, knives, scissors, locks, spectacles, needles, beads, and tinsel, looking-glasses, paper, and clamped boxes of all sizes, gold embroidered stuffs, and cochineal. The trade in the latter articles by this route is, I imagine, decreasing, for now Russian manufactures are had chiefly from the port of Reshdt. They are of very indifferent quality, but extremely cheap, and appeared to find ready sale.

The price of provisions in Meshed is very moderate, as will appear by the following extract from a table of prices current, made during our residence in the city:

Eight Irâk reals = 1 tomaun of Irâk, or 13*s*.
One Tabreez mun = 7 lbs. English and a fraction.

	Reals.	Muns.
Bread (average price)	1	5
Dearest cost, 1 real 3 muns; cheapest, 1 real 12 muns.		
Barley	1	10 to 15
Kau (chopped straw, used as food for cattle)	1	25
Rice (from the vicinity of Toos, or from Boojnord)	1	1 to 1¼
Mutton: In winter, when the sheep are at their folds . . .	1½	1
Mutton: At other times . . .	1	2

About one hundred sheep, or two hundred lambs, are daily killed in Meshed. Beef is eaten only by the poor classes; occasionally camel's flesh is sold. Very many of the pilgrim's eat no meat, living upon bread and cheese, and curds or fruits.

	Reals.	Muns.
Fowls: For one (dear)	0⅓	—
Fowls: A pair (cheap)	0½	—
Cheese: In spring and summer	1	2
Cheese: In winter	2	1
Clarified butter	2	1
Turnips, carrots, gourds, and cucumbers .	1	10
Beans	1	5
Onions (according to season)	1	5 to 10
Grapes and melons	1	10
Fine apples	1	5
Peaches, pears, and quinces	1	2
Rock salt (from Neshapoor)	1	10
Tallow and oil	1	1
Firewood: Pistachio, brought from a distance	1	8 to 10
Firewood: Common sort.	1	per camel load.

Much of the province of Meshed is fertile, but its produce being insufficient for the demands of the city, grain is imported from Neshapoor and from Koordistaun. Many of the householders, who profit by baking bread and sending it into the streets for sale, keep stores of grain to be provided against failure of supply from without.

The people of Meshed chiefly drink water which is conducted to the city by canauts. At each main gate there is a large and deep reservoir, and within the city are many more. There is scarcely a house without a well, but the water is rather brackish.

The average price of a camel at Meshed is from forty to forty-five Irâk reals. These animals are had from the desert; some from the Serruxees, but more (through the medium of the Koords) from the Tekkah Toorkmuns, who breed them in great numbers. The Koords also breed these animals for sale, as do the Gôklan Toorkmuns.

Horses are generally scarce at Meshed itself, but from the Koords many could be procured. Merchants at Astrabad calculated that the Yimoot Toorkmuns could furnish annually one thousand horses, at the rate of twenty tomauns a head, among which there would be animals worth no more than ten, and others worth as much as from forty to sixty, tomauns each. The Koords could provide yearly about 2500 at a somewhat cheaper rate, as they rear many more than they themselves need, and could get them from the Gôklans or Tekkahs.

Mules are dearer at Meshed than at most other places in Persia.

The mean heat of Fahrenheit at Meshed, from the 28th of June to the 13th of September (in the shade, at the hottest time of the day), was 89°. The mercury rose one day to 98°, and it did not fall lower than 76°. When we quitted the city, towards the middle of September, the nights had become exceedingly cold. The winter here is very severe; much snow falls.

The reason of the troops coming from Koordistaun and Heraut was not known, until Meerza Mousa, after sundry interviews with the chiefs of both armies, went to their camp, and marched with them into the desert to fight the Toorkmuns. It was on the 14th of August that they marched: fourteen days afterwards, the allied troops returned ingloriously, looking all very weary and disconsolate. It appeared that after making a feint of marching upon Serrux, and thereby inducing the Toorkmuns of that place to retire into the desert, they had gone northerly, in the direction of Dereguz, spent some time in firing at a mud fort, and lost one hundred and fifty men in skirmishes with the Toorkmuns; and that then, finding themselves short of water and food, they had returned hastily to Meshed to escape starvation. Meerza Mousa, who had been taken to the seat of war much against his inclination, rode into the city "with the air of a man who had lost his father," and, soiled as he was with travel, went at once to vent his sorrows at the tomb of the Saint Reza. A crowd soon assembled at the shrine, and from a looker-on we heard what had passed. It came out that the chiefs had quarrelled about the plan of operations, and the Vuzeer, declaring that if his suggestions had been attended to they might have swept the infidels from off the face of the desert, wept in admitting that these had set them at nought; while he hinted that much of the failure might be owing to their having allied themselves with one set of unbelievers against another. The minister's aim was to get out of the scrape with good grace, and his reputation for wisdom gave him the day against the Koord and Affghaun chiefs, who told their stories to no purpose.

It was now announced that the Affghaun army would in a few days return to Heraut, and travellers in that direction prepared to journey under its protection. It may be well here to describe the occasion of this army's coming to Meshed, and in order to do that, it will be necessary to glance at the history of the Affghauns.

The great empire which Ahmed Shah Doorraunee founded A.D. 1747, fell to his grandson Shah Zemaun, in 1793; but the latter was deposed and blinded, after eight years' reign, by his half-brother Mahmood, who owed his rise to the bold enterprise of Futteh Khan, chief of the powerful Doorraunee tribe of Baurikzye, whose father had been executed for treason by Zemaun Shah, and who satisfied at once his revenge and ambition, by dethroning that monarch, and making himself Mahmood's vuzeer. The usurper's reign was short and unsettled; military force alone upheld him till the summer of 1803, when he was deposed in a religious tumult at Caubul, and Prince Shoojah-ool-moolk, full brother to Zemaun, was raised to the throne by the people.

Shoojah kept the throne till 1809. Mahmood, who, by his brother's clemency, had only been confined at Caubul, was unfortunately allowed to make his escape thence. He fled to Futteh Khan, who had retired to his castle at Girishk on the Helmund, and that daring chief did not rest until he had again made him king. Shoojah, who deserved a better fate, was fain to fly from his country, and finally to seek an asylum in British territory, within which he has since lived with his family.

Mahmood was again nominally king at Caubul, but Futteh Khan, in the capacity of grand vuzeer, ruled the kingdom as though it had been his own, strengthening his authority by placing many provinces in the hands of his near kinsmen.

The growth of this man's power was so rapid, that the fears of Mahmood and of the heir-apparent (Prince Kamraun) were excited: they conceived that he aimed at supreme power, and consulting only their jealousy, they cruelly assassinated the man who had done so much for them.

The immediate consequence of this inconsiderate act was that all the kinsmen of Futteh Khan revolted and made head against Mahmood. This weak king delayed long in marching his troops to quell the rebels, and when at last he neared their clans, was afraid to engage them. Finally he became suspicious of those around him, and put the seal upon a series of unaccountably foolish acts, by deserting his army suddenly by night, and flying with his son Kamraun by a direct road to Heraut. With the exception of the latter province, the whole of Affghaunistaun fell into the hands of Futteh Khan's brothers, who portioned it into petty governments, and ruled, two or three in concert, at the different seats.

The relative situations of the Royal and the Baurikzye families have remained the same up to the present time, but the Affghauns have lost, to the Sikhs, Cashmere and all their country east of the Indus; the Sindees have become independent; the Beloochees nearly so; and on the west, the domestic troubles of Persia have alone prevented that country from encroaching upon its fallen neighbour.

In this part of Asia, the right of "the strongest" is sufficient reason for dispossessing a man of his country; but the Persians do not want excuse for taking Heraut, seeing that they claim it as the ancient capital of Khorassaun. Towards the end of Shah Shoojah's reign, the Cujjer naib at Meshed compelled a payment of fifty thousand rupees from Prince Hâdjee Ferooz, Suddozye, then governor at Heraut; and later still, in 1819, Prince Hussan Ali Meerza sent an envoy from the Holy City formally to desire that the supremacy of Futteh Ali Shah, his father, should be acknowledged at Heraut. This demand was resisted by the Affghauns more stoutly than was expected, and a battle was fought in consequence, but neither party conquering, the question rested there. Kamraun, however, is constant in giving tribute to the Shah of Persia: he disguises it under the name of a present, and the Persian monarch allows him the title of Shah; but Kamraun must feel, as the Persians do, that there is more courtesy than sincerity in these relations, and if (as, if he lives, he doubtless will) Abbas Meerza secures the succession to his father's throne, it is very probable that he will add Heraut to his dominions, if the politics of Affghaunistaun remain in their present state.

The ex-Shah Mahmood died at Heraut in the winter of 1829, and Kamraun, succeeding to the name of king, bethought him of attempting to recover his country. The misrule of his rebel brothers at Candahar gave him hopes of success there; but he feared lest while he should be absent against the Doorraunee capital, his only place of retreat, Heraut, might fall into the hands of the Persian Khorassaun chieftains. He therefore made friendly overtures to the most powerful man among them, Reza Kouli Khan, Koord, and through him sent amicable professions to the Shah of Persia. Reza Kouli Khan was at issue with the Toorkmuns, and he being a subject of Futteh Ali Shah, Kamraun affected to testify his regard for the Persian monarch, in sending the army in question to co-operate with the Koords against his majesty's enemies the Toorkmuns. This was good policy; for it conciliated the Shah of Persia, directly obliged the powerful Koord chief, and was calculated to produce a very favourable impression for Kamraun in his own country, as we observed when we reached Heraut, where it was bruited about that "the Shahs of Affghaunistaun and Persia had formed a never-to-be-ended friendship, that their allied forces had gone like a strong wind over the desert, driving the Toorkmuns before them, and that Shah Kamraun would presently march to take possession of his capital," &c.

In return for the assistance of the Affghaun troops, Reza Kouli Khan sent a son, with five hundred Koords, to give aid and countenance to Kamraun's projected attempt upon Candahar; and he moreover, it was understood, engaged to be a check upon the Khan of Toorbut-e Hyderah, or upon any of the Persian Khorassaun chieftains who might threaten Heraut during the absence of the royal army.

Still we heard nothing from our friends, but anxious to travel the dangerous road between Meshed and Heraut under escort of the Affghaun troops, we redoubled our exertions to obtain money. Seeing that the merchants of the city distrusted my story, I caused the Syud to write in my name to the Vuzeer, saying that as the letters which I had brought to the Prince and him were testimonies of my rank and character, I begged the favour of his vouching for the same, that I might obtain from some merchant money to continue my journey. The reply of this cautious diplomatist is worthy of insertion, and I only regret that I cannot translate it more in the spirit of the original.

"TO THE VERY EXCELLENT, THE EXALTED IN RANK, &c. &c.

"By the fortunate head of the Kebla* of the Universe, to whom the lives of the world are a sacrifice, it is an oath,—that, in this country, such a merchant as you seek will not be found. Had the fulfilment of your wishes been within possibility, compliance with your request would have been a pleasure. On all matters write your wishes, that I may do your bidding."

Though he had treated us civilly when we called upon him, the minister had not given himself any pains to show us attention, never having once rendered me the compliment of sending to inquire about my health. He felt conscious of his remissness in this particular, for the next morning, when the Syud attended at the levee, he received him very affectionately, and taking a pen from his scribe's hand, wrote on a small slip of paper what follows.

* The Kebla is the point to which men turn when they pray; here used in an hyperbolical sense to signify the Shah of Persia, a monarch towards whom the eyes of the Universe are supposed to be directed.

"O SYUD OF MINE!

"If the very excellent Mr. Conolly reproaches me, it is not, I confess, without apparent reason; but God knows that a multiplicity of business has kept me in bondage, and I did not inquire about his wellbeing, knowing that *you* were with him. The sum of your need, God can witness, I possess not; and in this country, cash is like the *Oonkâ*, a bird which flies so fast that it is not seen. You, who have the tongue of eloquence, convince your friend of my sincerity."

When our affairs were at the worst came relief: not that which we expected, nor altogether such as we should have chosen, but still assistance which, considering our situation, we were very grateful for. Our good friend the Aukhoond-zadeh met with a young merchant about to visit his relations at Heraut, who, after much persuading, agreed to pay our debts, and take us with him to that city, on condition that we despatched an express messenger to Tehraun, and bound ourselves not to leave Heraut until he should be satisfied. We could only bind ourselves with promises, which are too common in these parts to be thought much of, but the Aukhoond boldly offered himself as our security, and though he could hardly have raised half the sum he pledged himself for, the merchant was assured by the confidence that he reposed in us.

Gholam Reza was the name of the Yezd merchant:

I do not remember it out of any regard for the young man, for his character was a compound of meanness and knavery, and we were truly glad when we were freed from his claims. As a preliminary, he made us agree to purchase his horse for seventeen tomauns, because it did not suit him to keep it. To no purpose did we protest we had already a horse too many, and that his animal was not worth a third of seventeen tomauns; he had made up his mind, he said, to get rid of the beast, and surely we ought to oblige him, if we expected him to oblige us; logic that there was no disputing. For two hundred tomauns, which we wrote to desire might be immediately paid into his agent's hands at Tehraun, he agreed to give us one hundred and forty, but he paid us in light money, and in such small instalments that we never felt any richer; he took advantage of us in every petty way possible, and as a conclusion to match his preliminary, kept back part of the cash until we agreed to allow him the use of the horse he had sold us all the way to Heraut.

We wrote pressing letters to our friends, to the Persian minister for foreign affairs at Tehraun, and to our friend the Parsee merchant, requesting them to pay our debts and send us more money; these letters we gave into the hands of a cossid, a Cashmerian, who engaged to go on foot to Tehraun in twelve days, and to follow us to Heraut, at the same rate, as soon as he should receive an answer. As the only means of performing this labour, he said, he would put himself upon a diet of bread soaked in clarified butter and white sugar.

I was not insensible of Moollâ Mohummud's great kindness, for he showed it in very many instances; but in this particular one, I could not help perceiving that a second motive gave a spur to his zeal. He could not, as indeed none of these people can, conceive it possible that a European should incur the danger, labour, and discomfort of such a journey for the mere love of locomotion, and he therefore satisfied himself that I was travelling for political purposes. Remembering the occasion of a British ambassador's coming to the court of Shah Shoojah, he fancied that I had been sent to report upon the land, and that by assisting me on to Heraut, he might gain the favour of Shah Kamraun. I do not exactly know what his thoughts were, but they were something of this sort, and he early made a point of introducing us to Abbas Khan, a Persian nobleman in the service of the Shah Kamraun, who was at once his pupil and patron. This young nobleman, who held a command in the Affghaun army, showed us every civility, begging that we would consider his marching establishment as our own, and expressing a hope that he should be able to serve us on our reaching his home.

Having now the means of continuing our journey, we prepared for it, the Aukhoond-zadeh assuring us that we might travel as though we were packed in cotton. A friend and protegé of the Syud's, who, having a slight knowledge of medicine, as Asiatics practise it, wished to perfect himself in the science, proposed to accompany us to Hindoostân; and, as his object was a laudable one, and he was a good cook, we agreed to take him with us. In the room of Meshedee, who would remain to see the last of us, we engaged as a servant a Mohummudan native of Lahore, who having come to Meshed on a pilgrimage, had been kept there a year or two by want of means to return home.

On the 10th of September we went to take leave of the Vuzeer, who, it was busily reported, was about to accompany the Affghaun general to Heraut on a ceremonious visit to Shah Kamraun, that people might see how good an understanding existed between the royal families of Persia and Affghaunistaun. Meerza Mousa, however, was not now inclined to go upon any such errand, and to evade compliance with the Affghaun general's request, was shamming sick. We found him in the middle of a very large garden, seated on a small terrace with several Koord and Affghaun gentlemen, and surrounded by a crowd of idlers and domestics. Near him was seated a man with the title of Hakeem Bâshee, said to be a very learned doctor, late from Bokhara Shereeff, before whom were two trays, containing, we were told, fifty-two drugs, a portion of virtue from each of which was considered necessary to form a whole, that would remove the indisposition under which the minister laboured.

Meerza Mousa seemed to think we had come to dun him, and was so surprised when told that we had found the merchant we sought, that he looked rather foolish, but quickly recovering himself, he assumed an affectionate air, and heartily congratulated us. "Agha!" were his words, "travel where you will, you have a *bukht** which will carry you on: by the life of the Shah you have! The Inglis," he said to his company, "succeed in whatever they undertake: see this man! he has come (how many thousand fursukhs is it?) all the way from Frang, and now, Inshallah! he will go on safely to Hindoostân. Khan!" addressing an Affghaun nobleman seated opposite, "this friend is consigned into your hands."—"Inshallah!" was the reply, — a word which, according to the emphasis laid upon the different syllables, is by Persians made to express various meanings, but which the Affghauns, out of respect for the word, commonly use without any meaning at all. Ask a man how old he is, and the odds are he will answer,—"Please God, thirty," or thirty-five, as may be; how many sons he has?—"Please God, half a dozen;" and one person asking another about his village, will say,—"That is a nice place of yours, Inshallah!"—to which the answer will be, "*Bulli Inshallah!*"—"Please God it is!" But to take leave of the Vuzeer: he lavished fine speeches upon the Syud and me, which my friend was not backward in returning, protesting that we were so

* Fortune.

overpowered with the recollection of his many kindnesses, that we had not words to express our sense of them. "Well then," said the minister as we arose, "you will ride with the Khan to-morrow?"—"By your favour, we are engaged to accompany Abbas Khan, who has charge of the rear-guard."—"Better still, better still; go then, and God keep you! Khan! these are confided to you; have a special regard to their comfort on the road, and see them safely forwarded to Candahar!"—"By my eyes and head, Vuzeer!" was the answer, and we took leave.

CHAPTER XII.

March with the Affghaun army from Meshed to Heraut.

We rode from the Heraut gate of Meshed at sunset, on the the 13th of September, 1830, in company with the Aukhoond-zadeh and a dozen others, under the escort of Abbas Khan and fifty troopers, the rear-guard of the Affghaun army. A moollâ of the city accompanied us a few hundred paces from the walls, and then, halting, began to recite the Azan: "Allah Ho Acber! Ushudo un La Illah Il Illah!" &c. We drew bridle for a moment, and then moved on, leaving him standing in the middle of the road with his hands raised in prayer for us. Meshedee-Norouz now took an affectionate farewell of us, wishing us luck in our journey, and breaking a pot of water after us to ensure it. A little further on we halted, while Abbas Khan went to take leave of the Koord chief, whose tent was pitched within the square of a large caravansera. On the roof of the building were picketed several horses, and around it to a considerable distance, were encamped the chief's men, horse and foot, a martial but wild-looking tribe of men. We rode over a plain, about twenty miles S.E. by E., to Tungul Shoor, a spring of very brackish water, in a ravine under a bare hill, near to which the Affghaun army was encamped. It was midnight ere we arrived, and we rode about the camp, among horses camels and sleeping men, in what appeared the vain hope of finding the servant whom we had sent on with our property, till, aroused by the shouts which the newly-arrived party were addressing to their friends in the dark, he came to seek us with a torch, when being conducted to our baggage, we lay down in our clothes and slept till morning.

At daybreak a gun was fired, and by sunrise we were on our march. The troops consisted of four thousand Affghaun cavalry, one thousand Soonnee Hazaureh horse (serving Kamraun), and five hundred Koords, under the "Pisser-e-Eelkhaneh," the son of the Lord of the Tribes: the artillery comprised four light guns and twenty camel swivels. The prospect of travelling so unsafe a road in security, had caused a large kafilah to assemble: there were one hundred and twenty camels bearing covered kajavahs, which were chiefly occupied by women and children, many others laden with food for man and beast (for we carried every necessary with us), mules and ponies, similarly charged, and a crowd of horse, donkey, and footmen; every man paying a tax to the generalissimo, as the price of his protection.

On the march, the kafilah kept one line—about twelve camels abreast where the country was plain; the Affghauns marched in dustehs (regiments) on one side, and far off, in all directions, the Hazaureh horse kept a look-out. We travelled all day south of south-east, over a plain in which were scattered low hills; six miles from our resting-place we saw on our right, distant three miles or so, the caravansera of Sungbust, a stage on the usual kafilah road. Eight miles beyond were two ruined brick reservoirs, partly filled up with rubbish. We met with no water, and felt the want of it much, for the sun was hot and the dust choking, and the water of Tungul Shoor had not been kept by many on account of its brackishness. Few seemed to know any thing about the route which we were taking; the professed reason for deviating from the usual one was Kamraun's regard for Futteh Ali Shah, and his fear lest the march of troops might injure the Shah's province of Khorassaun; but as in marching up, the Affghauns had taken the liberty of supposing part of it to belong to Mohummud Khan of Toorbut-e Hyderah, and had wasted his* lands accordingly for an old grudge, the Sirdar got less credit for his delicacy than for his

* A man of Abbas Khan's, who was detailing the incidents of their march up, said, "The Karaes must eat barley-bread this year, for please God we trod every blade of their wheat under foot; but," added he, "we injured ourselves as much as our enemies,—curse them! for many of our horses died from feeding upon the standing corn."

prudence; for it was rumoured that the Toorbut chief had leagued with the Serrux Toorkmuns, to fall upon the Affghauns on their return.

After thirty miles of plain country we entered gravelly hills, and, a mile further on, came upon the bed of a small river, which was nearly choked by long green grass: the little water that was in it was soon rendered muddy by the crowd which rushed to quench their thirst, and learning that our resting-place was still seven miles ahead, we rode on.

The road now was very narrow, through hills; our horses had carried us ahead of the kafilah, and when after dark we reached our ground, we heard that the Sirdar had ordered a halt where we first found water, in consequence of the camels being knocked up. The few who had food shared it: the Aukhoond-zadeh was up, and his interest procured us some boiled rice; there was plenty of good water, and the loan of a horse-rug enabled me to sleep comfortably through the cold night. We lay in a small circular valley, divided by the same shallow stream which we had first met with, the bed of which was here also filled with high green grass. I had fallen asleep, and awaking suddenly, was startled by what appeared to me a supernatural appearance: several large lights shone around our camping-ground, high up in the air, and at one of them seemed to stand the shadows of human figures. It was not till, rousing myself, I looked attentively at the appearance, that I marked the outline of the hills, which the extreme darkness of the night had obscured, and saw that several fires had been lighted, by which men were standing. These were beacons to show the Sirdar where we were, and they were kept burning until return signals were made by the other camp.

15.—Halt. This spot was called Huftauseaub, or seven mills, perhaps because water-mills were worked here formerly. The troops and the kafilah came up about ten o'clock, and halted for the day. Shortly after arriving, the Sirdar called before him the Hazaurehs who had headed the march of the day before, and accusing them of having pushed on with intent of separating the kafilah, in order that they might carry off stragglers, he ordered some of their noses to be cut off, and others to be severely beaten and turned out of the camp. In the evening tattoo was beat, and a crier went through the camp, by order of the Sirdar, to threaten the life of any one who moved from his quarters, or who presumed to push on ahead during the march.

16th.—Twenty miles half a point east of south-east, over successive ranges of parallel hills. This day the march was without order, for the road was narrow, and all endeavoured to press forward. Attached to the Affghaun force were four guns, three twelve-pounders and a smaller one, mounted each on a very heavy carriage, drawn by six indifferent horses, which were ridden by gaunt Indians, dressed by way of uniform in tight red cotton clothes. In the early part of the march, a gun rolled gradually back from near the top of a hill, the riders beating their half-choked nags with large sticks, and screaming to urge them up the ascent, the crowd the while fighting to make their way back, to escape being crushed; and some troopers sent to remedy the confusion, but increased it, by beating indiscriminately those within their reach. At last, gradually ascending, we came to hills so steep that the heavy carriages could not be dragged up them; so the nearest camels were seized and unloaded without ceremony, and the guns being unshipped, were packed upon them; the carriages were sent round by an easier pass to our left, and they reached the ground as soon as we did. The Aukhoond-zadeh and some others, with the majority of the Affghaun troops, took a road to the right of ours, which, by their description, must have been an easier one: they met with water, which we did not. We crossed the highest of the parallel ranges eleven miles on the road, and, descending gradually, halted by another small stream, flowing from us, called Beraush, where there was plenty of green forage for the cattle.

17th.—Nineteen miles, by a tolerable road (on a descent), through narrow grass valleys between the bases of the hills: water in plenty after the first ten miles. The last six miles of our road lay on the bank of a broad bed without a name: good water in sufficiency, and plenty of forage; name of the spot Tymunnuck. Hardly any of our camp had travelled this route before, and we could find no one to tell us what bed this was. I conceive it to be that of the Herirood, the water of which is so largely drawn off for cultivation in the valley of Heraut, that it can hardly, even in spring season, flow in any quantity thus far north. Some Herautees, whom we asked, said they did not think that it was the bed of the Herirood, but they evidently had never before thought on the matter: we certainly crossed the bed of the Herirood nearly fifty miles further south, where it was dry, though there were springs here and there; and if the valley of Heraut was formerly cultivated as it now is, the Herirood river could hardly have run so far north as it was thought to do by former geographers. We learned that there is no scarcity of water in these hills, and, on the last day's march, we saw vestiges which showed that different spots had been inhabited and cultivated: the soil commonly yielded good grass, which, wherever there was water, grew luxuriantly with full flowery tops.

18th.—After five miles we wound out of the hills by a defile, and on the plain, in the distance, saw the small town of Toorbut-e-Shaikh Jam, three or four miles in advance of the branch, or Toorbut range, and bearing about seventeen miles south of our resting-place. We marched altogether thirty miles, but our road took a sweep to the westward, bringing us up to a point called Kaul-e Hussanabad, distant from Tymunnuck about twenty-five miles south-south-east half east. The hills which we had quitted were on our left, running down to Heraut; under them was a dry bed, which I take to be that of the Herirood.

Toorbut-e-Shaikh Jam is now a town of two hundred houses. The town was named after Shaikh Jam, a saint of repute, whose remains lie buried in a beautiful garden. This Shaikh Jam has been confounded with a man who lived after him, Shaikh Abdurahmaun, known by his poetical name Moollâ Jam-ee, or the Moollâ of the goblet, who wrote the poem of Youssuf and Zuleika (Joseph and Potiphar's wife), and other affecting love-stories, the best of which is that which details the sorrows of Lylee and Mujnoon, the Thisbe and Pyramus of the East. Their loves, as all true loves are, were crossed by cruel friends: Mujnoon pined away to a very shadow, so that the birds sat on his shoulders, not knowing him to be a man, and the wild gazelle did not lift up her eye from grazing when he approached. Lylee too fell very sick: the physicians could not tell her disorder, but they ordered her to be bled, and so much sympathy was there in Mujnoon's love for her, that, although he was far distant at the time, when her vein was pierced he also felt a pang, and a stream started spontaneously from his arm.—Mortal love can go no further!

The town has decayed ever since the Toorkmuns got the *entrée* of the country. In 1825, Allah Kouli Khan of Khiva came with an army and chuppaoed the country round, carrying off the inhabitants of two or three entire villages, and inducing many to leave the neighbourhood for fear of a similar visitation: the place when we passed, though nominally belonging to the Shah of Persia, was held very independently by a Hazaureh chief. The plain had been cultivated to some miles extent, by means of several small canauts of good water: luckily for the husbandmen, only the straw of their crop remained upon the ground: it had been chopped small and piled in stacks, but these were quickly thrown down, and there were few who did not busy themselves in carrying off loads before the troops should come up. The Moollâ Hossein (once quoted as having come to Meshed in the train of the Aukhoond-zadeh) who was riding near us on a wretched horse, which carried him, a wife, and a large bundle, at first, out of regard for our opinion, reprobated the act of appropriating the cultivators' property, but seeing that no one listened to him, and that the troops were fast coming up, he did not trust himself to look at us, but jumping from his nag, made for the nearest heap, and for want of a cloth in which to pack the spoil, took off his cloak, which he filled with many armfuls of the straw, using the sleeves to tie up a load which he added to the already great burden of his horse. "Hallal bood," he said in apology to us, "it was lawful; in another minute the soldiers would have swept the field; besides, it was probably the property of infidels."

When we rode up to our ground, we found many

of the Affghaun troopers engaged in catching black partridges which were in an extensive field of long grass. Parties stationed themselves in and round this, and when they flushed a bird, they frightened it with shouts from one to another, till exhausted by its flight, it fell to the ground and was taken up with the hand. More than twenty birds were thus caught here.

19th. — Thirty miles to Tummeenauga. The country over which we marched this day was plain; the soil chiefly sandy and heavy, with here and there patches of dark saline ground, on which lay a thick crust of salt. We rode without finding water for twenty-six miles, to the Herirood, or Heraut river: the greater part of the bed was dry and pebbly; in some places were pools of water, rendered so brackish by lying on salt soil, that some of the horses would not drink at them. Crossing the bed, we rode four miles nearly on a line with it, and halted where there was a spring of excellent water and much long grass. Near the river was an old caravansera, built by Toomaun Aga, a wife of Ameer Timour, from whom the name Tummeenauga.

20th.—Sixteen miles to Teerpool. The country was plain, and the road ran nearly parallel with the Herirood, about three miles from it. Eleven miles on the way, we passed through the deserted town Kousân, or as it is named in old books, Kousavee, the fort of which place is mentioned as having held out against Chengis Khan; the town had only been forsaken three years before, on account of the constant inroads of the Toorkmuns: there was a very fine caravansera, scarcely a brick of which had been displaced; the roof of the houses had mostly fallen in, but in some of the gardens the fruit-trees had not been destroyed, and they flourished among the ruins. The contrast touched even some of our party: *haif ust*, they said, "it is a pity," and I heard one Sheah friend add to another in a confidential tone, "but Inshallah Taullah, Abbas Meerza will come to Khorassaun, and burn the fathers of these Affghauns and of the Toorkmuns, dogs as they both are."

The spleen of my Kuzzilbash companions was frequently excited, for no particular danger being now apprehended, the Hazaurehs and many of the Affghauns marched in what order they would, and the Persians, being unable to go far without halting to take a whiff of tobacco, were sure, the moment they produced a pipe, to be surrounded by a crowd of horsemen, who would stay to partake of it just as though it had been their own. My friend Keramut Ali, who was of a very peppery temperament, took these freedoms ill, and was disposed to refuse his tobacco to strangers. One morning, as we halted for a moment to smoke, an Affghaun also stopped his horse, with some others, and waiting till the pipe had been lighted and handed to the Syud, addressed him coolly with—"Brother! guests before the master!"—"And who made you a guest?" was the angry answer.—"A Mooselmaun needs no invitation to the pipe of another," said the stranger, now also angered; "but I suppose you are a Sheah, and if so, and you come to introduce your notions into Khorassaun, perhaps we shall cut you as small as your tobacco;" so saying, he snatched the calleoon from the hand of our companion, drew a very long whiff, and then superciliously holding out the pipe that it might be taken from him, rode on at a walk, with an air that said,—I give you no thanks.

Three miles beyond Kousân we crossed the dry bed of the river; again, after a little distance, our road brought us across it, near to a bridge of six arches, a mile from which we encamped, where there was plenty of excellent water, and good forage. To-day another duty was levied upon the men and beasts of the kafilah, on account of the Hazaureh chief, who had guarded us on the march, and furnished night-watches. This tax was very roughly extorted from those who demurred paying, a party of Hazaurehs going round with some of the Sirdar's men, armed with heavy whips, which they were not slow to use: some who resisted their demands were severely wounded. We saw a man struck to the ground who was for some minutes supposed to have been killed; the women of his family set up a wail, and a body of men went to the Sirdar's tent to complain, but the general learning that the man had come to his senses again, dismissed the suitors, advising them to pay what was required, and so avoid such accidents.

About nine at night we were roused from sleep by a messenger from head-quarters, who said that the Sirdar wished to see me; so although at a loss to guess the cause of this ill-timed summons, the Syud and I rose, and followed the messenger through the camp to an open tent, under which were assembled the generalissimo and his staff. Sirdar Yar Mohummud Khan did not receive us either with much politeness or dignity: he was on a low bedstead, leaning his length on one arm, and scratching himself with the other: from his couch to the entrance of the tent sat a semicircle of Khans, among whom, after the Syud's salaam alikoom had been answered, he motioned that we should take place, but no one seated there seemed inclined to acknowledge his inferiority by making room for us. The Syud, seeing at a glance the place he was entitled to, walked directly to it, and stood quietly before two men, till they parted to let him in. I, not having the pretensions which his descent gave him, occupied a dubious post, near Abbas Khan, but behind the line.

The Sirdar whispered something in the ear of Abbas Khan, probably to ask how much civility he was to bestow upon me, and then our friend said, "The Sirdar bids you welcome." "May the condescension of the Sirdar not diminish!" was the Syud's answer, on which the great man took the conversation upon himself. "You are?" "An Englishman."—"From whence?" "England."—"And travelling?" "To Hindoostân."—"You have been in India?" "Some years."—"And you left it?" "On account of my health."—"By what road?" "By sea."—"And why did you not go back by sea?" "So great," answered the Syud for me, "is the name of the Affghauns in his country, that he desired to see and know them; besides, the land route is the shortest."—"Good," said the Sirdar, and after a moment he added, "Khoosh omedeed," "You are welcome." An Hazaureh Khan now in rather a supercilious manner asked me if I was not a Christian, and on my answering in the affirmative, begged that I would explain my religion, root and branch; but the Syud excused me from this, by saying that I was neither sufficiently well-versed in divinity nor in the Persian language, and so their inquiries were turned upon "the land of the English," of which they had most confused ideas, Abbas Khan, the only one who pretended to a knowledge of European countries, not understanding whether London was in England, or England in London, or whether they were not both in Hindoostân. "What does your tribe in India?" asked a stoutish youth who proved to be "the son of the Lord of the tribes?" "We possess it."—"How possess it?" "Our king orders the government."—"Does he strike coin?" "The coin of the country has not been altered, and rupees are coined as before." The exclamation of "wonderful!" and an incredulous smile and stare, were the rejoinder to my last answer, and the young chief evidently conceived that I was equivocating, for in the opinion of Asiatics, the right to coin money is the chief prerogative of a ruling power, and our having refrained from using this privilege, has doubtless caused much misapprehension among eastern people generally regarding the nature of our government in Hindoostân.*

The company evidently disbelieved me when I said that India was nearly four months' sail from the throne of the king of England, and at no time, much less on so short an occasion, would it have been easy to explain our system of government to them. To one question put by an Affghaun nobleman about the Indian government, I replied by asking whether he did not remember the circumstance of Elphinstone Sahib's coming ambassador to Shah Shoojah-ool Moolk. "*Sahib!*" muttered an Hazaureh chief to his neighbour; "are they called Sahibs?" and he looked as though he thought that dogs would be a fitter appellation.

If I had not expected great civility from these men, I had at least thought that they would be aware of the consequence of our nation; but I now found that we were confounded with other Frangees of the unknown world, and scarcely more esteemed than known. There is an indomitable pride about Asiatics, which not only makes them indifferent to a knowledge of European nations, but which, when they have been forced into the acquaintance, still

* Since the publication of the above, our coinage has been introduced into British India.—Note to Second Edition.

makes them shut their eyes to every conviction of their own inferiority: flatter or beat them, they still look down upon you. The Affghauns hate the Persians very cordially, but still it was evident that they were galled to think that even these heretics had been conquered by the infidel Oroos. I was often asked whether the Russians really had got the better of the Persians, as it was said, and once, in a company of Affghauns at Heraut, when I mentioned that the Muscovites had routed Abbas Meerza's army, one of the assembly said very sincerely with a sigh, "Ah! if *Sheerdil Khan* had been there with his three thousand lords of the sword and stirrup, he would have given a different account of the Oroos."

While we were seated with the Sirdar, an officer came in to report that the sound of a musket had been heard not far from the camp, upon which one hundred men were ordered out to the side on which the kafilah lay, and the patrols were ordered to be alert, on pain of losing their ears and noses. The Sirdar's manner was gracious to us when we rose to depart. "Now that we are acquainted," said he, "you will ride with us on the march; we mount when the gun fires;—*khoosh omedeed.*" We returned suitable acknowledgments, but did not avail ourselves of this invitation, for I was shabbily dressed, and badly mounted, and did not for other reasons wish to make myself conspicuous.

Sept. 21.—Sixteen miles to Rosanuck, by a plain good road. Half way was Shubbush, a small mud fort, immediately about which was a little cultivation, walled in for fear of the Toorkmuns. The bastions of the fort were open on all sides, and within them were fixed horizontal windmills, each turned by five or six light mat-sails. Rosanuck is a well-sized village. Ghourian was said to bear seven or eight miles south-south-west of us, concealed by the hills, in the direction of which several fortified villages were visible. From Rosanuck to Heraut the distance is forty miles: on the right of the road from Ghourian to the city is an unbroken line of fortified villages, so that a traveller may halt where he will. Fifteen miles on the road from Rosanuck is Shikkeewan; close to it Mummeezuck, a village with a strong little fort. We rested here an hour, and for one small piece of copper, the lowest coin current, we purchased as many fine grapes as two persons cared to eat. We rested on the night of the 22nd at Séher Keis, a little fort fifteen miles from the city. Here they had actually the conscience to levy another duty upon the kafilah, on account of the governor of Ghourian, who had license to tax all travellers through his province, and no one was allowed to proceed to the city until he had paid his share.

On the morning of the 22nd we rode into Heraut: villages, and well-watered fields and gardens, crowded upon each other as we advanced into the valley, and our road lay through them to the very walls of the city. Long before we reached the town, we were met by parties of the inhabitants, who came out to welcome friends; but most of these were disappointed, the astrologers having determined that an auspicious hour for entering the city would not occur for four days. We met in the crowd a merchant with whom we had made acquaintance at Tehraun, and under his guidance proceeded to a caravansera in the city, where, as we would not engage a cell for six months, they put us into a dark and filthy hole off the range of chambers, which smelt so abominably that it was distressing to be in it. The Syud, "accoutred as he was," went out at once to search for better lodging, but was met by a servant of Abbas Khan's, whom that nobleman had kindly sent to tell us that he had ordered a small house to be cleared for our reception.

24th.—Finding it impossible to sleep in our cell, I spread my bed in the gallery which ran round the chambers, and slept comfortably till, aroused by a kick in the back, I looked up and saw an old Affghaun Moollâ standing over me. "Have you no shame," he asked, "to be sleeping an hour after prayer-time?—get up." I assured him that I was very unwell, and needed rest; but he authoritatively insisted upon my removing myself and my bed out of sight, and I had nothing for it but to obey him.* I was alone in our cell later in the morning, when two men entered, one in the dress of a Syud, and seating themselves without ceremony, addressed

* The Soonnee Moollâs of Heraut are few, but they are great disciplinarians, and so zealous, that on Fridays they beat their congregations into the mosques, if they are not disposed to go of their own accord.

several impertinent questions to me. The Syud was the one who chiefly spoke; he addressed me in the Hindoostânee language, desiring to know why, having set out for Bokhara, I had come down to Heraut. I declined giving an account of myself to strangers, upon which he said that I must recollect having seen him at Astrabad, when Gholam Ali Shah (an Indian derveish) and he had visited us, to make arrangements for travelling to Khiva together. I did recollect the circumstance of two Indians having called on us the day that we quitted Astrabad, but this man's face was not familiar to me; however I did not deny that I might have seen him, and thereupon he proceeded to tell me what had happened subsequent to our departure.

"When you went," he said, "and it was known that you were a Russian, there was a hue-and-cry after those who had been seen to communicate with you; the Shahzadeh killed Gholam Ali Shah, and beating me within a little of my life, took to the value of one hundred tomauns from me, after which he turned me out of the town, as this man who was with me can testify; was it not so?"—"Bulli," answered his colleague, "Yes, it was just so."

Had this attack been more covert, I should have been alarmed at it; but I felt so secure, as to be amused at their rascality, seeing that they had fairly outwitted themselves, and therefore replied ironically, that I felt pleasure at being able to inform him that his friend Gholam Ali Shah was alive and well, we having dined with that person on our return from the desert; that with regard to his own particular loss, I could only regret that he had come (as in the present instance) uninvited to visit a suspicious person, and strongly recommended his taking himself off quickly, lest a similar disaster should again befall him.

This fellow had left Astrabad at the same time that we did, and therefore knew not of our having returned; but seeing that he had overshot his mark, he assumed a bullying tone, said he knew who I was, and what my object was in travelling; that I was in a country where life was held cheap, and that as a few words from him would have the effect of endangering mine, I had better not provoke him, but at once pay the money that he claimed. I now felt the want of assistance against this villain; the Syud and his protegé were away with our servant, arranging the house which Abbas Khan had lent us, and the odds would have been against me in a quarrel (an infidel against a Syud), therefore I assured him that we really had very little money, but that of what little there was the Syud kept the keys, and that if he would favour us with a visit on the morrow, we would talk the matter over; with this he was obliged to be contented, and so took his leave.

25th.—This morning we removed into Abbas Khan's house, the upper part of which, consisting of two rooms separated by a small open passage, we occupied, picketing our horses in the court below. About noon came the strange Syud, according to my invitation: I had prepared my companion to receive him, and accordingly, the moment that the man reached the head of the stairs, Karaumut Ali went forward to meet him, led him to the highest seat, and quite oppressed him with asking after the state of his health. No sooner did the stranger open his mouth, than my friend addressed a florid compliment to him, "How strange and delightful it was that they should have met in Heraut again!—How little a man knew what fortune had in store for him!" &c.

I saw by the flush on the stranger's countenance that this could not last long, and presently, as if determined not to be worried out of his self-possession, he assumed a determined countenance, and asked the Syud if he knew the reason of his visit. "Something I have heard," answered the Syud, "but kindly indulge us with a full detail of your wishes."—"Then I wish to know, shortly, if you intend to restore what you caused to be extorted from me." "As shortly, then," said the Syud, altering at once his tone and manner, "we do not; and for several good reasons, Agha, the best of which is, that if we had one hundred thousand tomauns, you should not touch the value of a copper coin of them. Brother! we are no fish for your net; so be satisfied with the assurance, and do not waste time and roguery which you may employ to better purpose elsewhere." The man's face actually became livid with rage, and when he could find utterance, he said in a choked voice,

"You do not know me that you contemn me; perhaps when you have been dragged before the Shah, and skinned with whips, your tone will be different; we will have you to the ordeal of the oven,* and then it will be seen what sort of a Syud you are, leading about a professed infidel to spy all countries." "Not know you!" retorted my friend, now fairly roused, "not know you! are you not that beggar to whom I gave half a real in charity at Astrabad? Dog of a bad breed, who have now turned to bite the hand that fed you! Go! man without honesty! go thief! go rascal! go! I spit upon you." The dialogue now became shorter, both being enraged to such a degree, that they abused each other in the most unmeasured terms. "Pay me two thousand tomauns," screamed the impostor; "help against robbers!"—"Seize him!" returned the Syud; "I recognise a man who murdered my father, and stole ten thousand tomauns." Our Persian friend and our servant came in at the noise, when seeing that it would bring a crowd in upon us, we all set upon the fellow, and thrust him down the narrow staircase, he, as he was borne down backwards, a step at a time, venting the grossest abuse upon us and our ancestors, and swearing to return presently to play the very deuce with us. Some hours elapsing without our hearing more of

* A hot experiment upon a person's virtue, answering to our ancient test of walking upon hot irons. If Monsieur Chabert should fancy travelling in these countries, he might pass for a Syud of the first order.

him, the Syud went out, and calling upon Hyder Kouli Khan (Shumloo), a Persian nobleman in Kamraun's service to whom we had an introductory letter, he mentioned the circumstance. The Khan kindly sent a man to remain at our house, but we dismissed him late in the evening, feeling satisfied that our enemy had thought better of his attempt.

We had made a party to go the next morning to visit the shrine of a famed saint, buried four miles from the city, therefore being awakened from sleep, and seeing a person standing in the passage in which I lay, I thought it was the Yezd merchant, and spoke to tell him that he had come too soon. Receiving no answer, I raised my head, when I saw a small party of men at the foot of my bed, and was aware that they had come from the roof, by a small flight of steps down which others were still descending. Had my sword been near me, it would have been a mere bravado to draw it against such numbers, and as they were now round the bed, I sat up, and asked the reason of my being thus broken in upon, at which one having an air of authority, called me rascal, and giving me a poke in the stomach with a long stick, bade me rise and see. "It is the kotwâl," said the man, seizing my wrist at the same time, and a second one placing himself on my other hand, they led me into the room in which slept the Syud, whom I found standing on his bed, held by the wrists by two or three armed persons, and threatening all the intruders with the vengeance of Shah Kamraun, for whom we had letters.

There had been talk about the felek* and sticks to beat us, but at the Syud's words our hands were loosed, and the armed men stood across the door, while the kotwâl seated himself and ordered lights. Our terrified servant ventured up from the court in which he had been sleeping, and lighted a lamp at a lantern which they had brought with them; I then observed our visiter of the morning, who, leaning forward, said in a low sarcastic tone to the Syud,—"*Have you seen? can I make good my words?*" He, and three or four others who were respectable looking men, sat down near the kotwâl; we also seated ourselves, and the magistrate proceeded to examine us *à la Dogberry*.

Keraumut Ali, who had recovered his temper, was not to be daunted by the kotwâl's high tone, and answered with an air of great nonchalance to the queries put, that I was an English officer travelling to India, no Russian, and no thief to be broken in upon at midnight, against all law and decency; that he was a Syud of Hindoostan, and my fellow traveller: as for that *goorumsauk* (scoundrel), said he, "who has come to forswear himself, let him look to his own skin."

"Now for *your* story," said the kotwâl to the Indian. "Bulli!" answered this villain, "by your

* A bar of wood to which a culprit's feet are fastened, so as to expose the sole when he is laid on his back to be bastinadoed.

excellent leave I beg to state that I knew these men six months ago. (Would to God I had never met them, I should not then be as I am.) I was at Damghaun, I beg to state, about to set off with a kafilah, when these men, and another who is not with them now, came up to me and asked what I was cooking; I replied kitcherree (a dish of rice and peas), upon which they invited me to eat with them, saying that they would treat me to better fare. I at first declined, but they pressed me much, so I went, I beg to state, and they gave me sweetmeats, which as soon as I had eaten I felt my head go round, and my eyes grow larger and larger, and I became without sense. My companion also partook, as he will tell you," looking round for his ally, who apparently not well pleased with the part he had been brought to play, had taken place among the men at arms, and whom we now noticed for the first time. "A whole day and night," continued the Indian, "we lay stupified, and when we came to ourselves, the kafilah was not; our horses were picketed near, but the prisoners were gone, having taken with them a carpet bag, in which were eight hundred tomauns, two muslin caps, and a piece of kimcob. I saw no more of them till the day before yesterday, when I recognised them as they rode into the town, and having ascertained their residence, for I beg to state that they have changed their lodgings more than once, I laid my request before your consideration! Further, what shall I petition? my case is in your hands, to recover pemoney, or to deal with these men as seems most fit to your excellent judgment."

"Ullah!" said the kotwâl, at the end of this wild story, "is it thus that a traveller and a Syud is robbed? Bring forward their effects, mayhap some of the stolen property may be forthcoming."

"What is the Darogha's name?" asked the Syud, with perfect self-possession, of one who sat near. "Meerza Agha," was the answer. "Then, Meerza Agha," said my friend, coolly, "you have no law for what you are going to do, that is, if the men of Heraut are Mooselmauns: we are no *shraubee kabaubees* (revellers on wine and kabaubs), that you should take us by storm, and do offence to your dignity by clambering in by the roof of our house. That man has told nothing but lies; we never were at Damghaun, for we came by the direct road through Mazenderaun to Astrabad, where he saw us; if you suspect us, bring us and our accuser before the Cazee in open day, but do not forget that we are guests of Abbas Khan, and that violence to us is offence to him: further, before you treat this man with indignity, know who he is, and see a letter which we have for the Shah."

This letter, which had been given me by Sir John Macdonald, was directed to Shahzadeh Kamraun, news of Mahmoud's death not having reached Tabreez when I started: the kotwâl, looking at the superscription, pronounced it a forgery, and throwing it from him, proceeded to the examination of our effects, causing search to be made even into the pockets of our dresses, and under the corners of the carpets. Had we been thieves, there was nothing in our baggage to prove us such; we were not possessed of a sous, scarcely of any thing worth one, and except, in his estimation, a rather superfluous quantity of shirts, the kotwâl found nothing to call forth an exclamation. Two or three books which lay on a shelf, were handed down to Meerza Agha by one of his obsequious myrmidons as they hunted about the room, and one of them chanced to be a receipt-book for Indian cookery. "Ah!" exclaimed the kotwâl, when he he had looked into it, "hence the receipt for that intoxicating food which took away the senses of this unfortunate person; say, O man! what are these?" But the Syud, seeing the silliness of our inquisitor, and observing that his own address had produced a favourable effect upon those who attended, took the book, and adroitly quizzed the magistrate, reading out receipts for well-known good dishes, and hinting that if they had been at all injurious in their effects, Meerza Agha would not have been in such good case: a servant of Abbas Khan's too now coming in, and, I imagine, warning him confidentially who I was, the kotwâl said, with an affectation of dignity, that he would have the matter sifted on the morrow, and that we were not to consider ourselves at liberty to leave the house until he authorized us to do so. We had an opportunity of showing our civility by letting the party out at the door, but we had reason to regret that they did not retire as they came, by the house-top, as some of them cut the blankets from our horses' backs and carried them off.

This outrage having been committed in the house of a nobleman high in favour with Shah Kamraun, we guessed who had ordered it, and the next day recognising as men of rank, two of those who had accompanied the kotwâl, we had no doubt upon the subject, and resolved to sit down quietly under the affront; indeed, we were congratulated upon it by our friends, who assured us that we might now travel where we would, since no one could possibly suppose us possessed of any thing valuable, if the kotwâl had not found it. I need scarcely say that we did not consider ourselves bound by that worthy's arrest, and that we were no more troubled either by him or by the Indian. The latter, we learned shortly after, having made the place too hot to hold him, had taken himself quietly away, and gone, it was supposed, to Candahar; intelligence which only interested us so far as to make us resolve to be on the look-out for a rascal whose villany we might not be able to defeat where we had no patrons.

The Syud had in the city of Heraut a long intimate, and very excellent friend, Hadjee Moollâ Ramazaun, a Sheah divine, who, for his great age and his good character, was looked up to by every body in the place. We called upon the old gentleman, and he carried his kindness so far as to promise to introduce me properly to the Sirdar after his entry, so as to ensure me good treatment, and the means of intercourse with the Shah if I desired it. "It is perhaps the part of Abbas Khan," said the old Hadjee, "seeing that you are his guests; but he was my pupil, and dare not be offended with me; moreover, as I am an old man, and probably, save the mark! as much in the esteem of the Sirdar as any one, my introduction may serve you most. Have you any present to offer the Sirdar? any thing uncommon? 'Yaik cheesee, Yaik taroofee,' a something or other; a compliment, just to mark your respect: all men like to be approached with an offering, let it be ever so trifling, and, between ourselves, the direction of most affairs here rests with Yar Mohummud Khan." The only things that we possessed, capable of being offered to so great a personage, were a few penknives, and some cases of fine gunpowder. These the Hadjee said would be sufficient to show our wish to be attentive, and he undertook the delivery of them.

27th.—Early this morning a great Peshwaz went out to meet the army and welcome it to the city. The Sirdar hit the exact minute for entering the gate, and proceeded at once with the chiefs of the army to audience of the Shah, making their salutes to him as he sat in open durbar. Moollâ Mohummud was in high spirits, for he and his father-in-law had been the astrologers called upon to determine the fortunate hour, and the generalissimo had been so favourably *accueillé* on his return, that he had promised to give our friend a fine colt. "I thought you took an oath against ever wearing boots again," said the Syud jocularly to him. "I did, and I will be true to my word."—"Then what good will the colt do you?"—"Oh! I will give it to one of the khans here, who will return me something more in my way."

About sunrise on the morning of the twenty-eighth, we went with Hadjee Moollâ Ramazaun to see the Sirdar. At the outer portal of the minister's quarters we met three servants, one of whom carried on his back an elderly and respectable-looking man, who had been beaten on the soles of his feet until he could not stand upon them. In great pain as he evidently was, he did not forget the respect due to our old friend, ordering his bearer to stand on the side of the path to let the Hadjee pass: the latter shook his head, and on our inquiring what fault the man had committed, we were told that he had been in the habit of beating an obstreperous wife, as he considered her, who petitioned the king, and obtained a royal mandate for her better treatment; but the husband, like a good Mohummudan, choosing rather to be guided by the law which authorizes the faithful to beat their wives *à discrétion*, corrected his lady for her next fault, upon which she sought the refuge of the Shah's harem, and his majesty ordered her spouse to be beaten as we saw, for disregarding his injunctions. The woman, once within the walls of the Shah's harem, could never pass it again, and if the man cared in the least for her (as it is to be presumed he did, by his taking such trouble to correct her), he was thereby punished, not to say that he was more than sufficiently so, by the scandal of his wife's *bona gratia* divorce, and doubtless the Hadjee shook his head because Kamraun had exercised his power at the expense of the law; but it was amusing to an European to hear what, according to our civil code, would be considered a commonly just interposition of authority, stigmatized as an act of unwarranted interference, an impeachment of the rights of man.—"Agha Jan," said an acquaintance to whom we related what we had seen, "*Een zoolm ust!*" "This is oppression!"

The Hadjee led us through several enclosed courts into a small one, at a door leading from which were seated a couple of withered eunuchs, who, after a little demur, allowed us to pass into a paved square, in which were the quarters of the Sirdar's brother, a singularly manly and handsome nobleman, whom we found superbly dressed in shawl cloth, seated at the head of a select company, entertaining them with an account of the events of the late campaign, romancing considerably, as was to be expected from a man so connected, and who had not taken part in the expedition, telling how "the troops of the Shah had gone to the assistance of the troops of the Shah of Persia," and how, Inshallah, they had gotten themselves a name all over Iran,

&c. We sat here long, in expectation of the Sirdar's coming out, and then our old friend, leading us down into the court below, bade us stay there while he went to speak privately with the minister. During the half-hour that we were kept here, the court was gradually filled by those who had influence enough to obtain the entrée, and some feroshes, bringing in bundles of long willows, cut them into proper lengths, and threw them into a basin that occupied the centre of the court, to keep fresh till any one should be ordered to receive the bastinado.

At last Sirdar Yar Mohummud Khan came out, attended by a few particular friends, the chief of whom was Hadjee Moollâ Ramazaun, who, beckoning us to keep near him, desired a ferosh to look to us; a necessary precaution, for the great man was presently lost in the crowd who hurried round him to offer their compliments: he took some to his bosom, and gave his joined hands to the less distinguished, moving across the court the while, as well as he could, to a flight of steps which led to a large upper room: the crowd pressed after him with little regard to order, and but for the assistance of the ferosh, we might not have obtained place in the apartment. When we were all seated on our heels, nearly as many as the room would contain, Hadjee Moollâ Ramazaun, who was on the right of the Sirdar, sat up, and with a manner which was rendered peculiarly impressive by his venerable appearance, gave thanks for the Sirdar's happy return, and prayed for a blessing upon him, the company joining in the wish, passing their hands down their beards at the conclusion, and repeating severally, "*Ulláho Ukbur.*" Then the Sirdar was particularly greeted by friends among the company: "*Shé raughlé Sirdar! Sirdar, shé raughlé.*" "You are welcome, Sirdar." He answered them nearly in the same words, and looked round the apartment, nodding kindly to those who met his eye.

When we saw Yar Mohummud Khan in camp, he struck me as rather a course, vulgar-looking man; looking at him now, as he sat, handsomely dressed, in the seat of honour, he appeared to be a person of considerable dignity: his thick black beard had been combed out to its length, and a pair of large dark eyes animated with the pleasure that he felt at the attentions lavished upon him, gave an intelligent expression to what otherwise would have been a heavy countenance. He was now at the pinnacle of court favour; premier, and commander-in-chief; and his brothers held all the good appointments that Kamraun had in his gift. When we inquired if the Shah was going to march upon Candahar, we were answered, "That depends upon the Sirdar; we shall see what he will advise." Our audience did not last long; the Hadjee's rising to take leave was a signal for the rest of the company to retire, and we dispersed to our homes. Our friend told us on the way that the Sirdar was well disposed towards us, and that he would take an early opportunity of explaining to the Shah who I was.

In the evening we went to see Abbas Khan, whom we found engaged in the ceremonious task of receiving a c wd of visiters of different ranks, "*deed wo bâz deed*," as they term it, or the interchange of visits; a person of any consideration, returning home from travel, being formally waited upon by all the respectable men of the place, whose visits to a certain extent he is obliged to return.

Among the men of degree seated with him, Abbas Khan introduced us to the Attâr Bâshee, or apothecary-general, a man so entirely in the confidence of the Shah, that he was scarcely ever out of the private apartments in the palace, honour which, to look at his wasted figure and sunken eye, he had earned at some cost. He must have been a man of merit, for he contrived to enjoy the favour of the Shah, keep on good terms with the minister at war, and please all classes of the people. His original rank was that of a druggist in the city, in which capacity he enjoyed a consideration which eventually led in a singular manner to his rise. When Prince Hadjee Ferooz Oodeen, after a long rule at Heraut, was seized and plundered by Futteh Khan, his chief officers, fearing lest their effects should be confiscated privately confided their valuables to the care of the druggist, who, it was thought, would not be suspected; but Shahzadeh Kamraun coming to Heraut shortly after, received intimation of the circumstance, and set about possessing himself of the wealth. The Attâr was asleep in the interior of his house one night, when he was broken in upon by a party of thieves: he awoke at the noise of their entrance, and would have given the alarm, but glancing at the intruders, he saw that Kamraun was one of them; so covering his head with the bedclothes, he lay quiet, and suffered them to break boxes and carry off what they sought. From that time he had gradually risen to dignity, and a short time before, having watched Kamraun through a dangerous illness, he had quite won the favour of the monarch, who, it was said, trusted him with all his secrets.

It so happened that our Persian companion, Agha Hossein, was related to the Attâr Bâshee, and as he had told our history, the minister bowed graciously when Abbas Khan introduced us, and took charge of the letter for Kamraun which had been rejected by the kotwâl. The latter worthy was seated among the visiters when we entered, and appeared ill at his ease when Abbas Khan introduced me as an Elchee from the great Elchee at Tehraun, a gentleman of distinction, his friend and guest, and the Syud, as a man of the highest acquirements, and a person in every way to be esteemed. My friend's eye sparkled at the opportunity, and in the most cutting manner, yet with an air of studied politeness, he told our host that we were already so fortunate as to know the kotwâl, he having conferred upon us the honour of a visit only the second night of our arrival; and he quizzed the magistrate with so much address, that though the man could have stabbed him for his sarcasms, he could not well openly take exception at the words. A young Affghaun nobleman named Shumshoodden Khan, a favourite of the Shah's, who had married his said beautiful sister, occupied the seat next to the Attâr Bâshee: he appeared to enjoy the joke much, and doubtless so did our host, though he was too well bred, on such an occasion, to show resentment for the indignity put upon his guests.

My coming caused the conversation to turn upon Frang, which they understood to be a different country from that inhabited by the Oroos. In comparison with the Russian, I found that neither my countrymen, nor the people of any other European nation, were considered of consequence: indeed some conceived from his title, IMPERATOOR-E-AZUM, "The Supreme Emperor," that the Russian Autocrat gave the law to the kings of Europe. Wonderful things were asserted of the Oroos, particularly about their military deeds. Shumshooddeen Khan, who engrossed much of the conversation, among other things, told the company that no fort could hold out against this people, for that they never stopped at a ditch, marching soldiers into it until it was filled, and so on over their heads to the storm; and our host, whom I had credited for better sense, said he understood that on a certain occasion provisions falling short in his army, the Generâl-e Oroos gave orders that fifty thousand men should be killed and served out as rations. "*Ullah ho Rubbee!*" ejaculated an old Affghaun gentleman, "God is my protector! Is it possible? why they are cannibals, and must have a larger army than Timour had."

I could scarcely believe Abbas Khan was not speaking in jest, but he seemed quite serious, and I really believe mentioned the anecdote to illustrate the discipline of the Russian army: certainly his company credited the story; but what bounds can be set to the credulity of men who believe that the Chinese are such skilful mechanics, that they can make horses which will go for two or three days, and sell them as real animals? Abbas Khan made us return to dinner, and was as good as his promise at Meshed, establishing us in the house which had been emptied for our accommodation, frequently seeking our society, and endeavouring to make our time pass agreeably.

I will now take a slight review of the country which we passed through coming from Meshed. Allowing four miles an hour for the average of horses' march (which is little if any thing in excess, as the horses amble), we travelled 232 miles from Meshed to Heraut. We fell in with the usual kafilah road when we got out of the hills before Toorbut-e Shaikh Jam: the distance by the latter route is said to be sixty fursukhs, or 240 English miles, and having in my journal shown the country from Toorbut-e Shaikh Jam, I may here content myself with describing from native information the road from Meshed to that place.

The first march is to Sungbust; six and a half fursukhs. The mountains are crossed easily; at Sungbust there is a caravansera, and "grass and forage for one thousand horses."

The two next marches are to Hadeera and Khireabad, uninhabited places, where there is water. The fourth day's march is to Mahmoodabad, a small Hazaureh town of two hundred houses, and the fifth takes you to Toorbut-e-Shaikh Jam. Thence kafilahs usually go, *viâ* the reservoir of Kaufir Kullah, to Kahreeze, also a town or village of two hundred houses, inhabited by Hazaurehs, remarkable for the excellence of the melons grown there, two of which, we were assured by many persons, were not a bad load for a mule, and which, a man protested to us, were so full of juice, that if a rider galloped his horse within two miles of the ground in which they were cultivated, they would burst!—this is like the "come eat me" plum-puddings of fairy land. From Kahreeze the road goes by Kousan and Shubbush to Rosanuck, or to Ghourian, and so on to Heraut.

Travellers by this route for the most part carry their own provisions: formerly, as stated in a preceding page, the great road lay on the west of the hills, *viâ* the towns of Toorbut-e Hyderah and Khaff.

Coming the latter way from Meshed, you travel

two fursukhs to Toorook-e Baulah, or upper Toorook, two miles or so beyond which you commence the ascent of the great hills. The kotul is steep, but not so difficult as that of Durrood, for Tukht-e Rahwans,* and camels bearing kajavahs ascend it; whereas also the kotul of Durrood is barely passable in winter from the snow, this road is open all the year, and guns might be got over it. The summit of these mountains is a very broad table-land. The road is hilly to Shereefabad, the first stage from Meshed, a village of forty houses, where is a caravansera and much good water. From Shereefabad to Khaff the road is easy, and water is had in plenty. At Khaff the soil becomes sandy, water scarce and brackish: you march thirty-two miles, without meeting with water, to Dâna Karât; sixteen miles beyond the latter place is a spring of indifferent water, and then you are twelve miles from Ghourian. From Ghourian to Heraut the distance is ten fursukhs, nothing but villages and gardens all the way.

From Toorbut-e Hyderah to Ghourian there is another, and, as far as regards water, apparently a better road,—*viâ* Dowlutabad, Himmutabad, Kullah Agha Hussan, Sheher-e Noh, Meshed Reza, Tauyeabad, and Kousan. There is also a road from Shereefabad to Sheher-e Noh, avoiding Toorbut-e Hyderah; *viâ* Robat-e Suffeid, Nusr Kullaush, Butroo, and Checkmauk. According to the information we re-

* Litters carried by mules.

ceived, there are forts and a little cultivation at all the stages on the first road. Sheher-e Noh is a small town. Neither the relative distances, nor the directions of these places could be clearly ascertained: I troubled myself considerably in the attempt to fix them, but no two persons of whom I inquired, had the same idea of distance. One traveller, more honest than the rest, said in answer to my particular inquiries about stages, when he had given me a route which was prolonged some thirty miles beyond what it possibly could be, "Khoda donud Agha!"—"God knows, sir, how far it was; sometimes we went slow, sometimes fast, we travelled in fear of property and fear of life, and my only thought was to get to the end of the march." I mention the names of these places, because they are at least points where water may be had, and they may serve as a clue for subsequent inquirers with better means.

These roads do not appear to oppose many difficulties to the march of troops: the country is level, water is in sufficiency, and even now the country west of the small branch as far south as Khaff could send considerable supplies to commissariat points. The capabilities of Persian Khorassaun must not be judged by its present condition, for it is in its worst state: much of the country is naturally fine; it has been rendered desert by the turbulence of its chieftains, and by the inroads of Toorkmuns, but these are both causes which may be corrected, and if they should be, the province assuredly would in a great measure recover itself. The roads once rendered safe would be thronged, the country would be repopulated, and plenty would take the place of barrenness.

END OF THE FIRST VOLUME.